Evaluating Comprehensive State Welfare Reform:

The Wisconsin Works Program

Editors:
Burt S. Barnow
Johns Hopkins University

Thomas Kaplan
Institute for Research on Poverty
University of Wisconsin — Madison

Robert A. Moffitt
Johns Hopkins University

The
Rockefeller
Institute
Press

Rockefeller Institute Press, Albany, New York 12203-1003
© 2000 by the Institute for Research on Poverty,
University of Wisconsin — Madison
All rights reserved. First edition 2000
Printed in the United States of America

The Rockefeller Institute Press
The Nelson A. Rockefeller Institute of Government
411 State Street
Albany, New York 12203-1003

Library of Congress Cataloging-in-Publication Data

Evaluating comprehensive state welfare reform : the Wisconsin Works program / editors,
Burt S. Barnow, Thomas Kaplan, Robert A. Moffitt.
    p. cm.
  Includes bibliographical references and index.
  ISBN 0-914341-72-3 (pbk.)
    1. Public welfare--Wisconsin--Evaluation. 2. Welfare
recipients--Employment--Wisconsin--Evaluation. 3. Evaluation research (Social action
programs)--Wisconsin. I. Barnow, Burt S. II. Kaplan, Thomas. III. Moffitt, Robert.

HV98.W6 E93 2000
362.5'8'09775--dc21
                                                                99-042252

ISBN: 0-914341-72-3

Table of Contents

Acknowledgments

The chapters in this volume were originally written as papers for a national conference on the evaluation of state welfare reforms. The conference was held in Madison, Wisconsin, in November 1996. The Joyce Foundation and the Charles Stewart Mott Foundation provided generous financial support for development of the conference papers and for the conference itself. Conference participants too numerous to mention provided insightful comments on the papers and the issues they raised, and helped greatly to improve the quality of the papers. The editors especially acknowledge Robinson G. Hollister, Robert G. Lovell, Demetra Smith Nightingale, Werner Schink, and Daniel H. Weinberg for their written comments on the conference.

Foreword

The Nelson A. Rockefeller Institute is pleased to publish this volume of papers on methods for conducting research on state welfare reforms. The papers are focused on welfare policy changes made in Wisconsin. Much of course has happened since the November 1996 conference for which the papers were prepared. State legislation enacting Wisconsin's welfare reform — called "Wisconsin Works" (W-2) — was passed five months prior to the conference. At the time of the conference, the national welfare reform law had just been enacted, actually three months before in the Personal Responsibility and Work Opportunity Reconciliation Act (PRWORA) signed by President Clinton in August 1996. This federal law created the Temporary Assistance for Needy Families (TANF) program that replaced the Aid to Families with Dependent Children (AFDC) program. The TANF program went into effect nationally in October 1997.

The November 1996 conference participants knew about the purposes and main features of W-2, but they did not know how it would be implemented. Participants also did not know how reforms in other states would develop as a result of the national welfare reform law. As many of the Wisconsin conference participants expected, and has since then become apparent, W-2 is the most radical and activist welfare transformation among all the states. One indication of this is the dramatic caseload declines that have occurred. In February 1999, there were approximately nine thousand W-2 cases for people receiving cash assistance. (An additional 3,300 were receiving services only.) This represents a decline of 90 percent from the peak AFDC caseload of 1986. Although much of this decline occurred before the introduction of W-2, post-implementation declines continue to be striking.

There also has been a substantial organizational transfer of authority in Wisconsin from the state's equivalent of the U.S. Department of Health and Human Services to the equivalent of the U.S. Department of Labor. This change ratifies the philosophical transition of W-2 from an income-support to a work-focused program.

W-2 has altered the culture of most county-level administering agencies in Wisconsin. The program is now located in one-stop job centers that provide a number of employment related services to the entire community, not just the poor. Front-line W-2 workers are "Financial and Employment Planners" (FEPs), not income-maintenance or eligibility specialists as in the past. The signs on offices signal that participants are applying for a job.

W-2 emphasizes the centrality of work from the first contact participants have with the system. The first W-2 check comes only after a period of work or other assigned activity and does not vary with family size. W-2 is also distinctive for its reliance on private agencies to provide jobs and other services. In nine of Wisconsin's 72 counties, W-2 is operated by private agencies under a contract with the state. The main county where this is the case is Milwaukee, where over 80 percent of W-2 participants reside. Contracting agencies, both private and nonprofit, have the same responsibilities as public W-2 agencies for services, which include the assignment of eligibility in one of four program tiers for W-2 that reflect different degrees of job readiness. The exception to this is that public agency staff members have to give formal approval for benefit recipiency.

The promptness of financial penalties is another characteristic that makes W-2 different from the way the "new welfare" operates in many states. With the exception of W-2 participants with children younger than 12 weeks, assigned activities begin right away under W-2, and failure to participate results in an immediate financial penalty. Other states also have participation requirements and penalties for failure to meet them, but often allow a grace period after program entry before reductions in cash assistance occur.

Compared to many states, W-2 places minimal emphasis on the idea of a "social contract" whereby the state and the public assistance recipient agree on reciprocal obligations, the one side (the state) to make opportunities available and the other (the participant) actively to pursue those opportunities. W-2 provides services to program participants — child care, health care, and job-searches strategies, etc. But the focus of W-2 is on the participant's obligation to follow an employability plan, or if considered ready for an unsubsidized job, to secure one.

The de-linking of related social programs from one's welfare status is an important change in the new welfare. A good example of this in Wisconsin is the treatment of child support. W-2 families keep all child support paid by an absent parent on their behalf. This marks a decided change from the policy that existed under AFDC and still exists in most states where a family keeps $50 per month of the child support paid on the family's behalf and the rest is deducted from the cash-assistance benefit.

Participants at the November 1996 conference knew about many of the features of W-2 that make evaluation of the program's impact challenging to say the least. The discussion in these papers of how one might study the effects of W-2 is of course most relevant in Wisconsin. But they are of interest nationally as well. Many of the same research challenges arise in other states. Important impacts of W-2, and this is true in many states, affect people not in the program, and in some cases who never were, but who would have received benefits under the AFDC program if it still operated as it had previously. This special challenge of determining the impact of W-2 and other state welfare reforms on people who are "_diverted_" or "_deflected_" from welfare cash assistance is addressed in several papers in this book.

New welfare-to-work programs such as W-2 give extensive flexibility to case managers and in so doing allow geographic variation within the state. The resulting situation, which in research conducted at the Rockefeller Institute we call "_second order devolution_," is widespread throughout the country. Capturing the impacts of so much variation is not easy. Several conference papers emphasize this local diversity as well as the continuous nature of change under Wisconsin's welfare reforms.

The conference organizers for this volume believed from the outset that experimental evaluations would be less relevant than in the past. Despite the views of many participants on the merits of experimental designs, it has become increasingly apparent that such studies cannot be the main method for assessing new state welfare and job programs. Only one evaluation underway in Wisconsin (an evaluation of the full pass-through of child support) has an experimental design.

Historically, there has been a lively interest in welfare research in Wisconsin. The response to W-2 is no exception. At a conference in Racine, Wisconsin, held in November 1997, one year after the conference was held at which the papers in this volume were presented, researchers and agency staff met to coordinate W-2 evaluations.

Earlier, in 1996, Wisconsin Governor Tommy Thompson created the Management and Evaluation Project (MEP) chaired by J. Jean Rogers, head of the state's Division of Economic Assistance, which runs the W-2 program. The vice chair of the panel is Michael Wiseman, a senior researcher at the Urban Institute and formerly a faculty member at the University of Wisconsin in Madison. Governor Thompson also appointed a National Technical Advisory Committee. Wiseman and Lawrence Mead, a political scientist and welfare policy expert on the faculty of New York University, serve on the technical advisory committee as well as on the MEP group. Members of the technical advisory group are listed at the end of this Foreword. The Management and Evaluation Project has endorsed and supported a number of evaluation projects for W-2, and state officials are actively working with a wide range of policy researchers.

I want to express appreciation to Burt Barnow, co-author of the introductory chapter in this book and co-editor of the volume, for helping to arrange for the publication of this book and also Thomas Kaplan and Thomas Corbett for their assistance. Michael Cooper, Director of Publications at the Rockefeller Institute, supervised the production of this book.

Richard P. Nathan
December 1999

Members of the National Technical Advisory Committee are:

- ❖ Eugene Bardach, University of California at Berkeley
- ❖ Henry E. Brady, University of California at Berkeley
- ❖ George Cave, Consulting Economist
- ❖ Anna Kondratas, Urban Institute
- ❖ Larry Martin, University of Wisconsin-Milwaukee
- ❖ Rebecca Maynard, University of Pennsylvania
- ❖ Lawrence Mead, New York University
- ❖ Ronald Mincy, Ford Foundation
- ❖ Demetra Nightingale, Urban Institute
- ❖ John Weicher, Hudson Institute
- ❖ Michael Wiseman, Urban Institute

Introduction

Burt S. Barnow
Johns Hopkins University

Thomas Kaplan
Institute for Research on Poverty
University of Wisconsin – Madison

Robert A. Moffitt
Johns Hopkins University

In August 1996, Congress and the President replaced the 60-year-old Aid to Families with Dependent Children (AFDC) program with a block grant, Temporary Assistance for Needy Families (TANF). The new block grant, enacted as part of the Personal Responsibility and Work Opportunity Reconciliation Act, allowed states to transform their public assistance programs in many ways and gave them great discretion within federal rules to do so. Some states, such as Kansas, responded guardedly to their new policy flexibility, making only the changes specifically mandated by TANF (Johnston and Lindaman, 1998). These changes were not trivial; the new law, for example, limited federal cash assistance to a total of five years for each adult and required at least 50 percent of single parents who received the assistance to work full time by 2002. Yet other states used their new policy flexibility to craft still more sweeping changes to AFDC. In many of the more aggressive states, requirements for school attendance, work, or an activity that leads to work, along with modified policies for

1

adjusting family income according to family size, were bundled into packages designed to generate social messages that discourage dependency on public assistance, promote work, and influence family-formation decisions.

It has long been clear that Wisconsin would be one of the more ambitious states in welfare reform. An early draft of Governor Tommy Thompson's welfare initiative, Wisconsin Works (or W-2), was first circulated in the summer of 1995. The governor released his formal W-2 proposal in October of that year, nine months before the passage of the Personal Responsibility and Work Opportunity Reconciliation Act (PRWORA), which created the TANF program, and the Wisconsin legislature enacted W-2 into law in March 1996.

The W-2 legislation eliminated AFDC in Wisconsin and fashioned a replacement that was fundamentally and comprehensively different. Because the architects of W-2 believed that financial support should derive only from work, the new law requires W-2 participants to enter a work assignment immediately, with no grace period for the development and implementation of an employment plan. Because W-2 planners believed that clients should face the same constraints as the working poor, the new legislation includes immediate and sharp financial penalties for missed hours of work under W-2, makes families receiving W-2 child care assistance responsible for significant co-payments, and structures W-2 cash assistance so as not to vary by family size. Because program designers also held that W-2 participants should realize some benefits, as well as the constraints, available to the working poor not receiving public assistance, most W-2 participants under the new legislation receive all of the child support paid on behalf of their children (unlike the case with AFDC, in which all child support over $50 per month was taken out of the AFDC grant). Moreover, families gain access to W-2 through an agency that provides general employment and labor exchange services, not through anything called, or designed to look like, a welfare office.

Although Wisconsin is not the only state engaged in such comprehensive reform, W-2 is certainly among the most ambitious of the current state initiatives. For several reasons described later in this introduction, and more fully in some of the chapters that follow, comprehensive reforms present special challenges to evaluators and may require new evaluation paradigms. Researchers at, and affiliated with, the Institute for Research on Poverty (IRP) at the University of Wisconsin–Madison, which had helped develop the current paradigms 25 years earlier through an evaluation of a negative income tax program in New Jersey, believed that the W-2 program offered a worthy test of their ability to meet some of the new challenges of evaluating comprehensive welfare reform. A working group of IRP researchers began holding regular meetings in the summer of 1995 in an effort to develop a plan for the evaluation of W-2. After several introductory sessions, a set of core issues was defined and each subsequent meeting concentrated on one of those issues. The discussions evolved into papers which were first presented to a national conference on the evaluation of comprehensive reforms held in November 1996.

This volume contains selected papers from that conference. All the papers have been revised with the aim of offering a broader audience a discussion of general issues in the evaluation of comprehensive state welfare reforms and an application of that discussion to the evaluation of welfare reform in one state. The volume illustrates the many challenges researchers will face in evaluating such programs and makes specific suggestions applicable to evaluations both in Wisconsin and elsewhere.

This introduction has three remaining sections. Because this volume is first and foremost about the methodology of evaluation, the next section offers an overview of the different types of program evaluations that can be conducted and of several of the key issues that arise in any evaluation. While these issues are familiar to evaluation experts, they may not be familiar to those outside the field and to government policy makers. The issues summarized in this section will also provide a context for the individual chapters that appear in the volume.

In the subsequent section, the details of the Wisconsin Works program are outlined. Because the chapters in the volume all apply their general principles to the W-2 program, it is useful to have an understanding of the program at the start.

In the final section, we summarize the contents and conclusions of each chapter in the volume.

General Issues in the Impact Evaluation of Welfare Reform

The discussion in this section draws upon a long history of research on evaluation techniques. There are more detailed discussions of these issues in the many textbooks in the field (e.g., Rossi and Freeman, 1993). Our discussion pertains only to what is called "impact" evaluation, which is evaluation concerned with the effect of the program on the ultimate outcomes of interest, almost always outcomes at the individual or family level. (Chapter 2 contains a detailed discussion of outcome variables.) This type of evaluation is to be distinguished from "process" evaluation, which is concerned with assessing the effectiveness of the implementation of the program and in which, therefore, the outcomes of interest pertain to how well the program was put into place and its intentions realized in the field. Our discussion also explicitly addresses how each of the issues will have to be addressed in an evaluation of programs spawned by the PRWORA legislation, of which W-2 is one example.

Our overview addresses the following topics: (1) how to define the question of interest; (2) a classification of the different types of evaluation designs; and (3) data sources.

Defining the Question

In designing evaluations for social welfare programs, an evaluator must first determine the questions to be answered. Designs that are appropriate for answering some questions are often inappropriate for answering others. In addressing any particular set of hypotheses, there are five common questions to be considered:

❖ What is the intervention/activity of interest?
❖ What is the counterfactual to the intervention/activity of interest?
❖ What is the population of interest?
❖ What are the time frames of interest?
❖ What are the outcomes of interest?

For example, in many previous evaluations of welfare programs, the intervention studied has been a new job search, training, or employment intervention; the counterfactual has been an existing employment and training program or no program at all; the population of interest has consisted of volunteers or mandatory assignees to the "treatment" (that is, the new program or variation being tested) and has almost always consisted of individuals on the welfare rolls at the time of intervention (the general nonrecipient population has been excluded, by and large); the time frame of interest has typically run several years beyond the initiation of the reform; and the outcomes of interest have been the earnings, wage rates, and employment of the population as well as their receipt of welfare and amount of welfare payments. In a study of devolution resulting from PRWORA, many of these specifications are likely to change.

Activity/Intervention of Interest. Defining the activity or intervention of interest in the post-PRWORA environment raises many difficult issues. One is that the scope of the intervention must be much greater than anything tested in past evaluations. Devolution has already brought major changes to the AFDC program (including a new name), the food stamp and Medicaid programs, child care provision, and social services. Even if it were desirable, or possible, to focus solely on, say, the TANF program, the interventions already underway in most of the states are multifaceted and involve, most commonly, some combination of increased work requirements, heightened sanctions for failure to comply, time limits, financial work incentives, relaxation of AFDC-UP (Unemployed Parent) rules, family caps, and changes in asset requirements.

Disentangling the effects of interventions with multiple components creates what we term the "bundling" problem: The intervention is, in actuality, a "bundle" of different interventions, all of which are implemented more or less simultaneously. This will make it extremely difficult for an evaluation to estimate impacts of each of the individual interventions separately and to disentangle their separate effects. This problem can be overstated, however, because it is not clear that one should be interested in the impact of adding an individual component on top of the old program environment, or on top of the new environment after devolution. It is the argument of many advocates of devolution that the impact of the sum of the interventions is more than the sum of the impacts of each individually. To the extent this is correct, it is arguable that the first order of business is to estimate the impact of the bundle, and only secondarily to estimate the impact of the components; and it could also be argued that the impact of the components should be assessed against the new bundle rather than the old bundle.

Another problem is the infeasibility of conducting randomized experiments. In an experimental environment, it may be possible to test many of the major interventions with random assignment if it were desired to do so, although there are so many that the design matrix required would be very large. But if nonexperimental evaluations are the only options available, as we assume to be the case, then an evaluation must rely on "natural" variation — that is, on the choices that states and localities make. If this variation is very large relative to the number of states and localities, it may be difficult to infer impacts of individual components even if the impacts of bundled programs in a large number of states and localities are estimated.

The Counterfactual. The definition of a counterfactual is also problematic in the post-PRWORA environment because states and localities began implementing major changes in their programs before there was time to mount an evaluation. Consequently, it is too late, in a sense, to measure the "before" half of a before-and-after study. There are, however, two ameliorating factors in the problem of defining the "before." First, to the extent that it is possible to gather information on past behavior from historical administrative data, it may be possible to establish a baseline prior to the current changes underway in the states. Second, it is quite likely that the implementation of devolution will take many years and, more specifically, that the changes in the program from 1999 to 2001, for example, may dwarf anything that has happened by the end of 1999. If so, there is still plenty of time to measure major impacts because relatively little has yet happened. This possibility also has implications for an evaluation design, for it implies that a good evaluation must maintain the flexibility to accommodate itself to an evolving policy environment.

Population of Interest. Most past welfare evaluations have had as their population of interest individuals on the welfare rolls or some subset of them (e.g., JOBS-eligibles). However, in addition to the fact that the impact of the new reforms is likely to be broader within the recipient population (i.e., to affect a greater proportion of recipients), it is likely to have major effects in the nonrecipient population as well through well-known "entry" effects. Most observers expect these entry effects to be negative, i.e., that there will be *deterrent* effects. This is often explicitly intended by the policy makers implementing the programs and is often regarded by those policy makers as a desirable outcome. The expansion of the population of interest calls for a much broader population base for the evaluation than has been the case previously. This population might be circumscribable to some extent, for example, by examining only the poor or near-poor population.[1,2]

Finally, for some purposes it may be desirable to focus on particular subgroups of the population. For example, there is great interest in what effect time limits will have on AFDC recipients who exhaust their entitlement. It may be desirable to draw a special sample of near-exhaustees or to over sample such individuals.

Time Frames of Interest. There are several ways of considering the time frames of interest for the study. First, there is the issue of how long to track the sample or samples of participants. If time limits are included in the sites, it will be very desirable to track the research sample (or at least part of the sample) for at least one year beyond the point at which participants are terminated from the rolls. If five-year limits are imposed, this may be quite a long intervention. Rather different in spirit is the question of how long the time frame should be *prior* to the intervention examined. This is more a methodological question and we must postpone it to some extent to the discussion of alternative designs. One distinction worth making here, however, is that nonexperimental evaluations require, by and large, more historical data than do experimental evaluations because there is more need to control for the "histories" of the individuals and cities involved. In addition, as we noted previously, it may be desirable to construct sufficient historical data to get back to some defined "before" in any case.

Outcomes of Interest. At first blush, the outcomes of interest should be similar to the outcomes in previous studies: earnings, wage rates, employment, receipt of welfare, and amount of welfare received, for example. The broadening of the population we mentioned earlier, particularly to nonrecipients, requires that exit and entry rates be a part of the study of welfare receipt in this case. In addition, there may be interest in more aggregate outcomes such as caseloads and dollars spent on welfare.

The tradeoffs between different objectives may be more stark in the new environment than in the past, and it is worthwhile to be cognizant of that. By all appearances, the tradeoff between the goal of reducing the caseload, on the one hand, and increasing recipient well-being, on the other, is likely to shift more toward the former than has been the case in the past. Indeed, many policy makers are completely willing to accept reductions in recipient income and increases in poverty rates in exchange for caseload and cost reduction, particularly if it is achieved by altering the rules of the program in a way that is argued to be preferred by society. The notion of a time limit, for example, is partly based on the simple notion that only a certain amount of support should be given, regardless of the consequences.

Another implication of the current state-level interest in new "rules," "norms," and "expectations of behavior" is that implementation becomes more important, and is to some extent an outcome of interest in and of itself. If the major goal of current state-level policy makers is to require work while on the rolls and not to pay for more than five years of benefits or for additional children, and if these policies are aimed not at changing behavior but simply at enforcing what are asserted to be societal norms, then the goal of the program is merely to implement and enforce those rules, regardless of the consequences. That by itself may be difficult to do on a large scale, and it is not yet clear how successful states will be in that endeavor. But an evaluation design that ignores this point of view runs the risk of not answering the questions that some policy makers want answered.

A Classification Scheme for Nonexperimental Evaluations

Table 1 provides one type of classification scheme of the types of different evaluation designs, with a focus on the implicit counterfactual — that is, who is being compared to whom in order to obtain an estimate of the program effect. In nonexperimental studies, the estimation of a program, or "treatment," effect is necessarily based on a comparison of different individuals or groups of individuals who face, or have been exposed to, different types of programs or program characteristics. We shall term these "quasi-experiments," in line with traditional usage (Campbell and Stanley, 1966), in contrast to true controlled experiments. The table considers four different generic types of evaluations, and subcases within those: pure before-and-after designs, pure cross-section designs, designs which combine before-and-after with cross-sectional elements, and cohort designs. Each of the types of quasi-

Table 1
Classification Scheme for Nonexperimental Evaluations

Generic Type of Study	Specific Type of Study	Description
Pure Before-After		Units examined over time and outcomes measured; program has changed over time; attribute change in outcomes to change in program; can have multiple "before" and multiple "after" time periods
	Individual Units	Recipients or nonrecipients; in one area, most commonly; usually do not have a long time series; sometimes have subannual data and sometimes not
	Aggregates	Fixed geographic unit, usually a state; also called time series modeling; usually have relatively long time series and often have subannual data
Pure Cross-Section		Comparison of different units at a point in time (e.g., week, month, or year); program differs across units; attribute difference in outcomes across units to program differences
	Individuals Within Areas	Usually recipients only since recipient-nonrecipient comparisons usually not reliable; different individuals are treated differently; danger of selection bias
	Across Areas	Individuals or aggregates; danger of site effects
Cross-Section and Before-After		Combination of two; have units that are treated differently; measure outcomes of all observations over time
	Individual Units Within Areas	Different recipient or nonrecipients are treated differently; and treatment changes over time; permits "fixed effects" (or "differences in differences") as well as "autoregressive" models that use lagged variables ("history") to control for "heterogeneity"
	Individual Units Across Areas	Different recipients or nonrecipients in different areas with different programs, and program changes over time
	Aggregates Across Areas	Aggregate time series modeling but using multiple areas, usually states

9

Evaluating Comprehensive State Welfare Reforms:
The Wisconsin Works Program

Table 1
Classification Scheme for Nonexperimental Evaluations

Generic Type of Study	Specific Type of Study	Description
Cohort Design		Multiple birth or program entry cohorts who are each followed over time; program is changing over time; changes in cohort experiences are attributed to program change
	Individual Units Within Areas	Individual data on multiple cohorts within a single area
	Individual Units Across Areas	Multiple cohorts in multiple areas; can have cohort and area "fixed effects" by comparing cohort differences across areas
	Aggregates Across Areas	Possible if aggregate data can be disaggregated by age

Note: Each type can utilize administrative data, survey data, or both.

experiments in Table 1 thus makes a different type of comparison. It would be a wonderful state of the world if they all generated the same impact estimates for the same type of program, but this is unlikely to be the case because the threats to the design are different in each case.

Pure before-and-after designs simply follow individuals or groups of individuals over a time period within which a program change has occurred. The change in their outcomes is attributed to the change in the program. The threats to this design are of two distinct types: aging (sometimes called maturation or life cycle) effects, and systematic external changes in the environment. Aging effects might be ignorable for short periods, but over longer periods the change in outcomes may be affected by natural life cycle patterns. In programs with short average duration, such as food stamps, aging effects can be important even for relatively short periods. Also important are changes in the local labor market, in the neighborhood environment, etc., which occur simultaneously with the program change and which therefore confound the measurement of its effects.

If aggregate data are used, either at a state level or national level, this approach is usually termed "time series modeling" or "caseload modeling." Aggregation has very little advantage per se, but aggregate data are often available for longer time periods and for more cross-section units (see next generic type) than are individual, micro data, which puts them at an advantage. Particularly in a before-and-after evaluation, where reliance on stability of the local economic environment is so important, a longer time series can be invaluable in separating the influence of general economic events from the program change in question. Aggregate data are also often significantly less expensive to obtain than micro data, and they can be used to detect entry effects.

These evaluation types can be further distinguished by whether administrative data, household survey data, or both are used. Aggregate data on caseloads or wages can be obtained from administrative data, and individual data may be gathered from welfare records or wage records, for example. Again, individual data are generally preferred, but they are also usually available for fewer time periods and fewer areas.

The second type, pure cross-section quasi-experiments, are rare, even though they correspond most closely to controlled experiments. Comparing recipients to nonrecipients, different types of recipients, or different areas at a single point in time so obviously runs the risk of confounding program effects with other differences across individuals or areas that the method is almost never used. Instead, these types of comparisons are conducted when multiple periods of data are available, which falls under our third generic category of combined cross-section and before-and-after data.

This third generic category is, in fact, the most common type of nonexperimental evaluation and covers a large number of different subtypes. One classic method of evaluation is a comparison of participants to nonparticipants over time, using the history of their behavior to control for heterogeneity between the groups. However, while this method has a fairly long history in the evaluation of job training programs, it has almost never been used for the evaluation of welfare programs because welfare recipients and nonrecipients are generally thought to be sufficiently different to be noncomparable, even when observable histories are controlled for. Somewhat more common are comparisons among different types of recipients who are given different treatments (e.g., different employment and training programs), who are on waiting lists, or who are otherwise treated differently by the program. Fixed effects, autoregressive, matching, and other techniques are often used in this case to control for differences in histories between the groups compared.[3] However, the main danger with these methods is that the differential treatment accorded to different groups of recipients or nonrecipients is endogenous (to use the econometric term); that is, that the different groups being compared differ along unobservable dimensions which make them noncomparable. With a few exceptions, therefore, although it is possible that credible and valid comparisons of this type might be found, most of the types possible run a serious risk of selection bias by assignment to category.

More credible are combination designs that compare recipients, nonrecipients, or both together, in different areas over time, thereby making use of the variation in program type between areas to measure program impacts. Aside from poor matching of initial conditions, the chief threat to this design is again uncontrolled differences in growth rates or other time-related changes in the outcome variables across areas, which is the counterpart to the unobserved site-effect problem in the pure cross-sectional comparison across areas. Comparison-site or matched-site designs are aimed at reducing this threat by choosing areas that are similar in a few measurable dimensions, but such designs are not successful if the areas differ in too many other ways. In addition, implementation of this method requires that the programs in different areas are capable of being compared along some common measure or scale, which may be difficult for current program changes, which are diverse and complex and very different across areas.

This method can be combined with use of historical data on individual recipients and non-recipients; there is no reason that one cannot, or should not, attempt to control for as much individual heterogeneity as possible even though cross-area comparisons of changes over time are the ultimate source of impact estimate. The comparison of different areas over time can also be achieved with aggregate data on caseloads, earnings, or other variables. Here again the chief advantage of such an approach lies in the greater number of time periods and areas available with aggregate data. However, as with the use of micro data, this method requires that programs in different areas and over time be ordered along some dimension or small number of dimensions. The development of a program typology would be one step in this direction.

The final generic method presented in Table 1 is a cohort design which measures program impact by comparing the experiences of different cohorts who face different programs because they come into contact with the system at different calendar times. A well-known example of this method is the evaluation of the 1981 Omnibus Budget Reconciliation Act (OBRA) legislation by the Research Triangle Institute (RTI, 1983). RTI compared the welfare exit and employment outcomes of a cohort of AFDC recipients prior to 1981 and a cohort after 1981; the latter experienced the OBRA legislation in full. The differences in outcomes between the two cohorts was attributed to OBRA.

This method can be extended in many ways. Multiple cohorts over time can be used for the comparison, which, if they are prior to the intervention, permits the incorporation of changes in the economic and social environment. Cohorts across areas can be compared, with the treatment measured as the across-area difference in cohort differences. Historical individual data on the individuals within each cohort can be collected and used as controls for heterogeneity. In addition, we should note once again that administrative data, household survey data, or some combination could be used for any of these designs.

The use of recipients or nonrecipients as separate groups in any of these quasi-experiments deserves special attention. While use of recipiency as a defining characteristic is possible and desirable in many cases, it must be kept in mind that recipiency itself is self-selected and may consequently pose a threat to designs which stratify on recipiency. For example, comparisons of the outcomes of recipients in different areas or at different points in time within the same area, in order to draw inferences about the consequences of different programs or changes in programs over time, rely for their validity on the presumption that the population of recipients across areas or over time is the same in unobservable as well as observable dimensions. If this is not the case, differences in response may be the result of underlying differences in characteristics rather than of the differences in treatment. The same goes for comparisons of nonrecipients.

A reductionist position would be to only examine total populations of recipients and nonrecipients combined (or total populations of eligibles) across areas and over time. However, the gain in avoidance of selection bias has to be weighed against the loss of ability to pinpoint whether response is arising from recipients or nonrecipients, as well as having to rely on the alternative assumption that the two total populations are alike. This problem reflects a more general tension in nonexperimental analyses between a desire, on the one hand, to measure outcomes for narrowly defined subgroups of the population — not only for their intrinsic interest but also because it is easier to reduce the bundling problem, the narrower the subgroup — and the simultaneous desire to examine a large enough population to avoid separating the population into self-selected groups whose responses will differ because of unobservable differences in characteristics.

Data Sources and Issues

There are three general sources of data that can be used for the evaluation: aggregate administrative data, individual administrative data, and individual survey data. These forms of data are not simply substitutes, but can serve as complements as well — certain types of questions can only be answered with specific types of data. Thus, the question is not necessarily which type of data to collect for the evaluation, but which source or sources are needed to answer the questions of interest.

Aggregate Administrative Data. Aggregate administrative data consist of data collected by state and local governments for administrative purposes. Such data are generally available on a monthly basis and include total cases in the program, entries to the program, exits from the program (possibly by reason for exit), average benefit levels, and activity levels. They can be linked to demographic and economic data for the same area to estimate time series and determine the impact on caseload entries, exits, average number on the rolls, and benefit levels of program changes.

Aggregate data may be available only at the city or county level, but in some states it could be available at the office level. However, even if the caseload data are available below the city or county level, other determining variables that are needed for the analysis are likely to be unavailable below the local level. Thus, aggregate data are not likely to be helpful for any sub-city level analyses, for example.

Two advantages of aggregate data are that they are very inexpensive to obtain, and that they often go back for many years. In several states with which we are familiar, useful data go back to the early 1970s.[4] These are both advantages in carrying out evaluations. The low cost implies that time series analyses can be used to supplement other, more expensive approaches. Aggregate data are often available for considerably longer periods of time than individual case record data are maintained, and the longer period means that evaluations can capture the effects of a wider range of economic conditions than if only a few years are available.

A problem that affects both aggregate and individual administrative data is that the analysis is limited by what has been collected. If, for example, one would like to include the number of single poor female heads of households as an explanatory variable in the analysis, that variable may not be available. Likewise, some outcomes of interest may not be available in aggregate administrative data.

Individual Administrative Data. This type of data includes information maintained at the individual level on program participation and individual characteristics. Examples include benefits received in programs such as AFDC, food stamps, unemployment insurance, and supplemental security income (SSI). Because participation in these programs is generally conditioned on income, we can also obtain information on earnings, wage rates, and hours worked.

The time period over which such data are available will vary from state to state and program to program. Some states, for example, routinely discard unemployment insurance wage records after three years. Confidentiality statutes may pose access problems in certain states and programs.

Although administrative data are less expensive to obtain than household survey data (see below), they are not cheap to obtain either. Many states' records, even when kept in machine-readable form, are poorly organized and require a significant amount of matching, merging, and file creation. Files are often "dirty" in the sense of containing many errors and discrepancies which the administrative agency has not spent the time to correct. In addition, if the data are not in machine-readable form but only in raw hard-copy form, there is an extra series of steps in preparing a format for the data and then entering it either by human coders or scanners. Errors can be introduced at this stage as well unless sufficient resources are allocated to keep them at a minimal level.

Leaving these practical difficulties aside, the use of administrative data has some limitations from a design point of view as well. First, by definition, a study using administrative data is limited to the variables available in the data — there is no flexibility to add or modify data elements. Administrative data tend to be rather weak on demographic information, for example. Second, administrative data can only track individuals while they are in the system. To know anything about earnings of families who leave the welfare rolls, for example, IRS records or unemployment insurance wage records must be obtained (although this is not uncommon in many evaluations). Third, these two problems also affect the ability to gather preprogram information on individuals in the evaluation, some of whom were off welfare.

Survey Data. Surveys of individuals of interest have several important advantages over the two other data sources, but they also have several important limitations. Perhaps the most important advantage of surveys is that data can be gathered on any topic amenable to survey questioning, and this broadens the types of information that can be obtained enormously. Besides the usual questions on outcomes and demographic variables, surveys can seek to cover topics not covered (or at least not covered in depth) in administrative data, such as motivation, mental health, intelligence, education, detailed work history, and so on. In addition, a survey can be designed to cover whatever population is of interest, although broad coverage may significantly increase the cost. Thus, a survey can generate information on a comparison group that would not be available from administrative data.

There are a number of important disadvantages of survey data as well, however. Perhaps the most significant is that they can be very expensive, particularly when the focus is a low-income population. Major costs may be incurred in developing a sampling frame, for example. In addition, screening costs can be extremely large when only a small proportion of the population is sampled in an area. In some instances these problems can be avoided, but they may reduce the validity of the survey.

Another major disadvantage of surveys is that they can only gather data prospectively. Because of recall problems, it is not possible to use a survey to cover previous time periods. Thus, if we wish to compare a program starting next month with the current program, we cannot rely on surveys to gather data on a previous cohort. This makes it difficult to address the problem of the "before" with survey data.

Conclusions

The most attractive designs are those that combine cross-section before-and-after variation and utilize cross-cohort variation. In any evaluation, it is important that the threats to the particular design chosen be examined and that the data collection plan take this into account. Supplementing individual administrative data with survey data, for example, can permit checks for self-selection into recipiency; and supplementing an individual-level analysis with a time series analysis using aggregate administrative data can be used to check whether program effects are confounded with general trends. Although resource and time constraints obviously may limit such an ambitious data collection strategy, it should be regarded as a goal to be aimed for.

The Wisconsin Works (W-2) Program

Wisconsin's welfare reform plan, Wisconsin Works (W-2), is among the most aggressive of current efforts to "end welfare as we know it." The W-2 initiative, which eliminates AFDC and replaces it with cash assistance available only through work or participation in work-like activities, has several components. Participation requirements for low-income parents begin when the youngest child is 12 weeks old. The parents are assigned to a Financial and Employment Planner (FEP), who places them on one of four levels of a "self-sufficiency ladder" and helps and encourages them to move up the ladder to greater independence, as indicated on the grid in Table 2. The different levels have different grant amounts and also different time and participation requirements, as shown in the table. Small loans, which can be repaid in cash or community service, are available to help participants find and keep work. Two-parent families are eligible for all W-2 services if the families meet income and asset restrictions, although many services are restricted to the parent deemed most likely to be the primary earner. W-2 recipients in the two lower tiers technically receive a monthly grant, which drops by $5.15 for each hour of failure to participate without good cause.

Unlike the AFDC program, the level of W-2 assistance does not depend on family size, but only on the case head's hours of participation and level on the W-2 self-sufficiency ladder. Also unlike AFDC, W-2 is not statutorily identified as an entitlement. Participation in the overall program is limited to five years, the maximum period for which the federal government will support most participants under TANF. Each level on the self-sufficiency ladder also has time limits, with extensions possible on a case-by-case basis. Moreover, W-2 eliminates the previous practice under which child support income beyond the first $50 in a month goes to public agencies to reimburse welfare expenditures; most W-2 participants keep all child support paid on their behalf.

The W-2 program has a work-first emphasis and provides little support for formal education. The program does, however, offer child care and intends to offer health care assistance. The child care

Table 2
Key Provisions of W-2

Level of W-2	Basic Income Package	Time Required of Recipients	Program Time Limits	Estimated Child Care Co-pays ($/mo.)	
				Licensed Care	Certified Care
Unsubsidized Employment	Market wage + Food Stamps + EITC	40 hrs/wk standard	None	$101–$134	$71–$92
Trial Job (W-2 pays maximum of $300/mo. to the employer)	At least minimum wage + Food Stamps + EITC	40 hrs/wk standard	Per job: 3 mo. with an option for one 3-mo. Extension; total 24 mo.	$55	$38
Community Service Job (CSJ)	$673 per mo. + Food Stamps (no EITC)	30 hrs/wk standard; and up to 10 hrs/wk in education and training	Per job: 6 mo. with an option for one 3-mo. extension; total: 24 mo.	$38	$25
W-2 Transition	$628 per mo. + Food Stamps (no EITC)	28 hrs/wk work activities standard; and up to 12 hrs/wk in education and training	24- mo. limit, but extensions permitted on a case-by-case basis	$38	$25

Sources: K. F. Folk, "Welfare Reform under Construction: Wisconsin Works (W-2)," *Focus* 18, no. 1 (special issue 1996): 55–57, and presentation materials created by the Wisconsin Department of Workforce Development.

Note: Estimated child care co-payments are for a three-person family with two children in care and receiving no child support payments. To estimate child care co-payments, the Trial Jobs position is assumed to pay minimum wage ($5.15 per hour, or $858 per month), and the pay for unsubsidized employment is assumed to range from $6–$7 per hour, or $1,000–$1,170 per month.

19

benefit requires a participant co-payment, the level of which is based on family income and on the number of children in care. The co-payments are structured so as not to exceed 16 percent of family income and to be 30 percent lower for child care that has received county-level "certification" than for child care fully licensed by the state.

Wisconsin has also requested approval of a federal waiver to expand the current Medicaid program in a way that would serve most W-2 participants. Under the waiver request, submitted formally in January 1998 and approved to begin on July 1, 1999, the state would offer a new form of insurance, called BadgerCare, which would provide the state's current Medicaid benefits to a broader population, including all W-2 participants who do not have employer-paid insurance. Eligibility for the program extends to families with incomes up to 200 percent of the federal poverty line; those with incomes above 150 percent of the poverty line would pay a monthly premium of 3 percent to 3.5 percent of family income.

In general, the W-2 program reflects efforts by program planners to adhere to six core principles:

1. Parents without a disability should work, and should obtain no entitlement to cash assistance in the absence of work.

2. Expectations for success in the labor market should be high; custodial parents will live up or down to the expectations imposed upon them.

3. All cash benefits should be time-limited.

4. Government programs should provide child care and health care assistance to the working poor, defined in W-2 as families with incomes up to 200 percent of the federal poverty line, not just to public assistance recipients. (W-2 grants and employment assistance are available only to families with incomes below 115 percent of the poverty line.)

5. Those who receive grants and other benefits should face the conditions that affect the working poor: grant recipients should have to work; their first grant check should come only after a period of work; workers who receive public child care assistance and health care insurance should have to pay part of the

cost of their benefits; and program participants should receive all child support paid on behalf of their resident children.

6. Competition to meet selected outcome criteria, not government monopolies, should determine who administers public assistance. Key administrative choices ought not rest upon traditional relations between the state and its counties or traditional conceptions that only public employees should have access to sensitive information and control program benefits.

Although comparative judgments concerning TANF programs nationally must be imperfect, owing to the difficulty of understanding all of them in sufficient detail, at least three key features of W-2 are unusual and perhaps unique among state TANF programs. First, except for W-2 participants in the lowest tier of the program, the only income available is through work, and financial penalties for failure to work start immediately. Second, W-2 contains less social contract language in which the state and the public assistance recipient agree on reciprocal obligations — the one side to make opportunities available and the other to pursue those opportunities — than is the case in many states. The difference between Wisconsin and some other states in this regard is subtle but meaningful. W-2 certainly provides help to program participants, especially with child care and health care. Moreover, the administrative rules for W-2 require local agencies "in consultation with the W-2 participant [to] develop a written employability plan for a W-2 participant which includes the participant's W-2 employment position placement, required activities . . . and an unsubsidized employment goal." The state's W-2 policy document also allows FEPs to excuse participants from work requirements if child care is unavailable. But unlike many states, the FEP has complete discretion to make this determination of child care unavailability and complete authority to determine whether a participant needs a subsidized job. An applicant can appeal a decision of the FEP to the W-2 agency, which must rule on the FEP's decision within 45 days. Even if the appeal is successful, however, the applicant receives no back payment for the appeal period (Wisconsin Department of Workforce Development, 1997, p. iv-18). Although some FEPs may alter these emphases in their daily practice, the primary focus of W-2 is on the participant's obligations to follow the employability plan or, if considered ready for an unsubsidized job, to secure one. The emphasis is not on the responsibilities of the state or the W-2 agency to find them a job or train them for emerging opportunities.

The third atypical feature of W-2 is its treatment of child support. With the exception of 4,000 families included in a control group for evaluation purposes, all other W-2 families will be able to keep all child support paid on their behalf. This marks a change from the policy that existed under AFDC, when a family could keep only $50 per month of child support paid on the family's behalf. Any additional child support reimbursed the state and federal governments for their AFDC expenditures. Wisconsin is the only state that has chosen to pass through all child support to the resident parent. In fact, 30 states plus the District of Columbia have used their new flexibility under TANF to move in the opposite direction, keeping for the government all child support paid on behalf of a TANF family (U.S. Department of Health and Human Services, 1997).

The Chapters in This Volume

The chapters in this volume address both general evaluation issues and specific applications to the W-2 program. The initial chapters by Corbett, Cancian and Wolfe, Cain, and Haveman deal with fairly general issues, and the chapters that follow address W-2 more specifically.

In his beginning chapter, Thomas Corbett provides an overview of the evaluation problem. Corbett stresses that the evaluation problem in the current era of welfare reform will challenge traditional evaluation methods. He stresses that conventional impact analyses will be difficult to conduct because experimental methodologies will be impossible and nonexperimental methods will be, as always, subject to multiple interpretations. Moreover, he points out that process and implementation will be more important to welfare reform evaluation than they have been in the past. The reduced role of the federal government in evaluation is another significant feature of this round of welfare reform, according to Corbett. This implies that the varieties of evaluation strategies across states will be much greater than in the past and there is some danger of inadequate evaluation in some states. Finally, Corbett notes that the emphasis of the new round of welfare reforms on changing individual behavior provides another new, major challenge.

Corbett provides a useful history of the way in which the waiver process developed in the 1980s and the role of evaluation in that process. He then goes into great detail on the types of attributes that new welfare reforms are taking, and how they differ markedly from those in past reform efforts. Multiple characteristics of the welfare system are changed at the same time, and complexity will increase as different participants are treated differently. These developments make evaluation difficult, for they leave unclear the most desirable counterfactual, the appropriate unit of analysis, the target group of interest, the role of implementation analysis, and whether it is desirable or undesirable to capture local diversity and discretion in the evaluation. Corbett concludes by recommending the development of a common set of standards for evaluation, that expert review panels be formed, and that a strategy for diffusing information be developed.

In their paper, Cancian and Wolfe discuss the variety of different outcomes that might be considered in a welfare program evaluation and what constituencies exist for different types of outcomes, and they outline a number of trade-offs that arise in making these choices. Constituencies who have an interest in welfare reform outcomes include the affected families themselves, citizens, government officeholders, and program administrators, but also private charities, employers, schools and teachers, and members of the medical community. Because different constituencies have different interests, Cancian and Wolfe show that several trade-offs will arise. One trade-off is between studying a fairly narrow population that is served by the program vs. a broader population that is potentially affected. Many of the issues here are data-oriented because broad samples come from different data sets than those with necessary numbers of program participants. A second trade-off is between individual vs. community-based analysis. One example is that a new TANF program may have community-wide impacts that extend beyond the particular individual recipients affected. A third trade-off is between evaluation and monitoring, for evaluation is a causal inquiry which requires a well-defined counterfactual, whereas monitoring requires only collecting data on individuals over time. A fourth trade-off is that between a short and long time frame. Some income and labor market effects may occur quickly, but some effects (e.g., those on children) may occur more slowly.

Cancian and Wolfe apply these trade-offs to a consideration of four specific outcomes: work requirements, child care, child health, and family formation. For each they delineate a specific set of outcomes to be examined and whether each applies to a narrow or broad population. They then discuss the tradeoffs between individual and community-level study, between evaluation and monitoring, and between short and long time frames for each. Cancian and Wolfe conclude that priorities will have to be established given limitations in resources, and they offer the view that priority should be given to outcomes that can be simply monitored instead of evaluated, to outcomes that can be measured with administrative data, and to broad population outcomes that can be examined with existing national-level data sets.

Turning to the issue of evaluation methodology, Cain considers the usefulness of controlled experimentation in the new era of welfare reform. He begins by considering a traditional experiment with randomized experimentals and controls which tests the effect of a specific training program on welfare recipients. Two shortcomings of such experiments are that they would not detect entry effects and that they would not detect market-wide effects. Despite these drawbacks, such an experiment would be useful if the programs, populations, and outcomes are narrow and well-defined. However, the new welfare reforms are different and pose two major problems for controlled experiments, according to Cain. One is that the appropriate counterfactual of interest to policy makers is unclear, for the old welfare system is clearly not the alternative of interest, but it is not clear what other bundle of policies is. Another is that the effects of the new welfare are likely to be so broad in terms of markets, program services, and culture that any small-scale experiment will miss important outcomes and will yield inaccurate answers because the controls are likely to be affected. Cain points out other important issues in experiments that would create problems, including ethical issues, a sufficiently long time frame, the problem of continually evolving programmatic environment, and the lack of a clear-cut "before." Cain concludes that controlled experiments are not a practical method for evaluating the new welfare reforms.

Cain proposes instead that evaluators consider gathering longitudinal data across multiple states with different programs, while acknowledging the potential problems with cross-state comparisons. He proposes specific ways to control for confounding cross-state differences and to utilize the variety of programs implemented in different states. Cain ends up recommending evaluation within the traditional framework of a theoretically based nonexperimental study.

Robert Haveman investigates alternative designs for evaluating national welfare reforms as well. Haveman begins by noting the characteristics of the new welfare reforms that will create difficulties for national program evaluation — the fact that every state can design its own program, that state-level conditions will be changing at the same time as programs are implemented, that the speed of implementation will vary across states, and that the scale of the welfare within states is very large. Haveman then lays out the features of an "ideal" evaluation and develops basic principles for securing reliable evaluations. The latter include the need to specify precisely the counterfactual to the policy and that the outcomes under both policy and counterfactual be measurable. Haveman then uses these features and principles to consider experimental designs, comparison site designs, and pre-post designs. He concludes that experimental designs have a fatal flaw when applied to policies that change the culture in a state, for controls will be affected by that change as well. He also concludes that comparison site designs will run the risk of comparing noncomparable states, and that because all states have a "current policy" in effect, none provides an appropriate counterfactual. The pre-post design, while having the problem of separating program effects from other "state-of-the-world" changes, at least clearly identifies the with- and without-program groups and clearly identifies different policy regimes, or states of the world. Haveman then specifically considers the Wisconsin Works program and concludes that the pre-post is most feasible of the evaluation options, in part because the limitations of the experimental and comparison site designs are even greater. He ends his chapter by proposing a specific data collection strategy for a pre-post evaluation of the W-2 program.

The remaining chapters in the volume turn specifically to the Wisconsin Works program. The first chapter in this series, by Kaplan and Meyer, proposes in great detail a specific evaluation plan for the W-2 program. Kaplan and Meyer propose an evaluation built around six central impact domains — income, dependency, child care, child welfare, health status, and living arrangements and family structure — and propose a basic evaluation that focuses on individuals rather than other groups. Like Haveman, they propose a pre-post design and they also propose to rely primarily on administrative data for cost reasons, including tax, unemployment insurance earnings, W-2, and food stamp records. Then, for each of the six domains, they consider: (1) the likely effects of W-2 on those outcomes, (2) what data, comparison group, and analysis approach should be used, and (3) what issues and limitations would arise. For example, for the study of the impact of W-2 on income, they propose a variety of comparisons of W-2 and AFDC recipients before and after the implementation of W-2, both new entrants and current participants, and to compare the incomes of these groups for several years (up to seven) after the date they are observed on welfare. Thus, for example, they would compare incomes of 1988 AFDC recipients from 1989 to 1995 to the incomes of 1998 W-2 recipients from 1995 to 2005. To examine entry effects, they propose to draw two similar samples of low-income families based on Wisconsin tax records and to follow them in the same manner as the recipient samples. They then consider specific data issues such as the definition of income, definition of W-2 recipient, and what variables to hold constant in the analysis. They then conduct a similarly detailed treatment of the other five domains of interest. Kaplan and Meyer also consider several secondary outcomes, such as homelessness, residential mobility, health insurance coverage, and effects on children with disabilities.

Four papers on process analysis and data issues follow. The first, by Corbett and Boehnen, focuses on process analysis. Corbett and Boehnen distinguish process analysis from other types of evaluation and then consider the components of a process analysis, including a description of the implementation of the program, an analysis of the discrepancy between intended and actual sequences of activities, a participation analysis, as well as analyses of dosage or intensity, continuity of program engagement, program coherence, cross-site comparisons, and overall quality. They then outline the key institutional actors in the W-2 program at a very detailed level, down to the receptionist who performs gatekeeping functions, and the key procedural steps in the program, including signaling, gatekeeping, triage/plan development, participation/monitoring, review/adjustment, and exit/follow-up. Corbett and Boehnen also show the client and participant service flow in W-2. They then turn to local variation in implementation in Wisconsin and to the key problem of measurement of participant experiences and participant flow, and discuss a variety of data sources that might be used for such measurement.

In the next chapter, Holden and Reynolds also discuss process analysis. They list three reasons that a process analysis is an essential supplement to an "outcomes" evaluation: to validate that program services were in fact delivered in the way assumed in the outcome analysis, to determine why a program did or did not work according to the outcome analysis, and to promote replication of the program in the future and therefore the utilization of the evaluation results for future programs. Holden and Reynolds also list key specific questions that should be addressed in a process analysis, including whether administrative services were in fact in place, whether services were delivered to the appropriate target population, whether there was variation in program services and administration across sites, whether the delivery of program services changed over time, and whether program services can be validly linked to program outcomes. The authors then turn to a discussion of the W-2 program and stress the complexity of the program services and that service delivery is very likely to vary substantially across areas within the state. Holden and Reynolds list the processes that will be important to the outcomes studied by other papers in this volume and then discuss the data necessary for assessing process. They conclude that the data gathering for a process analysis of W-2 will be the most challenging part of the task.

The chapter by David deals with the issues in measuring income for the W-2 population and for a non-W-2 population with administrative records. David proposes to match the W-2 administrative data base with Wisconsin tax record administrative data for a basic data set. He then assesses the utility of these sources of cross-section and panel data on income and other characteristics and shows how a matched beneficiary data-tax return panel could be constructed from Wisconsin records.

The last five chapters in the volume consider different specific outcome domains in a W-2 evaluation. The first, by Sandefur and Martin, discusses alternatives for collecting and analyzing data on family structure, maternal health, and child health in the context of evaluating W-2. The authors first develop hypotheses regarding how W-2 should affect the outcomes of interest. Based on the changes from AFDC to W-2, they hypothesize that W-2 should lead to reduced out-of-wedlock childbearing; they conclude that the impact of W-2 on maternal and child health is ambiguous in direction. Much of the data that would be required for an evaluation on the topics discussed by Sandefur and Martin can be obtained from administrative data sources, but they conclude that several administrative data sources would have to be merged, that some additional data would have to be collected through surveys, and that the

National Longitudinal Survey of Youth (NLSY) includes many of the questions that would be needed for the evaluation.

Karen Folk and Marianne Bloch discuss how the child care services under W-2 can be evaluated. Folk and Bloch begin by noting that child care has been shown to be the greatest barrier to the employment of mothers of young children. They go on to note that an unusual feature of regulated child care in Wisconsin is the presence of a three-tier system of child care — licensed, certified, and provisionally certified providers. Folk and Bloch predict several effects of W-2 child care provisions. First, the strict work requirements of W-2 should lead to a large increase in the demand for child care that exceeds supply, especially in the short run. Second, the W-2 co-payment schedule may lower net income for some families relative to pre-W-2 levels. Third, the multi-tiered system can lead to changes in the quality of child care provided, but the direction will vary among families. The authors discuss the uses of various forms of administrative data, but they suggest that longitudinal data starting prior to implementation of W-2 will be required to fully answer the questions of interest. The more qualified licensed care facilities cost W-2 families more than certified facilities, so the W-2 recipients have an incentive to use the lower-quality care.

Daniel Meyer, Maria Cancian, and Emma Caspar describe the evaluation of child support under W-2 that they are undertaking. Wisconsin is evaluating the new policy under an experimental design in which the control group receives a smaller pass-through of child support. Because this component of the W-2 program is being evaluated with an experimental design, some of the problems encountered in evaluating the other components of W-2 are not present in the child support evaluation. They note, however, that some of the outcomes may take a long time to take effect. The authors note that outcomes of interest include formal child support, informal child support, paternity establishment, and earnings of both the custodial and noncustodial parents.

George Jesien, Caroline Hoffman, and Thomas Kaplan analyze the potential effects of W-2 on children under age three with developmental disabilities. Jesien and his colleagues note that having a child with developmental disabilities places additional demands on families' financial, time, and emotional resources. Of the estimated 7,000 families in the state with a child under three with a diagnosed disability, 2,250 will be required to meet the work requirements of

W-2. The authors suggest outcomes of interest include the ability of the family to remain together, the ability of parents to participate in the services and programs for their disabled children, and the health and well-being of the disabled children subject to W-2. The availability of good records on disabled children prior to the implementation of W-2 might permit a pre-post approach to an evaluation, but the authors state that such an evaluation would be complicated by other changes that occurred about the same time that W-2 was implemented, such as tightening of eligibility for supplemental security income (SSI) because of the Supreme Court's Zebley decision. The authors suggest three approaches to the evaluation: case studies on a number of families with eligible children, a panel study to trace developments of selected families with children with disabilities, and a review of administrative records.

The chapter by Mark Courtney discusses how to evaluate the child welfare services component of W-2. Courtney notes that W-2 is likely to have mixed financial effects on families needing foster care and related services. Some families will benefit from the greater earnings induced by the program, but others may lose income if they cannot or choose not to meet the work requirements of the program. Courtney raises some of the difficult issues that must be faced in evaluating the welfare services component of W-2. He notes that use of out-of-home care is one outcome of interest that should be easy to measure, but maltreatment of children, another outcome of interest, will be much harder to capture. Courtney then weighs the strengths and weaknesses of alternative evaluation strategies. Administrative data often have many advantages, but in this instance pre-W-2 administrative data on foster care entry and child maltreatment are not available. Given the data limitations, Courtney recommends that a panel study of W-2 children be initiated, although given the rarity of some of the outcomes of interest, the sample would have to be quite large to provide meaningful results. Finally, Courtney suggests that experimentation at the county level be considered.

References

Campbell, D. T. and J. C. Stanley. *Experimental and Quasi-Experimental Designs for Research*. Skokie, IL: Rand-McNally, 1966.

Johnston, J. M. and K. Lindaman. "Implementing Welfare Reform in Kansas: Politics and Administration." Paper presented at the Annual Conference of the Midwest Political Science Association, April 23, 1998.

Research Triangle Institute (RTI). *Final Report: Evaluation of the 1981 Amendments.* Research Triangle Park, NC: Research Triangle Institute, 1983.

Rossi, P. and H. Freeman. *Evaluation: A Systematic Approach.* Newbury Park, CA: Sage, 1993.

U.S. Department of Health and Human Services, Office of Child Support Enforcement. *Child Support Report.* Washington, DC: Department of Health and Human Services, December 1997.

Wisconsin Department of Workforce Development. *Wisconsin Works Policy.* Madison, WI: Department of Workforce Development, 1997.

Endnotes

1   To simplify the discussion, we ignore the AFDC-UP program here.

2   For some approaches, such as caseload modeling, it is not necessary to establish a population base for drawing the population of interest.

3   The method of "selection bias modeling," associated with a certain tradition in econometrics, is sometimes associated with these methods as well. However, it is in fact not a separate method from any of those presented in the table, each of which could be formulated as a "selection bias model."

4   The period that can be analyzed depends on more than just the availability of data. For example, New Jersey officials warned us that data prior to 1978 were of uncertain quality. Also, if the program structure changes in major ways, it may not be advisable to assume that the same model applies before and after the change. For example, the changes instituted by OBRA in 1981 may make it unadvisable to use pre-OBRA data in some states.

SECTION I

OVERVIEW AND OUTCOMES

1

The Next Generation of Welfare Reforms: An Assessment of the Evaluation Challenge

Thomas Corbett
Institute for Research on Poverty and
School of Social Work
University of Wisconsin – Madison

Introduction

The current era of welfare reform will profoundly challenge conventional evaluation methods and strategies. In turn, the evaluation community's response to these methodological challenges will inform what is learned from the explosion of experimentation now evidenced throughout the states. At the core of this debate is a concern that conventional protocols and standards for learning about what works no longer apply, at least in any universal sense.

The basic argument is simple. The existing standards for conducting *impact* evaluations based on classic experimental techniques may no longer be feasible nor warranted in those instances where change is ill-defined, ill-controlled, or ever-changing, and where the intent is to fundamentally alter the signals issued to program

35

operators and users. Nonexperimental and quasi-experimental techniques, on the other hand, are seen as always providing findings that are open to alternative interpretations, an unfortunate circumstance when one is attempting to apply science in arenas where norms and values are passionately held. In addition, standards for conducting *implementation* and *process* analyses increasingly are viewed as critical evaluative strategies given the complex character of recent reform initiatives. But we have no accepted standards for doing this kind of work, resulting in findings that lack comparability across studies and which often are viewed with suspicion. In short, the evaluation community may be required to rethink its tools and strategies if it is to respond appropriately to the challenges unleashed by welfare reform and related changes that are reshaping the social safety net.

Though W-2 is the object of attention throughout the papers in this volume, the purpose of this work is broader and more fundamental than exploring the evaluation of any single reform. We use W-2 as an expression of the new forms of reform and as the template against which we view the broader methodological and political challenges facing the evaluation community. It is a unique template, ambitious in scope and dramatic in immediate consequences.

W-2 reflects both the opportunities and risks embodied in the Personal Responsibility and Work Opportunity Reconciliation Act (PRWORA) of 1996. Under this new federal enabling legislation, states have greater flexibility in designing and managing their support programs for poor families with children. Greater flexibility brings increased responsibility and, given the nature of the new legislation, additional risk. There may be greater risk because, under PRWORA, the federal contribution is fixed and will certainly decline in value over time.[1] This suggests that states and local governments will bear the full fiscal risk of policy decisions *at the margin*, after the federal fiscal contribution is exhausted. Thus, states (or whatever level of government assumes ultimate program responsibility) will have a greater stake in obtaining a priori knowledge about the likely consequences of their policy decisions. If policy makers assume certain behavioral responses to a reform and guess wrong, they easily could incur substantial costs or be required somehow to ration services and benefits as budgets come under increased scrutiny.

In an environment of such change and challenge, program evaluations and other forms of analysis become critically important. Knowledge is more valuable in a devolved policy environment, since the decisions vested in local governments are both more complex and more consequential. But though the *value* of knowledge is greater, the *price* of obtaining knowledge also will increase. The federal government will neither mandate that evaluations be conducted, nor ensure that certain methodological standards be maintained, although it continues to play a role.[2] Many jurisdictions will hope to be free riders, letting others incur the fiscal and other costs of performing evaluations while accessing the results.

Complicating the situation is the fact that the next generation of reforms are designed to change behavior rather than simply provide income support, and thus require a whole new relationship between agency and client. As is described in detail below, the emerging reforms are complex, subject to continuing change, and often call for radical alterations in agency culture which, among other things, decentralize decision making and render management control more problematic.

No one, of course, really knows how welfare reform will play out in the long run.[3] States might continue to experiment with new policies and program forms, given that they are freed from most federal regulations, although the 1996 legislation turned out to be quite prescriptive. On the other hand, states might respond with less risk-taking behavior, given that additional fiscal risk is shifted to the states. A third possibility is that states will initially engage in innovative behavior, given that many will experience a fiscal windfall in the short term. After a while, however, they will become more conservative as the federal contribution declines in real terms.

These and related challenges to the evaluation community have come to inform discussions about program evaluative strategies.[4] Over time, interest in developing a coherent response to what might be called the evaluation challenge has emerged. We hope these papers are a small contribution.

The Context of Reform

The federal role in providing income assistance to poor families with children was established under Title IV-A of the 1935 Social Security Act, which provided fiscal resources enabling states to assist needy children without fathers. The states defined "need," set their own benefit levels, established within federal limitations the income and resource limits for eligibility, and administered the program. Title IV-A was not particularly controversial, as it accorded fiscal relief to hard-pressed states while retaining substantial state flexibility and control over the program. But increased federal regulatory oversight eventually followed, particularly in the late 1960s and the 1970s, when stronger rights were attached to beneficiaries and the benefits themselves came to be viewed as an entitlement. Though states always retained some program control — to set welfare guarantee levels, for example — the locus of control over policy development clearly had shifted to Washington by the early 1970s. Full federal control almost became a reality in the form of President Nixon's proposed Family Assistance Plan (FAP), which in effect would have instituted a federally guaranteed income floor under all families.[5]

Within a decade, the debate over where to locate program control was engaged once again. Since 1962, the Secretary of the U.S. Department of Health and Human Services has had authority to waive statutory program requirements to permit states to experiment with program elements in order to inform national policy about how to better achieve the objective of aiding children. Until the late 1980s, these Section 1115 waivers were seldom sought by states and rarely granted by federal authorities. That situation began to change, first with the passage of the 1981 Omnibus Budget Reconciliation Act, which gave states some flexibility in designing programs to move recipients from welfare to work, and then in 1986, when the Reagan administration began to encourage those states interested in pursuing waiver experimentation.

The use of waivers increasingly resulted in the devolution of program authority over welfare from Washington to the states. Rather than being granted primarily to add knowledge to national policy deliberations, by the 1990s waivers were being approved to accommodate state preferences concerning policy goals and program strategies. This transformation of purpose unleashed a torrent

38

of state activity and experimentation. In addition to the historical effort directed at enhancing the labor supply of AFDC adult caretakers through work-related policies and programs, other recipient behaviors became the focus of attention. These included personal decisions about marriage and cohabitation; decisions affecting family stability (e.g., divorce and other family composition changes over time); fertility decisions; and the quality of parenting. The thrust of reform activity was increasingly directed toward a new strain of social engineering: employing welfare innovations as strategies for influencing those behaviors society deems important.

Ironically, devolution of program and fiscal responsibility was an established fact, accomplished by means of the waiver process, by the time that the welfare bill was signed by the president. It could be argued that any remaining pretense to a national welfare policy, other than the procedural requirements associated with cost neutrality and certain evaluation requirements, disappeared some time during the first two years of the Clinton administration. Spurred by the rhetoric of the 1992 campaign to "end welfare as we know it," states became bolder in their waiver requests and the federal government clearly signaled that it would seriously entertain dramatic proposals for reform. States were exercising authority by the time PRWORA was enacted.

Since waiver-based activity may provide clues to future policy directions, salient trends from the pre-PRWORA period are worth review. First, the *scope* of waiver activity demonstrated just how extensive devolution was, even before it was formally legislated in August 1996. Over 90 percent of all states and the District of Columbia had obtained at least one approved waiver by that date. The new legislation provides that waivers already granted continue in effect for the duration of the originally granted time. Moreover, the *pace* of state level activity increased during this period.[6]

The *complexity* of state-based welfare demonstrations had also increased. In the early days, a state would request permission to modify a few provisions of the Social Security Act in order to implement one or two new ideas. In the years prior to PRWORA, the number of major changes to program parameters contained in a single waiver request would be in double figures. States increasingly would "borrow" ideas from other jurisdictions and bundle them together in complex reform packages. Delaware's Better Chance initiative, implemented in 1995, is an example of the increasing complexity in welfare waiver demonstrations. This program contained at least 18 major provisions, including a family cap, a 100-hour rule change, time limits, income disregards, a contract for program participation, changes in JOBS requirements, and school attendance and immunization requirements. The Virginia Independence Program, also implemented in 1995, bundles similar provisions, including term limits, family caps, a contract for program participation, as well as many other provisions intended to affect participant behavior.

Perhaps the most important trend evidenced in state demonstration activity involves a shift in program objectives. The demonstrations increasingly stress changes designed to alter critical personal and interpersonal behaviors with proposed welfare reform changes concentrating on helping (or obligating) people to play by society's rules: getting a job, getting married, making responsible fertility decisions, being a good parent, and obeying the law. For example, as late as 1992, only a couple of states had shown interest in the *family cap* concept, in which benefits are not increased when a mother has additional births while on AFDC. By the summer of 1996, about 40 percent of all states had actual or proposed family cap provisions and 18 states had (or had proposed) provisions that required minor parents on assistance to live with their parents or in a supervised setting as a condition of eligibility. Finally, about two-thirds of all states were involved in reforms that explicitly linked welfare benefits with good behaviors, such as students attending school regularly and parents ensuring that their children had all required vaccinations. Social engineering, using AFDC policy to inform and shape a variety of behaviors, had become a primary goal.

The outpouring of investigation associated with waiver-based demonstrations promised significant contributions toward understanding the dynamics of public assistance and for identifying empirically supported programmatic and management improvements. Prior to PRWORA, both Republican and Democratic administrations supported incorporation of an explicit evaluation scheme as a requirement for waiver approval. But we may never learn a great deal from those evaluations, for several reasons. First, many of the experiments in progress contain serious flaws in content and assessment strategy that, should they be completed, will diminish both the management utility and the internal and external validity of the outcomes. Second, PRWORA changes both federal and state incentives for experimentation in ways that diminish the likelihood that most ongoing experiments will be completed. Third, the character of future reforms may be so different from the changes examined in the past that the new demonstrations will not provide much proper instruction about how to proceed in the future — a true discontinuity in policy making.

It took a while for states to take advantage of the flexibility offered through a liberalized Section 1115 policy, but initially tentative experimentation became bolder as state officials gained greater confidence. Moreover, the political popularity of reform could not be ignored by the nation's governors. Whether justified or not, claims of state successes gained widespread media attention while national solutions, such as President Clinton's proposed Work and Responsibility Act of 1994, sputtered in Congress and quickly disappeared from sight.[7] If there was one implicit message that seeped through the policy community at this time, it was that the answer to various welfare conundrums lay outside Washington.

In the old welfare world (just a few years ago), change was limited and incremental and linear. The federal government preserved the basic framework of welfare and controlled the pace and conditions of change. The tools for learning from these experiments had been fairly well developed and standardized by a handful of the top evaluation firms.[8] The new world confronts us with a discontinuity in policy making and imposes new expectations upon the conventional methods found in the evaluation community.

The Next Generation of Reforms

The purpose of traditional welfare programs was to provide some measure of income support. The nominal objective was to redress economic need in the short run. The primary roles of operational personnel were to process information and to validate those data necessary to issue accurate checks to eligible families. The time frame was the monthly accounting period, each month representing a new and distinct set of calculations. Particularly in Wisconsin, where much of the actual case decision making had been automated as far back as the 1970s, little discretion remained in the system.[9]

There are some qualifications to this characterization of welfare administration. Various welfare-to-work initiatives had been around virtually from the time that AFDC had been transformed into an entitlement system in the late 1960s and early 1970s. These activities were, in theory at least, designed to change behavior. However, they often were viewed as tangential to primary welfare functions and were contracted out to service providers located outside the welfare agency boundaries. In all likelihood, the next generation of welfare will not be an extension of what we had in the past, but will constitute a qualitative change from what had existed just a few years before.

The change in organizational culture that W-2 requires can hardly be more pronounced and would probably be catastrophic had the alterations not been going on for a decade now. Among other things, W-2 moves toward a fully work-based approach to assisting low-income families with children, decouples related supports such as child care and health care and child support from the recipient's welfare status, reformulates the signals sent to the community by embedding what remains of welfare within agencies and systems designed to serve the labor market needs of the broader community, and introduces performance-based management incentives into the governance of welfare, including some privatization of key functions. But the specific provisions of W-2 are not what is important; rather, it is the fundamental ways in which traditional welfare has been reshaped on which we must focus.

When AFDC was enacted, the focus was on children. It was assumed that benefits paid for their well-being would enable them to stay with their caretaker (in the overwhelming majority of cases, a widowed female), an arrangement assumed better for the development of the child than substitute care (e.g., in an orphanage) or living with a working mother. By the mid-1960s, the reduction of income poverty became an explicit policy goal. Income strategies, such as the Negative Income Tax schemes, emerged; welfare was transformed into more of an entitlement. By the late 1960s, the focus had shifted to the caretaker, by now mostly women with children whose economic woes typically stemmed from a failed marriage or the failure to marry. The primary concerns were dependency and strategies for moving women into the labor market. The unit of analysis broadened to be the family, first in the form of child support enforcement reforms and later in a concern about adopting pro-marriage and pro-family policies. Most recently, there has been a subtle shift back to the children.[10] Although reform goals concerning the mother (or caretaker) and family remain, it is argued that what really counts are the longer-term prospects for healthy child development.[11] Emerging reform objectives do not fully replace prior goals. Often, they become part of the multiplicity of ends important to reformers.[12]

What sets the new generation of reforms apart is their focus on changing a broad range of personal, interpersonal, and community behaviors. Their emphasis on behavioral change, well beyond the goal of merely enhancing labor market attachment, is the most recent in an historical sequence of shifting and cumulating goals.[13] The emergence of new goals may suggest that new roles and organizational forms are not far behind.

Table 1 lists the attributes that might be said to characterize the new forms of social provision embodied within W-2 and other emerging programs. The benefits-oriented era of cash welfare was a simpler era in many respects. In terms of basic purpose, the goals were fairly limited — get a check out to eligible families accurately and, in some jurisdictions, efficiently. The target groups of interest were limited, mainly the adult recipients who provided the necessary data to process the checks, though on occasion the children might receive some attention. The worker-client orientation tended

Table 1
Emerging Attributes

Traditional	Emerging
benefits	→ behavior
unidimensional	→ multipurpose
limited targets	→ multiple targets
Process-oriented	→ outcome-oriented
Static	→ dynamic
uniformity-focused	→ multidimensional
bureaucratic orientation	→ professional model
Agency-dominated	→ mutual negotiations
vertical communications	→ horizontal communications
autonomous worker	→ collaborative worker
autonomous agency	→ transparent boundaries
risk aversive	→ risk taking

to be uniform, episodic, and routine. The basic recipient-worker relationship often was marked by distrust and suspicion. Getting involved with a recipient might interfere with the primary agency mission, the only one measured and rewarded through the quality control system — getting the checks out to the right families in the correct amount.

The emerging systems are quite different. They focus on individual, family, and community behavioral change, not income support. The new welfare systems will be behavior-oriented rather than income-oriented. By extension, the dominant treatment modalities will shift from income support strategies to service technologies. The new welfare systems will be dynamic rather than static. They take a family at a baseline status and actively work toward changing behavior and attitudes. W-2, for example, expects that participants will ascend the four tiers built into the system, moving up the tiers before "graduating" into the labor market and mainstream society.

The new welfare regimes will be longitudinal in character: Participants' status in the program will not be totally dependent upon their current monthly financial and categorical circumstances. The nature of their involvement will be determined, in part at least, by their experience in the program and the objectives set for (or with) them. Participants are viewed as being in a process and are subject to time limits, both within program components and in an overall sense.

The emerging generation of policy/program interventions are complex and typically introduce numerous changes simultaneously or introduce changes outside of the welfare framework.[14] The new interventions are also characterized by increased policy volatility (continuous change across time) and variability (significant differences across jurisdictions or agencies within a state). The new reforms intend to affect a more diverse set of actors. There are several target populations: adult caretakers, children, and noncustodial parents. W-2, however, is designed to change the attitudes and behaviors of those operating the program in addition to selected populations in the community (e.g., employers, child care providers, etc.). Thus, understanding what each of these groups "experience" is important.

The new welfare regimes will be craft-oriented rather than routinized. Under the old welfare, some of the decisions were fairly complex, but the basic intent was to treat all participants alike. The new reforms are designed to treat participating families as individuals, or in individualized ways. Many involve the negotiation of individualized "social contracts" or "individualized employment plans" and the new systems will be multidimensional rather than unidimensional. An extension of the principle of individualization is the notion that all participants will not proceed through the welfare experience in lock step. They are likely to be tracked along different paths.

The new welfare systems will be characterized by complex decisions that will require a good deal of professionalism and involve a good deal of discretion. And they will be labor intensive. The old welfare involved repetitive, routine decision making. The emphasis was on efficiency and accuracy. Participants who wanted help were referred to other systems. Not surprisingly, administrative costs often were less than 10 cents on the dollar of benefits issued. W-2 and similar reforms require intensive case management and active rather than passive participant-worker interaction.

Future Directions for Research and Policy Evaluation

If the above description represents the future, even in part, what are the implications for the evaluation community? The conventional approach to evaluation has been to change one or two parameters of the existing welfare program, randomly assign participating families into either an experimental or a control group, and to examine net outcomes by a limited number of measures that virtually everyone agreed was important. None of that holds any longer. The next generation of welfare reforms could well have its largest impacts through changing the social norms of society — by increasing the social stigma attached to childbearing out of wedlock, repeat childbearing among those already dependent on welfare, and childbearing among those unable to support their children. The arguments for many of the reforms relate to their power in promoting family values and work ethic. Thus from the parochial perspective of the states implementing the reforms, there is little reason to look beyond whether welfare rolls decline and whether fewer children are being reared out of wedlock. From a broader social view we ought to adopt a more comprehensive and longer-range research and evaluation plan involving multiple goals and assessment strategies.

Even the most basic evaluation issues must be reexamined. How does one establish a counterfactual? How are the correct criterion variables selected? How does one agree upon which target groups to examine? What is the appropriate unit of analysis, individual or case, or agency or county? How does one go about determining overall and component effects, or should we even worry about component effects? Should the implementation analysis be used in a formative way, if that increases policy instability and confounds the impact analysis? Should local discretion and flexibility be curtailed, so that the character of the intervention might better be understood? There are many puzzling questions that evaluators must confront in the future, not all of which lend themselves to simple technical solutions. As the need for good, empirical information increases, the cost and difficulty of obtaining those answers increase commensurately.

A future evaluation agenda should cover not only an assessment of the success of the reforms in meeting their central objectives, but also other possible consequences and the mechanisms through which both intended and unintended consequences occurred. For example, while traditional reforms and their evaluations focused on program participants, the new ones are intended to affect communities. In consequence, population and entry effects are of considerable importance. We also need to understand the context for the findings, in so far as this affects both their interpretation and generalizability to other settings.

As a way of viewing some of the evaluation challenges, we can organize the issues into three categories: major methodological questions; substantive policy changes; and alternate foci of concern, or units of analysis.

The major methodological questions are typically organized in three parts. First, we want to assess implementation and process. Carefully assessing how closely operations reflect policy intent is critical, particularly with complex interventions requiring complicated sequencing of tasks carried out by varied actors representing different institutions. Otherwise, we wind up with "black box" evaluations that are difficult to interpret. Second, we want to assess benefit/cost or cost/effectiveness ratios. Do benefits exceed costs or, at a given cost, do alternative strategies produce differential outcomes? Third, we want to assess "net" outcomes or impacts. This requires comparing outcomes for those exposed to the intervention with an appropriate control or comparison group (the counterfactual), created through random assignment of individuals, sites, or through statistical procedures designed to account for heterogeneity between groups.

The new social policy innovations are intentionally designed to affect several aspects (or domains) of the lives of those exposed to the program. This is a dramatic departure from the limited, linear framework within which earlier demonstrations might be understood. W-2, for example, is designed to effect changes in the following domains: labor supply, skill or human capital development (largely through increased labor force participation), health status, child care arrangements, fertility decisions, family formation and functioning, and child development. Each of these areas raises questions about what outcomes are critical, how the outcomes can be operationalized, what data sources exist and how good they are. Multiple domains also raise questions about interpreting results that may go in contrary directions.

The new reforms raise questions about the appropriate unit of analysis. Are we most interested in the adult caretaker, the family as a whole, the child(ren), the community, the workplace, the service providers? We envision different issues and challenges associated with measuring effects on the following: the adult caretakers(s); the family as a whole; the child, community, and the labor market; and institutional/service providers.

Process, or implementation, evaluations have traditionally been the stepchild of impact evaluations. They have become more important as a host of "black box" welfare-to-work evaluations done in the 1970s and 1980s raised questions about what really was being tested (if anything). But the craft of conducting implementation evaluations is still in its infancy. There are few accepted protocols for how to collect data on complex operational systems, or how to report the findings. The objectivity and comparability of process evaluations must be enhanced.

Impact evaluations, on the other hand, raise important questions about how to establish a counterfactual (no exposure to the program) when the state wants to saturate the county or state. States often have good reasons for this (interest in changing community norms, worries about administrative complexity, or migration effects, etc.). However, statewide programs do complicate the task of making causal inferences.

Recognizing that effects may be evidenced in different domains is one thing. Measuring changes in different domains is quite another. We have pretty good data on welfare utilization and wages earned (but not hours worked or fringe benefits) every three months. Data collection and quality, as well as the interpretability of data, become more problematic as we move toward broader measures. More thought must be given to how best to move beyond the conventional outcomes of welfare utilization, economic well-being, and labor force participation.

Conventional evaluations often have focused on one generation, the adult who is already a program participant (on welfare). Moreover, the focus is on the transition off assistance (or perhaps less reliance on welfare). The new reforms break many of the old conventions. They radically change the meaning of participation, alter the eligible population, and expect to transform community norms, individual and family behaviors, and agency cultures. At a minimum, this means more attention to community effects, entry effects, institutional effects, and perhaps even long-term effects on the low-wage labor market and other macro systems.

Some evaluation issues would cut across any classification scheme. For example, at all levels of analysis, there is the data question. Critical data may not exist, or exist in the right form, or be credible and reliable. The data issue will be explored in relation to the questions within the categories described above; revisions in extant data sources will be discussed; and new data collection recommended, where appropriate.

Next Steps

A number of analysts have been discussing a set of options for pursuing resolutions to the challenges facing the evaluation community.[15] Several strategies have surfaced so far.

Developing Common Standards and Practices

In the absence of a strong federal role in ensuring the application of rigorous methods to program evaluations, it has been proposed that a series of conferences and workshops be conducted to work toward a convergence of methods and practices in the following areas.

Common Terms and Definitions. Even when everyday terms are used, such as "case," or "successful outcome," or "full employment," or "noncompliance," great variation in meaning may occur. Without agreement on the meaning of terms, cross-state comparisons will be difficult.

Common Research Questions. All evaluations start with research questions concerning management and theoretical issues about which empirical information is desired. The questions posed inform all other features of the evaluation — choice of outcomes, choice of methods, and so forth. If a consensus (or movement toward a consensus) could be developed around a set of management and research questions, more comparability across evaluations would be likely.

Common Outcomes of Interest. Defining success in a devolved policy world will be a major challenge and a likely point of contention. Those who select the outcomes of interest and choose how to operationalize those outcomes greatly influence the political agenda of reform. Although local preferences should not be ignored, a core group of common outcomes, consistently operationalized, is needed to anchor state and local evaluations and permit analyses across jurisdictions.

Common Reporting of Findings. Several evaluations conducted by the Manpower Demonstration Research Corporation were influential in part because they reported findings in a predictable and understandable manner. More varied evaluations by an increasing number of evaluators are likely in the future, and standards for reporting results would be helpful.

Consensus Regarding Acceptable Methods. Both process and impact evaluations are difficult to do and both are important. There have never been agreed-upon methods for doing process

49

analyses; consequently, studies permitting cross-site comparisons are not common. Since the classic experimental design may no longer be the *sine qua non* for doing impact analyses, what alternatives are reasonable and acceptable for establishing causal inferences? Establishing minimal standards may not be a reasonable goal; moving toward such standards may be a necessary objective.

Developing "Expert" Review Panels

Program evaluations of reform initiatives will inevitably vary in quality and utility despite efforts toward some consensus. Consequently, it has been proposed that a pool of expert reviewers be established to examine the more important evaluations, for the following purposes:[16]

❖ To isolate which results and findings from an evaluation might be accepted with some degree of confidence. This would be an effort to sort out credible findings from those in which methods or management of an evaluation raise doubt.

❖ To identify and relate credible findings across diverse evaluations in order to build up a body of knowledge based on common findings in diverse program and situational contexts.

❖ To identify findings that seem contradictory and thus may constitute research and management issues that require further study. This is an attempt to identify the cutting-edge issues requiring analytic attention, articulate those issues that require additional study, and possibly suggest ways they might be examined. That is, the panel should push the envelope in terms of issue identification and resolution.

Methodological input is only one dimension of interest. We also want the consumer's perspective, and perhaps even input from the most common producers of program evaluations — the top evaluation firms. Thus, we potentially see panels drawn from academics, state evaluation and policy units, evaluation firms, and the federal government. Mechanisms for ensuring cross-panel communication would be developed. A critical review of current and future evaluations would both enhance their utility and help in the process of improving the next round of PRWORA-motivated assessments.

Information Technology Diffusion and Utilization

A general strategy involving the dissemination of information and "institutional" behavior modification should be developed. Selected target populations and behaviors might include:

❖ State officials. Develop increased appreciation for the necessity and value of evaluations, employ a common core of research questions and outcomes to increase the probability that cross-site comparisons are possible, use methods that permit causal inferences with some confidence.

❖ Evaluation firms. Move toward common terms, definitions, methods of reporting results. Move toward common ways of doing process and implementation analyses. Again, the issue is one of comparability and building up a stock of knowledge.

❖ Academics. Become more involved in policy and program evaluation activities. Develop increased ability to report findings in a way that allows researchers and their work to become more influential and useful to policy makers.

❖ Foundations. Develop common standards to look toward in making awards, improve the technical knowledge of program officers, increase interest in research and evaluation activities.

❖ Federal officials. Increase technical assistance role and continue to play an active, though perhaps less official, role in enhancing the quality of evaluations. Increase the use by federal officials and organizations of neutral, third-party experts to perform review and monitoring functions that can no longer be performed internally.

Influencing these target populations is partly a matter of continuous communication and contact. Dissemination in this context should not be confused with one-way communication of "fact." A coordinated effort to keep the evaluation agenda alive, to move toward common understandings and tools, and to communicate information useful to policy audiences may be what is required. The papers in this volume represent the efforts of one set of researchers struggling with the new welfare realities in one state. This drama will be repeated in state after state, locality after locality. If nothing else, these efforts should help others better understand that they are not alone in the frustrations they encounter as they attempt to explore and understand the next generation of welfare reforms.

Endnotes

1   Even assuming modest inflation rates, the $16.4 billion capped federal commitment may decline by 20 to 25 percent in inflation-adjusted terms over the course of the legislation.

2   On May 20-22, 1998, the Administration for Children and Families in the U.S. Department of Health and Human Services held a conference titled *Evaluating Welfare Reform: Forging Evaluation Partnerships*. Forty-nine states sent representatives. The federal government is still in a position to shape welfare evaluations, even if it cannot dictate how evaluations will be done.

3   While devolving authority over AFDC and other welfare programs to the states has promising features, the notion raises legitimate concerns; these are discussed in Thomas Corbett, "The New Federalism: Monitoring Consequences," *Focus* 18, no. 1 (special issue 1996): 3–4.

4   For example, see *Focus*, vol. 18, no. 1 (special issue 1996), "Monitoring the Effects of the New Federalism."

5   FAP failed, but welfare for the blind, disabled, and aged was largely federalized and the food stamp program was extended to all jurisdictions, creating what some regarded as an in-kind negative income tax.

6   For a discussion of welfare waivers, see Elisabeth Boehnen and Thomas Corbett, "Welfare Waivers: Some Salient Trends," *Focus* 18, no. 1 (special issue 1996): 34–37.

7   Clinton's proposed reform was submitted to several committees on June 21, 1994, after more than a year of development. The proposed legislation, including explanatory text, was 622 pages in length. It was too long and complicated to get a fair hearing in a Congress that was increasingly concerned with mid-term elections. The 1994 Congressional election results buried any hope for the president's proposal and dramatically shifted the debate.

8   Basically, the Manpower Demonstration Research Corporation, Mathematica Policy Research, Abt Associates, Urban Institute, and a handful of others refined basic approaches that had been developed partly at The Institute for Research on Poverty in the late 1960s and early 1970s, when the methods for evaluating the Negative Income Tax and Supported Work proposals were developed.

9   The Computer Reporting Network (CRN) was developed in the 1970s. Prior to that, the governing rules of welfare in Wisconsin permitted a great deal of discretion. CRN automated virtually all core decisions regarding the determination of eligibility and the calculation of benefits. Permissive language in the welfare manuals — the use of words such as *may* — were replaced by nondiscretionary words such as *shall*.

10 This shift was evidenced by the inclusion of child outcomes in the evaluation of the JOBS provisions included in the Family Support Act of 1988.

Child Trends, under contract to the Manpower Demonstration Research Corporation (MDRC), is focusing on this aspect of the evaluation.

11 For example, see Deborah A. Phillips and Anne Bridgman, eds., *New Findings on Children, Families, and Economic Self-Sufficiency: Summary of a Research Briefing* (Washington, DC: National Academy Press, 1995).

12 These subtle transitions are important to the reform debate and are not always fully appreciated. The debate has responded to the demographic earthquake evidenced in this country. Both divorce and nonmarital births have increased sharply over the last thirty years. In 1960, only 5 percent of births occurred outside of marriage. In 1993, the comparable number was 31 percent. In 1960, the divorce rate was 9 per thousand married women; that had grown to 21 in 1990. In 1970, less than 12 percent of all families with children were headed by a single parent (3.4 million); that percentage had risen to nearly 27 percent by 1994 (9.8 million).

13 Of course, the more traditional question has been the relationship between welfare and work, mothers and the labor force. The relationship between mothers and work also changed dramatically over time. At the inception of AFDC, less than one-quarter of all women were in the labor force, and mothers were disproportionately underrepresented. Societal norms did not expect them to work and many firms as a matter of policy encouraged mothers (or women who married) to leave. Over the post-war decades, the labor market participation of women in general, mothers in particular, began to rise, at some periods increasing by one percentage point a year. By the early 1960s, the question of whether welfare mothers ought to work had been engaged. By the 1990s, there was little debate on that point. Societal norms now accepted that mothers, even with young children, were obliged to be self-sufficient. Further, a host of welfare-to-work experiments had apparently demonstrated that such programs were feasible and at least modestly effective.

14 Simply put, welfare-type programs target benefits on the income and asset poor and on vulnerable families (e.g., single-parent families with children). Such targeting inevitably creates perverse incentives and so many recent reforms, including W-2, attempt to lessen the extent to which targeting is a policy attribute (e.g., the attempts in W-2 to decouple child support, child care, and health care from welfare status).

15 The key persons outside the Institute for Research on Poverty who are involved in these discussions are Larry Aber and Barbara Blum at the National Center for Children in Poverty; Howard Rolston, Ann Segal, Donald Oellerich, and Matthew Stagner at the U.S. Department of Health and Human Services; Rebecca Blank at the Joint Center for Poverty Research, Northwestern University and University of Chicago; and Barry Van Lare and Rikki Kramer at the Welfare Information Network.

16 Douglas Besharov, in fact, has launched such a review panel as part of his Welfare Reform Academy, located at the School of Public Affairs, University of Maryland.

2

Outcomes of Interest, Evaluation Constituencies, and the Necessary Trade-Offs

Maria Cancian
La Follette Institute of Public Affairs
School of Social Work
University of Wisconsin — Madison

Barbara Wolfe
Departments of Economics
and Preventive Medicine
University of Wisconsin — Madison

Under Title I of the welfare reform bill of 1996, which establishes the Temporary Assistance for Needy Families Block Grants (TANF), broad-based welfare reform will take place in most, if not all, states. Will state-based, comprehensive welfare reform be a success? How will we know? In contrast to limited policy changes with clearly defined goals, the critical outcomes of interest for current reforms are a matter of debate. Even setting aside problems of measurement and data collection, no clear consensus exists on how to define success. This paper begins to identify the outcomes of interest for evaluating the reforms that will take place in the wake of TANF.

Wisconsin has been a leader in welfare reform. The Wisconsin Works (or W-2) plan is substantially more developed than are the plans of most states. We use W-2 as a point of reference in the following discussion, but expect that most of the issues raised will apply to other states as well.[1]

Why a Broadly Focused Evaluation?

For a number of reasons, the outcomes of interest to evaluate current reforms will be broader than simply measures of impacts on welfare participants and their families. First, federal welfare reform legislation has moved primary responsibility for welfare design to the states. With block grants, states will have more freedom to design programs for needy families and will more fully absorb the financial consequences of their decisions. This raises a host of issues regarding the *fiscal and administrative responsibilities* of federal, state, and local governments. As the new system develops, evaluations will have to consider the impact at each of these government levels of programs that replace Aid to Families with Dependent Children (AFDC), JOBS, and Emergency Assistance.

Under the new program there is no individual entitlement. States are free to determine which families receive assistance and under what circumstances. This raises questions of *accessibility*. There is no longer an assumption that state residents are all guaranteed equal benefits, given equal income and family size.

Block grants mean greater state autonomy and variation in programs across states, raising issues of *interstate equity*. Historically, substantial cross-state variation in the level of AFDC benefits has occurred. Under the new legislation, program structure and eligibility standards are expected to vary even more substantially. In addition, because the 60-month lifetime cash benefit limit prevails across states, participants in a low-benefit state are not only receiving lower benefits, but are also reducing their opportunity to receive benefits in a higher-benefit state at a later time.

The scale and timing of work requirements increases the potential for important impacts on *labor market and social institutions*. TANF work requirements are substantial and some state plans call for most recipients to be employed almost immediately. Concerns have been raised about the potential impact of these initiatives on the low-wage labor market as well as on the market for child care. Because almost all recipients are expected to make dramatic behavioral changes over a short period of time, the potential for impacts outside the participant community are substantial.

Finally, the goals of welfare reform go beyond income support. TANF was designed to "reinforce appropriate behavior." The philosophy and goals of TANF emphasize work, support by both parents of their children, providing only requested or needed services, and reliance on market and performance mechanisms for program implementation. For example, in Wisconsin the program states that W-2 "will demand more of participants, but in the long run it will provide independence and a future." Proponents of W-2 and TANF have argued that welfare reform will encourage *substantial behavioral changes*. This suggests that an evaluation should include an assessment of the extent to which reforms achieve these goals.

Trade-Offs for an Evaluation:
Evaluation Questions and the Unit of Analysis

There are a very large number of potentially interesting outcomes. In part because the unit of analysis (e.g., individuals, households, or communities) and data needs differ according to the particular outcome, it will be necessary to prioritize. However, different constituencies have different questions, and hence are likely to be interested in alternative outcomes based on widely differing units of analysis. For example, analysts of welfare reform are interested in impacts on the population eligible (or formerly eligible) for AFDC, on all low-income persons, and on the general community. Questions concerning the fiscal and administrative aspects of welfare reform do not speak directly to the impacts on families, but are clearly of interest to citizens and government officeholders, especially in the context of devolution. Program participants also have an interest in evaluations of the impact of programs on their quality of life, while program administrators are likely to be interested in outcomes that capture the impact of the decisions they make at the local level. And there exist a number of other constituencies who have direct and indirect interests in the outcomes of reforms: private charities, employers, schools and teachers, doctors' offices and clinics are examples.

In sum, many constituencies are interested in the outcomes of welfare reform. However, they are not all interested in the same type of question. Their interests are sufficiently diverse that multiple units of analysis and approaches would be required to satisfy all constituencies. We expect that any evaluation of welfare reform will be done from the perspective of one or more constituencies and their interests will determine the outcomes examined. In determining the focus of evaluation efforts, a number of trade-offs will be faced. Below we distinguish four aspects of evaluations for which trade-off and alternative approaches will need to be considered.

Trade-Off 1: The Population Served vs. Broader Population

In order to understand the consequences of reform for the eligible and potentially eligible population, we require data on a representative sample of families who were previously eligible. However, since past as well as future eligibles form only a small part of any state's total population, very few of them appear in existing national data sets such as the Current Population Survey (CPS) or the Survey of Income and Program Participation (SIPP), or state samples such as the Wisconsin Family Health Survey. Even a very large general household sample would yield only a small number of eligibles and their children. Therefore, for those interested in this particular population, a special survey sample, or substantial oversampling of current welfare users, with some addition of low-income families and young teens at high risk of pregnancy, would be preferable. This sample or oversampling would allow studies of the impact of welfare reform on those most directly affected — recipients or would-be recipients. Simple statistical power calculations could be used to learn the needed sample size to observe even a small change in this group.

The sampling issue is even more critical for the study of smaller populations; for example, children with disabilities, immigrants with low incomes, or infants. For these groups, a household survey will have very limited numbers of observations. The bottom line on this is simple — the smaller the group within the total population, the greater the need to oversample the particular subpopulations to learn about impacts on this group.

On the other hand, in order to learn what proportion of the population uses any services, the type of jobs they enter, the performance of the labor market, etc., it is necessary to have a sample of all households — participants and nonparticipants. This will also provide the ability to analyze unmet needs in the population (such as medical care for a chronic illness, or adequate child care) as well as permitting us to observe *changes* in the level of unmet needs. For analysis of the state's overall population, the sample sizes of recipients and potential recipients are not very important. Hence there is a direct trade-off: The smaller the proportion of any group of interest (for example, disabled children), the greater the need to oversample, but the lower the value of the oversampled cases to the overall analysis. In considering this trade-off, it is important to recognize another complicating factor: It usually costs more per respondent to sample a targeted group than to conduct a general household survey.[2]

Trade-Off 2:
Individual vs. Community-Based Analysis

A second trade-off exists between using the local community as the basis of data collection versus a sample of individuals (households) across a state. (Both may oversample a targeted population or may focus on the general or only the low-income population.) Underlying conditions that may significantly influence the impacts of TANF are likely to differ across communities in measurable ways — level of unemployment, types of firms, amount and quality of child care, quality and availability of low-cost housing, ratio of medical doctors to population, for example. Resources allocated to TANF programs and the implementation of a program may also differ across communities. Hence an evaluation that considers program components and community conditions is likely to be a far better and more comprehensive evaluation. But, because collecting such data is expensive, not all communities would be included. Thus there is a trade-off between collecting data that is representative of the state versus those that could inform us about impacts in a local, county, or any smaller area in which we might have an interest.

Some of the outcomes that analysts, policy makers, citizens, and participants are interested in will affect children or their families across the state — for example, is the low-income population of the state better off along a variety of dimensions under a new TANF program than it would have been under prior policies? To answer this question, we need statewide representative data. Many government officials and analysts are instead, or also, interested in the effects of policy implementation and service provision at the state and community level on individuals (households) and/or on firms, schools, and other institutions. Related questions of interest include variation in the impact of a new program as a result of other environmental factors. For example, what is the impact in a community where there is near full employment, in rural areas or small towns, or in communities in which there is adequate child care versus those with waiting lists? To answer these questions and better understand differences across communities, data must be collected within communities or neighborhoods. Useful community data might include not only state data on services and implementation (such as the proportion of the participating population placed in private sector jobs within two months, or the waiting list for positions in licensed child care centers), but also information from such diverse organizations as employers, community organizations, employment offices, the school system, and private charities. Because these data are expensive to collect, there is incentive to consider only a few communities. However, it is difficult to evaluate statewide outcomes on the basis of data collected in a limited set of communities. In addition, concentrating on a few communities clearly limits the degrees of freedom in the analysis of the impact of community differences on the population(s) of interest.[3]

Trade-Off 3: Evaluation vs. Monitoring

A third trade-off exists between (1) evaluating the overall impact of the new program, (2) comparing implementation and impacts across communities, and (3) simply monitoring outcomes. Evaluation attempts to establish causal relationships; monitoring simply tracks various outcomes of interest. To evaluate the overall impact, we need measures of the counterfactual (i.e., what the outcomes would have been if the program had not been changed). This means we require data that capture the earlier outcome, adjusted to account for other exogenous changes that would have affected outcomes even in the absence of the new program. In cases where we can measure outcomes pre- and post-reform by means of administrative data or existing survey or other data, we will have some ability to evaluate welfare reform. In other cases data to establish an appropriate counterfactual may not exist, and an evaluation of the program impact will be far more difficult than a comparison across sites or simple tracking of outcomes over time. Cross-site comparisons and simple monitoring (i.e., tracking of performance measures over time) can give us important information on program implementation and effectiveness and on critical areas requiring further policy change. If we do not collect post-reform measures of outcomes because, for example, *pre*-reform period information is unavailable, we may omit outcomes that are of significant importance for a variety of audiences. Hence we may wish to compromise and not require that only outcomes that can be evaluated be considered, even though evaluation remains our primary goal.

Trade-Off 4: Short vs. Long Time Frame

Finally, the fourth trade-off involves the desired time frame. Some outcome measures would be useful immediately, such as labor market and income measures. Some, however, are longer-term in nature, such as the impact of reduced parental time on young children. To assess that full outcome, many years will have to pass (which makes data collection and any causal inference even more difficult). Moreover, for some outcomes, the short run and longer run may differ. In the very short run, with a full-employment economy the labor market outcomes may be quite positive; but if there is a subsequent downturn in the economy, these outcomes may change. Outcomes may also change over time because of program changes made to respond to unanticipated problems or changes in priorities of the state or local government. Even in the absence of program changes, outcomes may change over time. A sanction may be immediately deleterious to a family, but we may wish to know the medium- and longer-term outcomes. In any evaluation there are likely to be outcomes of immediate interest and those that must wait. In allocating resources for evaluation, a trade-off exists between funding an immediate evaluation versus a more comprehensive one that would require setting aside resources for future data collection and evaluation efforts.

Outcomes of Interest

These trade-offs will be faced to varying degrees in evaluating the variety of outcomes of interest. We now turn to a representative set of outcomes, and in each case consider the trade-offs identified above. We apply this approach to four areas: (1) work requirements, (2) child care, (3) child health, and (4) family formation. In each case we consider outcomes of interest to different constituencies and the potential importance of the trade-offs.

Much of the discussion that follows focuses on children. With the major changes demanded of parents, and resulting changes in parental resources, children in these low-income households are likely to be affected in significant ways. Children on average will spend less time with their parents, starting from young ages, and will spend more time in child care settings. Children of young mothers (under 18 and not married) not currently living with an adult or in a supervised setting will experience a change in living arrangements. Through added pressures, penalties, and uncertainties, more children may spend time with adults other than their parents, including foster parents. Locational mobility may increase, and with it, added uncertainties for the child. Requirements on parents, including increased working hours, may also affect a child's schooling as well as health status and medical care use. A broad-based evaluation would include outcome measures that attempt to capture these potential impacts on children.

The Effects of Work Requirements

TANF will require almost all participants to engage in near full-time work in order to continue in the program.[4] Under W-2 for example, there are four tiers of full-time work established in the "Job Self-Sufficiency Ladder": unsubsidized employment, subsidized employment, community service jobs, and W-2 Transitions. Time limits are associated with all except the top tier, and with the overall program. Clients will be directed to the highest tier in which they can participate, as determined by their Financial and Employment Planner.

Outcomes associated with work requirements that are of interest to many constituencies include participation rates, hours worked, stability of employment, and earnings and compensation. In the W-2 example, these outcomes would include the distribution of participants across tiers; the probability and timing of movements toward (or away from) unsubsidized employment and the stability of such employment; earnings, benefits, and work-related expenses; administrative efficiency and cost of community service jobs and W-2 Transitions, changes in wages or job availability for low-wage workers not participating in W-2; and the availability, productivity, and cost of labor for firms.

Labor Market Outcomes Are of Interest for All Low-Wage Workers, for TANF Participants, and for Selected Groups. Primary outcomes of interest for TANF participants include the probability of initial success in securing a private sector job and the probability of maintaining such a job, as well as the timing of moves between jobs that are fully private and those that include some public sector intervention. In the case of W-2 these include moves between community service jobs and subsidized and unsubsidized private sector employment for those who begin their work experience in tier three, community service jobs. A variety of measures of compensation such as earnings, the availability of health insurance and other benefits, and work-related expenses are also of interest. The extent to which these outcomes differ across participant groups will be important in evaluating the adequacy of client evaluation, placement, and support services. For example, work requirements for mothers of young infants suggest that we may wish to pay close attention to outcomes for this group, which constitutes only a small fraction of the general population. At the same time, the timing and scale of work requirements raise the possibility of impacts on the general labor market, especially the market for low-wage workers. Concerns have also been raised about the potential for subsidized employment and/or community service jobs to displace current employees. Assessing these outcomes will require data on nonparticipants, especially but not exclusively low-wage workers. Thus, assessing work requirement outcomes will require consideration of the trade-off between collecting a broad sample and oversampling participants and/or particular groups of participants.

Outcomes at the Individual and Community Levels Are of Interest. Some work outcomes, such as total earnings and benefits, and proportion of participants in private sector jobs are of interest at the individual level and on a statewide basis. However, there are many outcomes, particularly those relating to the implementation of work requirements and the availability of planning and support services, for which community-level outcomes may be of equal or greater interest. For example, in Wisconsin, both individual and community-level differences in the type of initial job placement and the probability and timing of transitions between tiers are likely to be influenced by local labor market conditions (openings, type of firms, etc.). Thus, not only individual but also community-level data will be important in assessing work requirement outcomes.

Feasibility of Impact Evaluation, Cross-Community Comparisons, and Monitoring Varies Across Outcomes. By linking administrative data from the AFDC, TANF, and unemployment insurance (UI) programs, we can trace the earnings of program participants and other workers before and after implementation of TANF programs. UI records allow us to trace the earnings of all individuals who work in covered employment and to learn how these earnings vary over time and across employers. We might then use a pre-post design to evaluate the impact of a TANF program on such outcomes as earnings and employment stability among participants and other workers. In many cases these data are available on a county basis, allowing cross-community comparisons as well. Nonetheless, evaluating the impact of work requirements on the well-being of the eligible population will be more difficult owing to the absence of information on individuals who may be discouraged from applying for TANF sponsored services. This may be a particular problem for younger persons just finishing their schooling.

Short-Term and Long-Term Outcomes Are of Interest. TANF in many states requires a large and immediate transition to work. The feasibility of this approach and the nature of administrative and labor market incompatibilities are clearly of interest. It will be important to examine the extent to which wages and earnings increase over time and the potential for work experience alone to lead to improved economic status, especially in light of the retreat from long-term training and education and an increased focus on immediate job placement and experience. Employment patterns of continuing AFDC recipients and new entrants are expected to be substantially different, further suggesting the importance of long-term evaluation. Long-term changes in staffing and proprietorship of TANF agencies (which ultimately may influence their cultures and functioning) are also important. Finally, most states are currently enjoying very strong macro-economic conditions with very low rates of unemployment. It will be important to evaluate the effectiveness of work-based TANF programs over the business cycle.

The Effects of Child Care[5]

TANF work requirements will increase the time children spend in child care. TANF programs such as W-2 change eligibility for state-subsidized child care, the types of child care providers that may be used, and the cost of care to participants. The availability of increased child care dollars and regulations, such as one in Wisconsin stating that no mother with a child under age six will be required to take a job unless child care is available, is a clear incentive to rapidly increase the supply of child care providers. To expand availability of care, Wisconsin has developed a new category of "provisionally certified" providers who will not be required to undergo child care training and who will be reimbursed at a lower rate. Thus, there are reasons to expect a supply of lower quality child care.[6] W-2 requires co-payments that are figured as a percentage of the family's income. Because co-payments are lower for certified as opposed to licensed care, there is an incentive to place children in lower cost (lower quality) care.[7] In addition, any rush to increase the supply of formal or regulated care may lead to problems with the quality of the providers and/or facilities, at least in the short run.

Child care outcomes are of interest to diverse constituencies, including those concerned with effects on children's well-being, with the effects of child care availability and cost on TANF employment transitions and related costs, with the effects of availability and quality of child care on the general population, and with effects on the working conditions and wages of child care providers.

Outcomes of Interest Include Availability and Quality of Child Care for All Families, for TANF Participants, and for Selected Groups. TANF work requirements will substantially increase the demand for child care, especially for care of very young children (whose mothers were previously exempt, but must now work at least half time once the child reaches a specific age. In Wisconsin, mothers must work 30 to 40 hours when the infant is 12 weeks old). In addition, changes in the child care subsidy structure, which provides a subsidy up to 200 percent of the poverty line, will also increase demand for child care. Because of the timing and scale of the increased demand for child care, and given the incentives of the new co-payment structure, TANF may affect the quality and availability of child care for nonparticipants as well as participants. Thus, outcomes of interest include not only the availability and quality of child care for TANF participants, but also for other low-income families and all families with children. Also of particular interest is the availability of child care for children with special needs. In assessing data collection priorities for the evaluation of child care, we will face the trade-off between collecting a statewide representative sample of households (which might allow us to assess the impact on child care among all families) or oversampling particular groups (which might allow us to assess the impact on children with special needs, for example).

Outcomes at the Individual and Community Level Are of Interest. A primary outcome of interest is the effect of care on child well-being, including such indicators as total time in care, ratio of providers to children at any one time, and stability over time and adjustments to child care. Also of interest is the use of informal care, and the probability and consequences of older children being left without supervision. The availability, cost, and convenience of child care also have important implications for the ability of parents to work and to have sufficient income to cover other expenses. Collecting individual data will be necessary to evaluate these outcomes. However, community-level outcomes are also of great interest. These include the supply of child care by type, the success of TANF agencies and community steering committees in each state in coordinating child care services, and the interaction of public sector agencies, employers, community organizations, and private charities. Community-level data will be necessary to evaluate these outcomes. Thus, in assessing data collection priorities for the evaluation of child care we will also face the trade-off between collecting individual or community data.

The Feasibility of Impact Evaluation, Cross-Community Comparisons, and Monitoring Varies Across Outcomes. In a number of states, including Wisconsin, reliable baseline data are available on the regulated child care market, including enrollment, open slots, new facilities, and closings. Administrative data are also available on the use and cost of subsidized child care for low-income parents. These data are generally at the county level. A pre-post design might therefore be used to evaluate the impact of a TANF program such as W-2 on the general regulated child care market and on the demand for subsidized care. Cross-county comparisons could also be made, comparing for example services in rural and urban areas. However, no systematic pre-implementation data exist for unregulated care. We also lack state baseline data on individual-level outcomes. This limits the ability to do an impact evaluation. Nonetheless, these outcomes may well be of sufficient importance to warrant data collection, if only to monitor outcomes.

Short-Term and Long-Term Outcomes. The availability of an adequate supply of child care in the short term is important, especially in light of time limits. Short-term outcomes related to child care administration, coordination, and the implementation of a new category of providers will also be important in assessing the need for change. However, many outcomes are long term in nature: The impact of child care on child well-being, school readiness, and later life outcomes can only be assessed over a long term. Other outcomes may change over time: The quantity and quality of child care may be expected to adjust over time in response to increased demand, the new structure of co-payments, changes in child care workers' wages, and the new category of providers. The evaluation of child care will involve outcomes with a variety of time frames.

Effects on Child Health

The changes resulting from welfare reform may also affect the health of children in a variety of ways. This discussion includes factors that may influence health directly and the measures of health that may capture other changes. Health-related outcomes of interest include child health status, nutrition, and ability to participate in school; parental availability to monitor health, take children to the doctor, and provide support to children with special needs; and the demand for health services and access to and costs of regular and emergency care.

Outcomes of Interest Include Measures of Health of Children Directly Affected, of Children Who Are in Contact With These Children, and Parents and the General Public. Studies of children in low-income environments find that they are more likely to be exposed to lead paint, to obstacles that can cause injury, to adults under stress who may engage in endangering acts, to poor nutrition, and to emotional stress. For children in families participating in TANF, other factors may come into play. Increased demands on the time of parents in TANF may reduce their use of preventive medical care for their children, may increase the use of child care and of schools for ill children (as parents go to work instead of staying home with an ill child), and may reduce the provision of healthy food. One outcome that should therefore be monitored is the health status of children in TANF covered families.[8]

On the other hand, secondary health problems may also occur: Higher rates of illness among "TANF" children may lead to increased health problems among the children with whom they come in immediate contact, at child care centers or school.

Finally, all of this may mean a change in demand on health care providers, including a demand for a change in hours of operation, an increase in the demand for services for acute illnesses, and related expenditures by Medicaid and perhaps private insurers. Increased illness may also affect the operation of child care centers and of schools.

Among the *overall population* we might collect data on the proportion of persons by groups (especially children) who have health insurance coverage, who report excellent, good, fair, or poor health for their children, the proportion of children ages 1 through 4 who are fully vaccinated, the proportion of low-weight births, and accident and injury reports from hospitals or police. These data should be able to capture broader impacts of W-2 on children's health status.

Outcomes at the Individual and Community Level Are of Interest. Health can be measured by anthropometric indicators such as height and weight-for-height, and by surveys of parents questioned about the general health of their child and more specifically about use of emergency rooms, etc. Some of these data are collected in existing surveys,[9] but these surveys do not contain a large sample of low-income children. Nonetheless, health status could be measured at the individual level if medical records on these children were made available.[10] Community-level data would be of interest because supply factors, such as the ratio of providers relative to the population, and the use of paraprofessionals, counselors, and other support personnel by provider groups (clinics), may all influence utilization of care and the follow-up use of medication. Responses to changes in demand, such as changes in hours of operation, are likely to affect changes in utilization, if not health itself. On the *community level* there exist such measures as a greater incidence of injury seen at hospitals, or greater or reduced congestion at medical facilities, which could be measured through average waiting times for care and obtaining appointments.

The Feasibility of Impact Evaluation, Cross-Community Comparisons, and Monitoring Varies Across Outcomes. Most of these measures of children's health could be collected for children in the pre-TANF period by using medical records, vital statistics, existing surveys, and the like. Measures such as days of school missed (average daily attendance), proportion of children with a diagnosed physical and/or mental disability, proportion of children with a learning disability or proportion in special education may be obtainable from administrative or school records in a selected set of communities and could be obtained for the pre-implementation period. Birth records could provide data on low-birth-weight infants; hospital records could provide data on the use of emergency rooms.[11] However, even if we lack resources to collect the data necessary for a pre-post evaluation, certain health outcomes, such as emergency room use, are of sufficient importance to warrant collecting these data for monitoring purposes.

Short-Term and Long-Term Outcomes. A number of short-term outcomes will give us information on the immediate effects of a TANF program on child health. We might expect to see changes in days of school and/or child care missed, in the proportion of ill children in these settings, in the rate of injuries, and in the use of medical care in communities that include a high proportion of participant families. Still other outcomes are of interest in both the short and longer run: for example, we should be interested in measures that would capture both short- and long-term effects of increased stress on children. These data could be gathered in surveys of parents, teachers, and child care workers. Other changes resulting from TANF may take far longer to have an impact. Only over time should we expect to see effects that reflect nutritional changes, which are indicated by anthropometric measures.[12] Similarly, among children aged 1 through 4, the proportion without immunizations, or with an incomplete set, may gradually change over time. And the proportion of the low-income population with health insurance coverage may change as parents change employment patterns, or as children's or family's eligibility for Medicaid is lost.

Effects on Family Formation

One of the philosophical principles behind welfare reform is to encourage parents to be responsible for their children. Another principle, explicit in the federal reform bill, is to reduce teenage parenting, nonmarital parenting, and in particular nonmarital teenage parenting. The national legislation requires teenage mothers to live at home or with a responsible adult in order to receive any benefits and moves away from the restrictive criteria under AFDC that gave benefits primarily to single-parent households. Under a number of welfare reform plans, including W-2, both two-parent and one-parent families are eligible for assistance. Noncustodial parents whose children live in families eligible for TANF services may themselves qualify for a variety of services. TANF programs may also have a family cap, under which benefits (cash benefits in particular) do not increase with the birth of additional children. And a teen's parents may face requirements concerning the care of any children born to their underage child. All of these programmatic changes are expected to change incentives with regard to family formation.[13]

Outcomes of interest with regard to family formation include living arrangements — whether married or not, whether cohabiting in a stable relationship, whether living with one's parents or other adults. We would also wish to collect measures of subsequent fertility, such as delaying or foregoing subsequent births. Among noncustodial parents, we would like to know whether involvement with their children has been influenced by the change in welfare reform.

Measures of Family Formation. Outcomes of interest include measures of family formation among the population most directly affected (single mothers with limited assets and income), teenagers who are potentially eligible for services, noncustodial parents, and selected subgroups of the general public. Among the primary variables of interest under family formation is the rate of teen out-of-wedlock fertility among the "at risk" population. This population includes those who have already given birth as an unmarried teen as well as younger teens living in low-income communities.

70

We might also wish to collect data on teen fertility, teen out-of-wedlock fertility, and out-of-wedlock fertility for the entire population and subpopulations of the state, since such data are readily available over a long period of time. They would also serve as a type of control for changes in fertility rates that might be due to other events and changing circumstances within the state.

Another measure of considerable interest is the time parents spend with their children. Of particular interest is involvement of fathers in their children's lives. This might include measures of paying support for and of time spent with the children and other contacts (phone calls, attendance at school and sports activities, etc.). We would concentrate on the fathers of children who are eligible for W-2, but might also wish to include children who have lived in households on AFDC prior to the change in the law. If society is successful in increasing the involvement of fathers in the lives of their children we might expect to find this reflected in the broader population, and so would like measures of a noncustodial parent's time spent with children who are growing up in single-parent households, and with children who began life in a single-parent household, as well as the proportion of children living in single-parent households.

Individual and Community Outcomes Are of Interest. We may wish to compare individual data on marital status, childbearing, and living arrangements of TANF participants with a state's past AFDC recipients. In particular communities, or zip-code areas or census tracts, that have high rates of participation in welfare-related programs, it would be useful to compare rates of out-of-wedlock childbearing by women's ages over time. TANF includes substantial funding for abstinence education programs as well as financial incentives for states that reduce nonmarital childbearing. To evaluate the effectiveness of education programs and other efforts we would need to collect indicators of education and attitude changes at the community level.

The Feasibility of Impact Evaluation, Cross-Community Comparisons, and Monitoring Varies Across Outcomes. The easiest data to collect, and for which historical data exist, are administrative data from birth certificates, containing information on mother's age, whether the mother is married, race of mother, and whether she had previous live births. The mother's county of residence and city, village or township would allow aggregation of these data to the community level. Also easily collectable are rates of marriage by age and county. Similar information exists for divorce and annulments. The data on these certificates also include presence of children and award of custody. In Wisconsin, data from administrative records and surveys of parents are available from the Wisconsin Court Record Database (WCRD). These data have some limitations,[14] but might serve to construct a baseline. Collecting data on the amount of time absentee fathers spend with their children is more difficult. However, there are a number of data sets that might provide approximations of the time allocation before W-2. For example the WCRD parent surveys include questions on contact between children and noncustodial fathers in Wisconsin, and the Panel Study of Income Dynamics (PSID) has a long history of asking such questions. For time allocation after W-2, survey data would be necessary.[15]

Short-Term and Long-Term Outcomes. We can observe short-term effects on teen fertility, marriage rates, divorce rates, and the parenting role of the noncustodial parent. Over time, however, the patterns may change. In all of the family-formation measures, the short-run response may be smaller than, and even of different direction from, the long-run response. For example, if the teen nonmarital birth rate is reduced in the short run through a variety of targeted programs, they may change the culture as well as contraceptive knowledge, which will further reduce such births. If fathers allocate more time to their children, their relationship may be closer and would increase over time. However, if the father feels that too large a proportion of his earnings are allocated to the child, or the child's demands are too great, this allocation of time might decline in the longer run.

Conclusions

Because resources are limited, choices will have to be made regarding the principal outcomes of interest. These cover a broad range, from the effects of employment requirements on participants, to effects on child well-being and family income, to child care quality and availability across the entire population. Some important outcomes may be evaluated using existing or easily available administrative or survey data; such evaluation should clearly be pursued. However, to gauge important effects of welfare reform, some new data will be required. In deciding what data to collect, all the trade-offs must be recognized. Should data be restricted to eligibles, or also include near eligibles, or focus on special groups, such as families with a disabled child, or be spread to the entire low-income population? Should the database attempt to link outcomes to community opportunities and structure, to the structure and personnel of the service programs, and to local nongovernmental organizations, making the community the organizing basis for data collection, or should the database cover the state more generally? What can be learned about the state's programs if the community approach is followed? Should only those impacts for which we can construct a counterfactual be included, or are there outcomes so important that we wish to measure them regardless of their evaluation potential? Over what time period should we measure these outcomes?

Resources for evaluation are clearly limited. Prioritizing is essential but difficult. Different constituencies would make different choices. We would emphasize (1) those aspects that can be evaluated rather than simply monitored (but not to the absolute exclusion of important effects not available for the pre-reform period); (2) those impacts that can be evaluated using administrative data (which will of necessity emphasize the target population rather than the overall population or near eligibles); and (3) broad measures of well-being in the overall population that can be drawn from existing, large-scale data sets such as the CPS. We view the major choice remaining to be made in evaluation design as the choice between a panel survey of the low-income population of the entire state versus a community-based panel survey of the low-income population; within these, choices involve focusing on a particular group of interest (e.g., children with disabilities) versus a larger sample of the low-income population. Because of the potential importance of differences in service availability, job opportunities, and other community-level factors, we argue for a community-based panel survey.

Endnotes

1   As noted throughout, we draw extensively from the background issue papers on W-2 prepared for the Institute for Research on Poverty conference on Evaluation of Comprehensive State Welfare Reform.

2   This occurs whenever prescreening is required to identify sample members. Thus if the population to be oversampled is potential eligibles and young teens, a household screen would be required to locate such individuals. If the targeted population is those of permanently low income, a screen is also required. If the targeted population is instead current recipients of services, this need for prescreening is removed, but locating the population may itself increase costs. In order to reduce survey costs, clustering is usually used, which raises another related issue. If the screening or selection of the targeted populations is done in clusters, costs are reduced, but so is the "usefulness" or representativeness of the sample. In effect, by clustering, the degrees of freedom are limited so that the "effective" sample is less than the number of observations.

3   One approach that has been used in a number of studies, particularly in the health area (the Rand Health Insurance Study, the Epidemiological Catchment Area Study), has been to select communities as the first basis for data collection. They can be chosen with a probability that is proportional to the size of their reported AFDC cases, for example. Within the community, agencies can be selected and within this, those who use the agencies can serve as the basis for the selection of a random sample. Or, a random sample from the community can be drawn (with oversampling as determined by the choices discussed above). Employers within the community can also be randomly selected or selected based on a probability of employing low-skilled workers. The use of data based in communities allows study of the impact of services provided, the labor market, etc., on outcomes of interest. The negative consequence of this design is in limiting understanding of the broader consequences throughout the state. And it is not clear if community studies can be pooled for analysis. If there are only a limited number of sites — say 4-6 — there would be too few degrees of freedom to characterize the system. And, if data were pooled, we would need to have accurate weights on individuals in the community-based samples to represent the state, and it is not at all clear what would serve as the basis of these weights.

4   A federally established time schedule sets up minimum levels of participation in terms of hours and proportion of participants.

5   This section draws on the companion chapter by Karen Fox Folk and Marianne Bloch, "The Evaluation of Child Care Services under the Wisconsin Works Program (W-2)."

6   A frequently used definition of quality of day care refers to the training of the provider and the ratio of children to provider. A more fundamental def-

inition would include caring and stimulation of learning. These are more difficult (and costly) to measure.

7   There is a 30 percent differential, on average, between licensed and certified care. This means, for example, that a family with an income level below 70 percent of the poverty line would pay $40 to place two children in licensed child care but $28 to place the same two children in certified care; at the poverty line, a family would be required to co-pay $114 for licensed care compared to $80 for two children in certified care.

8   The health outcome of specific groups may be of particular interest; for example, infants and children with disabilities may be especially vulnerable to the impact of new work requirements for their mothers.

9   Existing surveys include the SIPP, which has sampling units within the state, including Milwaukee, and the Wisconsin Family Health Survey, covering the whole state.

10 Data on children covered by Medicaid could be obtained from the computerized collection of Medicaid records. Using these data or hospital data, we could analyze the proportion of children with categories of diagnosis usually related to accidents or violence. Medicaid data would also permit analysis of immunization rates among the covered population. Records of low-birth-weight infants in low-income areas or to mothers living in certain areas could be collected over time to see if changed policies affect the probability of low birth weight and hence the health of infants (and their future health). An indicator of emotional or mental health is a child's ability to engage in activities that are age-appropriate, such as playing with other children. Once children are in school or in preschools, teachers' records might provide such information. (In many cases these data may at the community rather than the individual level.)

11 For more on these options, see the chapter by Sandefur and Martin. A preferred strategy might focus on children enrolled in Medicaid, using computerized Medicaid data on a variety of indicators of health and medical care use among this population. Alternatively, a sample of children in TANF families might be identified, their medical care provider approached, and permission requested to obtain medical records for a specified period of time, including some years prior to welfare reform as well as after. This might be much easier among a random sample of children covered by Medicaid or for cases in a hospital than if a large number of individual providers or HMOs have to be contacted. Nevertheless, it might be possible to do a case study with the cooperation of a limited number of HMOs serving the low-income population, or serving a sizable number of families covered by Medicaid.

12 Because anthropometric measures reflect nutrition over a length of time, collection of items such as height and height-for-weight at an early point in W-2 would serve as a measure of nutrition prior to W-2. Measures several

years later would be post-W-2 measures. Unfortunately, however, this effort would be relatively expensive.

13　The welfare reform programs, particularly W-2, change incentives in complicated ways. For example, the ability to get benefits (services) as a two-parent family may make it attractive to marry. However, a noncustodial parent may now get benefits, which would seem to make it more attractive to be a noncustodial parent.

14　The database contains records of divorce and paternity cases from 21 Wisconsin counties. However, these data may be limited because of the small sample of AFDC-eligible cases.

15　As discussed elsewhere in this volume, such data will be collected as part of the survey undertaken for the W-2 Child Support Demonstration Evaluation.

SECTION II

GENERAL
EVALUATION
STRATEGIES

3

Controlled Experiments in Evaluating the New Welfare Programs

Glen G. Cain
Department of Economics
University of Wisconsin–Madison

Introduction and Conclusions

Controlled experiments, also called social experiments, are a method of evaluating welfare reforms that have been used extensively, especially since the passage of the Family Support Act in 1988, which authorized programs to increase the employment and self-support of welfare mothers. Gueron and Pauly (1991) present an extensive and generally favorable discussion of many of these evaluations. A brief summary of all completed controlled experiments involving employment programs for recipients of Aid to Families with Dependent Children (AFDC) is contained in Greenberg and Shroder (1997). Depending on how one defines the subject of welfare reform or work-related programs aimed at AFDC recipients, at least fifty controlled experiments on these subjects are listed and summarized in Greenberg and Shroder. Writing in 1992 about the evaluation research of welfare and training programs, Manski and Garfinkel state that, "In the past decade . . . analysis of social experiments has become the new orthodoxy, dominating the evaluations commissioned by the federal government and by the major foundations" (Manski and Garfinkel, 1992, p. 12).

It may seem natural, then, to propose the method of a controlled experiment to evaluate the new welfare reforms that are now being implemented in every state as a consequence of the revolutionary change in federal welfare policy embodied in the Personal Responsibility and Work Opportunity Reconciliation Act of 1996 (PRWORA). By ending the entitlement to the income support offered by AFDC, that act virtually requires adults in AFDC families, and those who would have become participants in the AFDC program if it were still in existence, to become self-supporting. For most of these families, self-support requires finding and holding a job, which was the primary goal of the many programs that were evaluated by controlled experiments in the previous decade.

This paper reaches a contrary conclusion, which is that a controlled experiment is not a practical method for evaluating the new state welfare systems. Controlled experiments remain a valuable tool for evaluating component parts and incremental changes of the new programs, but observational (or nonexperimental) studies of the new state welfare programs are likely to be the appropriate, although imperfect, method for evaluating the new programs as a whole. Some suggestions for using this method are offered below. Two main reasons for my negative conclusion may be stated briefly. Detailed explanations will follow.

First, most social experiments have "'pilot tested' major innovations in social policy" or "have been used to assess incremental changes in existing programs" (quoting Greenberg and Shroder, 1997, p. 3). None have been used to evaluate such large-scale economic programs as federal minimum wage laws, federal tax legislation, or even state-level versions of these programs. The major exception to this generalization may, in fact, prove the rule. The U.S. Department of Labor's evaluation of the Job Training Partnership Act, beginning in the early 1990s, included a large experimental design that turned out to be difficult to implement, and the validity of these experimental findings have been contentiously debated. See the criticisms of the experimental evaluation by Hotz (1992) and Heckman and Smith (1995). Even in his staunch (and to me, persuasive) defense of controlled experiments, Gary Burtless (1995, pp. 79-80) pointed out several weaknesses of this particular experiment.

Although the experimental findings reviewed by Gueron and Pauly (1991) were accepted and influential among government policy makers (see Fishman and Weinberg, 1992), a major difference between these experimental programs and the new state welfare systems is the small scale of the former and the very large scale of the latter. Indeed, the small-scale experimental programs themselves have been subject to questions about their "external validity" — that is, whether they truly represented the process and outcomes of a permanent program that would be universally available to the full eligible population. (See Manski and Garfinkel, 1992, and Garfinkel, Manski, and Michalopoulos, 1991 for a general discussion of the problem of external validity.) The special problems in attempting to carry out a controlled experiment with an ongoing state welfare system are discussed below.

A second serious problem that looms in the background of evaluating the new state welfare programs is the uncertainty about the appropriate counterfactual. The question of whether the new system is working well or poorly must be posed in conjunction with the question: Compared to what? The "what," the counterfactual, that is of greatest interest to policy makers is some feasible alternative program. In most evaluation studies that use controlled experiments, the alternative to the experimental program is the status quo. I doubt, however, that state officials view a return to the old system as an alternative to the new system, particularly since restoring the old is not under their full control, given the PRWORA legislation. Instead, comparisons between or among states are more policy relevant; that is, relevant to the question of what changes need to be made to improve the new welfare system of the individual state. In a controlled experiment, however, what would the experimental (alternative) welfare program be? What would it look like if the old system is ruled out? The question has received no attention by state government officials because none (to my knowledge) has proposed using a controlled experiment.

In arriving at my pessimistic conclusion about the viability of a controlled experiment, I recognize a troubling distinction between a comparison of the ongoing state program with (a) a counterfactual that is useful for scientific analysis and (b) a counterfactual that is useful for policy analysis. Certainly, there is profound scientific interest in whether the new state programs are working well or poorly compared to the old system, and the interest is by no means confined to economic historians. A comparison to the old system also has the virtue of specifying a well-defined counterfactual, but it has limited policy usefulness. In contrast, the counterfactual of some "viable alternative welfare program," is highly relevant to policy, but it remains to be defined. Clearly, the choice of a counterfactual also arises in evaluating the new state programs by observational studies.

The rest of this paper is divided into three parts. The first examines a conventional example of an experiment in welfare reform to illustrate both the potential power of the method and standards for achieving a good evaluation. The next part deals with specific problems in using controlled experiments to evaluate the new state welfare programs, with references to Wisconsin's new welfare program, to illustrate several problems that are likely to face other state evaluations. The last part briefly discusses evaluating a state's new welfare program with observational data from different states.

The Controlled Experiment as a Standard

In its conventional application, the controlled experiment tests some new program to allow a comparison of its outcomes with those of the existing system. Consider an experiment to determine whether a training program increases the employment, earnings, incomes, and other outcomes for welfare mothers. Typically, a sample of welfare mothers would be selected and randomly assigned to either a treatment group or a control group. The treatment group is eligible to receive the training, while the control group continues in the existing welfare system without access to the training program. The goal of the experiment is to measure what the outcomes would be if the experimental program were made a permanent part of the welfare program and were made available to all welfare mothers. The sample for the experiment is drawn from the population of welfare mothers, including new entrants who would also be randomly assigned to the treatment and control groups.

Assume this experiment has the following three positive features:

1. The training program in the experiment is similar to what the program would be if it were extended to the entire population of welfare mothers. Similarity refers to the content and quality of the program, including the quality of the facilities, administrators, trainers, and so on. We may then assume that the treatment group's response to the experimental training is similar

to the way welfare mothers would respond to a permanent (nationwide or, perhaps, statewide) training program applied to all welfare mothers.

2. The treatment and control families are followed for a sufficient length of time to determine the post-training and long-run outcomes under study, using household interviews and other sources of data, such as administrative records. Persons and families in the treatment or control groups who move would be followed and surveyed in their new locations. Both features, (1) and (2), contribute to the external validity of the experiment; they are necessary to achieve unbiased estimates of the relevant outcomes of interest — the full (or long-run) benefits and costs of the permanent training program.

3. The third feature is that the proposed training program is voluntary in the sense that the mother's eligibility to receive welfare benefits does not depend on participating in the training program. In the experiment, those who choose not to participate, as well as those who drop out of the program, would remain in the treatment group for purposes of comparison with the control group. Allowing the training program to be voluntary removes a possible ethical objection, which is that mandatory training could make some of those randomly assigned to the treatment group worse off compared to the control group. The control group and welfare recipients who are not in the experiment do not receive the training, but neither do they risk losing welfare benefits if they do not participate in the training program. If the proposed permanent program were, in fact, mandatory — requiring participation in the training program to receive welfare benefits — then the experiment would also have to have that feature; otherwise the experiment would not test the proposed program. The ethical objection to an experiment involving mandatory training may be overruled, but I mention the issue because it arises later.

Now consider two potential shortcomings of the design of the training experiment. One is the fact that if the experimental training program were adopted as a permanent part of the welfare system, the population of new entrants might change. If the training program were notably rewarding, some women who would not have entered the old welfare system might decide to enter the new system. Conversely, if the training program were, say, mandatory and onerous, some women who would have entered the old welfare system may not enter the new system. The experiment would not detect these outcomes because the experimental training was not imposed on all new entrants to the welfare program. (See Moffitt, 1996, for a discussion of the need to account for entry effects in program evaluations.)

A second, widely acknowledged shortcoming in evaluating training programs by means of a small-scale experimental program is that a full-scale program is likely to have an adverse effect on the overall low-wage labor market by substantially increasing the supply of low-wage workers. Without measures to increase the demand for low-wage workers, the expected market response to the increased supply is a decline in wages and other conditions of employment of low-wage workers and an increase in their unemployment. Almost all low-wage workers are not on welfare, so this population was not, and could not have been, studied to determine its response to the experiment.

Neither of the two weaknesses just discussed implies that the experiment would be a futile endeavor. Rather, the message is that an experiment can answer some, but not all, important questions. As described above, the experiment offers persuasive evidence of the ability of a replicable training program to affect the earnings capacities of welfare mothers. The experiment's central questions and its intended policy decision are well defined; namely, how do the outcomes from a welfare program that includes a training program compare with those of the existing system, and should the existing system be changed to include the training program? The first question is fundamentally scientific; the second question is fundamentally political. The experiment permits the measured change in outcomes to be attributable to the training program rather than to changes in the economy or to various characteristics of the women in the treatment group. The experiment also provides most of the information needed for a benefit-cost analysis of the training program, which is essential for the policy decision. The experiment's measure of gains from the training would probably require a downward adjustment to allow for the smaller expected gains in a permanent program, because of the marketwide supply effects from the full-scale program. The costs of the full-scale program, on the other hand, might be adjusted downward in anticipation of economies of scale.

Note that the experiment could also provide information about the child care arrangements of the children of welfare mothers who undertake training and obtain jobs. Indeed, a child care program might have been included as another component of the experiment. If it were included, however, the experiment would not be able to measure whether a full-scale child care program would affect marketwide prices and other conditions of the child care industry. Similarly, the training experiment could provide information about whether women who left the welfare system obtained health insurance. Alternatively, health insurance could have been another component of the experiment. If the experiment consisted of three components — training, child care, and health insurance — then all the outcomes being studied should, in general, be attributable to the package of the three components, and assigning the causal effect of any particular outcome of the experiment to one of the components may be unwarranted. But such individual attribution of causality is not necessary if the full-scale permanent program matches that which was carried out in the experiment. The method of controlled experiments in evaluating changes in welfare programs is appealing in many settings.

Can a Complete Change in a State's Welfare System Be Evaluated by a Controlled Experiment? A Pessimistic Appraisal

In describing the evaluation of the hypothetical training program, emphasis was placed on the clear policy decision at issue: whether or not to adopt the training program in the welfare system. What is the comparable decision at stake in evaluating a new state welfare system? The question may be answered with a negative: No one appears to be saying that if the new systems fail, we will go back to the old system. The old system was part of a national program that has been repealed and replaced, so the closest a state could come to this alternative and still operate within its legal boundaries would be to use its block grant money to install a system with as many features of the old system as current legislation permits. Perhaps a state could request permission — a waiver — to conduct an experimental program that consisted of the old system. As stated above, a comparison between the new and the old has great scientific interest and appeal. But unless returning to the old is a realistic policy option, it is difficult to see much public support, let alone enthusiasm, for such an experiment. Admittedly, I am here expressing my judgment about prevailing political attitudes.

Several technical and logistic problems face a controlled experiment, in which the old system is the treatment program and the new system provides the control group. I see five important problems, which I subjectively rank from least serious to most serious.

Ethical Issues

Evaluating the new welfare reform by means of a controlled experiment may raise ethical objections if the random assignment to the treatment group would make some families worse off than participating in the ongoing new welfare program.[1] The ethical issue does not arise if the new welfare program in a given state is unambiguously less desirable to welfare mothers than the old system, since the random assignment of some families to the old welfare system would be benign. In some states, however — Wisconsin is one — some features of the new system are beneficial; improved child care arrangements and Medicaid extensions to poor husband-wife families are examples. There may be ways of dealing with the ethical problem, perhaps by providing a lump-sum compensation that overcomes a family's opposition to participating in the treatment group, but such devices are complications and interfere with the integrity of the experiment.

Duration of Experiment

A second problem is that the experiment would have to be relatively long, five or six years, to represent behavior that matches the behavior of those who would be in the old welfare program, if the old program had continued to be the state's program or if it were reestablished. Long-duration experiments are more difficult to carry out and more expensive than short-duration experiments, but it is not the expense but the reason why a long-duration experiment is necessary that is source of the problem. To see this, consider the example of the training experiment. Here, the welfare mothers in the treatment group are in a training program that is expected to be completed in a year or so, and the effects of this on the participants' employment and earnings are expected to be revealed in one or two more years. The training program is to be adopted if the experiment shows it to be successful, and this decision can be made within three years after the experiment began.

If the experimental treatment were the old program, the relevant time duration for its participants varies from one to 20 years! Thus, to view the welfare mothers' behavior in the treatment group as representing what their behavior would be if the treatment (the old system) were in place, we would have to assume that they believed, or acted as if, their treatment were part of a permanent program. Perhaps the average time horizon for welfare mothers is five or six years, with some women expecting to be in the welfare system only a year or less and others expecting to be in it for 15 to 20 years. If the experiment lasted only a year or two, many women in the treatment group would not behave as if they were in the old welfare system. Instead, their behavior is likely to reflect their status in a temporary program, with the new welfare program as their soon-to-be destination. A time period of five to six years for a controlled experiment in which the old program is the treatment group is not an insurmountable problem, but it is a drawback, and a drawback that would be exacerbated if the old program is not seriously considered as an alternative to the new program.

Issues of the Transition to the New System

The third problem is that the new state welfare systems will not be in their steady-state mode of operation for some time, the length of time depending on many factors: the complexity of their systems, how radical the new changes are, the quality of the state agencies, the stability of their economic environments, and so on. Perhaps two years or so will have to elapse before the new welfare system settles into its normal, long-run operational status. A comparison between the assigned control group in the new system, which is starting up, and the treatment group in the old welfare system, which has a 60-year history, could be criticized as being not only unfair to the new system but meaningless. Again, contrast this evaluation of the two welfare systems with the evaluation of the training program discussed above.

The fact that the new state welfare programs will not be operating smoothly for some time is a challenge to any evaluation strategy, but the problem seems more serious if the evaluation is a controlled experiment that compares the old and new systems. If the evaluation of the state program were based on observational studies of other state programs, then at least the various state programs being compared would be in similar stages of development.

Variability in the Timing of Component Implementation

The fourth problem is that in many states one or more components of their new welfare programs have been under way for a year or more as a result of federal waivers that allowed the states to try certain reforms, such as requiring welfare mothers to seek and accept employment in order to receive welfare benefits. In these circumstances the old welfare system may no longer exist at the time when the experiment would begin. Assigning a treatment group of families to the old system will, therefore, involve families that are already altered ("contaminated") by exposure to and participation in the new program. The empirical question is whether there is a sufficiently large group of current welfare recipients who have been unaffected by the new programs and who, therefore, can be assigned to a treatment group (consisting of the old system) and to a control group (consisting of the new state welfare program). This obstacle to experimenting with the old system as the treatment group does not apply to all states. Some states made no changes in their old welfare system and others made minor changes that affected (and "contaminated") only small numbers of families.

The Old System's Environment May Change

A fifth problem with a controlled experiment that has welfare families randomly assigned to the old welfare system is that the state's economic environment is expected to change under the new system in ways that it would not have under the old system. Therefore, the outcomes of the treatment families (in the old welfare plan) are unlikely to represent what their employment, housing, child care, and other outcomes would be if the old system had been maintained. A clear example is the employment outcome. Under the old welfare system, a substantial fraction, perhaps 25 percent, of welfare mothers find a job that takes them off welfare during a period of less than two years of time on welfare. Thus, if the labor market for the (generally) low-skilled women in the treatment group did not change, then 25 percent of them would be expected to find jobs during this two-year period. However, we know that the pressure for welfare mothers to find jobs under the new welfare system will be great, making employment for welfare mothers in the treatment group (under the old system) more difficult and less rewarding. Assume only 10 percent of these treatment-group women find jobs and leave welfare. Assume further that 40 percent of welfare mothers in the new program become employed and leave welfare. The new system would look good compared to the old system by this criterion of success — a 40 percent success rate compared to a 10 percent success rate. But the new system's superior outcome is upwardly biased. The (hypothetically) true difference is 40 percent compared to 25 percent. If the old welfare system had been maintained, which is the counterfactual under study, then its welfare mothers would not have faced the expanded labor supply, and they would not have had the sharp drop in employment.

Although a similar weakness in the controlled experiment for evaluating the training program was pointed out, the problem is more severe here. The training treatment was not influenced by the behavior of women in the control group and the existing welfare system. Also, the crucial outcome was the test of whether the earnings capacities of the women in the treatment group were increased, and this can be measured whether or not there are marketwide effects of a full-scale permanent training program. Finally, the difference between the employment and earnings outcomes observed during the training experiment and the outcomes that would occur in the full-scale implementation of the training program seem minor and amenable to a modest adjustment.

Another and even broader type of marketwide effect of a new statewide welfare program, one that would not be present in an experimental program, is mentioned in the chapters in this book by Haveman and by Kaplan and Meyer: a societal "cultural change" in the ethos of and towards the welfare system. Compared to changes in supply and demand conditions in the market, the idea of a cultural change is potentially a much more serious problem for small-scale controlled experiments because it is difficult to define, to measure, and to take into account in adjusting the observed outcomes from a controlled experiment.

To gain some perspective on this issue, consider whether this claim applies to the experiments of negative income tax programs in the 1970s. Would the cultural changes that would occur if the negative income tax replaced welfare be so extensive that, for example, the labor-supply outcomes of either the treatment or control groups were incorrectly estimated? Economists would view this form of cultural change as a change in workers' tastes (or preferences) for market work brought about, for example, by a change in the attitudes and expectations of employers and other community groups. Is that likely? Perhaps the cultural change in the wake of the new state welfare system takes the form of certain institutional changes; for example, an expanded role by private charities. Again, we would need to examine how this change would bias the experiment's estimates of specific outcomes. Still another type of "contamination" is that people in the randomly assigned treatment and control groups will behave differently just because they are aware of the existence of each other. Again, this problem was not raised, as such, in the negative income tax experiments. Was this an oversight in the analysis? The famous "Hawthorne effect" — the proposition that experimental subjects alter their behavior simply because they are aware of being "experimented with" rather than because of the treatment, per se — was considered in the negative income tax experiments, but the program was considered sufficiently unobtrusive to avoid this problem. Perhaps this is the key issue: Is the change in the new program so dramatic and obtrusive that the entire community is likely to alter its attitudes toward the program's subjects and the institutions that deal with these subjects? It is a sobering question facing advocates of controlled experiments.

In summary, the obstacles to using controlled experiments to test new welfare programs against the old programs seem insurmountable. If the technical problems could be overcome, there would indeed be great scientific interest in the comparison between the two systems, but the fact remains that the old programs are not realistic alternatives to the new programs.

The best chance for a useful controlled experiment to test the new program against the old program exists in states that (1) have new programs that are decidedly less generous than the old program, (2) can carry out an experiment for at least five years, (3) have new programs that are relatively simple and can soon be operating at their steady-state level, and (4) can begin the experiment before the new program gets underway. The value of controlled experiments that test some reform or component of an ongoing program that has reached a state of normal operation remains, and there will surely be ample opportunities for these experiments in the future.[2]

Comparisons Among State Programs: An Alternative Evaluation Strategy

In evaluating a state's new welfare program, the programs in other states appear to have more policy relevance — although less scientific interest — than the old system in the given state. Cross-state evaluations may not produce a rigorous evaluation, in the sense of obtaining unbiased estimates of the causal effects of even the state program as a whole, let alone isolating the causal effects of the various components of the state program.[3] "Ball park" estimates are more likely. Nevertheless, the idea that the programs in other states offer alternatives, in whole or in part, to a given state's program is realistic and is in the spirit of the old tradition of viewing state programs as "experimental laboratories." Note that virtually all states would have programs in similar stages of development, so the comparison studies would not be biased by the factor of time-in-operation (point 3 in the above list of problems with a controlled experiment). A more guarded comment is that since the measure of an outcome from each state's program has a similar bias, any bias in the differences between (among) states is a second-order effect.

A preferred strategy for gathering the data for the evaluation requires longitudinal (panel) surveys across states, ideally before the new programs get underway (or soon after). With these data the analytic model commonly called "difference-in-differences" can be used.[4] Surveys, unlike administrative data, are uniform and easily comparable across states, cover a wider range of behavioral outcomes, and cover persons who are not in the records of the welfare system. Repeating a point made above, welfare changes will affect persons who are not "on welfare," especially persons with low wages and families with low incomes.[5]

The longitudinal surveys must continue over a relatively long period, perhaps six years. Many outcomes of interest occur after several years elapse, such as the effects of the mandatory terminations of welfare after a period of up to five years. Other behavioral outcomes, such as family composition and fertility, may take several years to appear. Also, a long-duration study avoids several biases that are likely to appear in the short run. The new programs will, on the one hand, improve over time in their performance as administrators learn what works. On the other hand, the program's performance will appear to decline because the administrators have every incentive to make the program look good in the first or second year by "skimming the cream." They will tend to find jobs first for those on welfare who are the easiest to place, and place their clients in jobs that are easiest to fill, such as low-level public jobs or jobs in subsidized nonprofit agencies.

Cross-state comparisons are natural, because the programs are legislated to vary across states, and all the inhabitants in a given state are covered by the same program. In contrast, if the evaluation design is based on within-state variation, such as variation across counties, these variations must be imposed as exceptions to the law. Therefore, the models used to explain variation in the outcomes among the counties would have to take into account the reasons for the differences in the county programs. Also, the comparisons across counties that have differences in their welfare programs will be biased by intercounty migration that is selective of families on the basis of unobservable characteristics that are themselves causal to the outcomes of interest. Interstate migration is less frequent, but it will also complicate the interpretations of interstate comparisons.

The diversity in state programs has good and bad consequences for evaluation. Wide variation in the program variables is useful in predicting and explaining outcomes. But some of the differences among state programs are effects of underlying variation in the states' economic and social conditions. For example, the large stock and flow of immigrants in California will partly determine the nature of that state's welfare program, so any comparison of outcomes between California and other states will have to take into account immigration as both a feature of California's economic conditions and as a reason why certain components of the welfare program in California are what they are. Depending on the context, immigration can be viewed as both a cause and an effect of California's welfare system.

A persuasive program evaluation based on cross-state comparisons is difficult basically because it ultimately depends on statistical controls not only for good measures of program differences but also for the levels and changes of the states' economic and social environments. Picking similar states to compare, controlling for state differences in observable environmental factors, and applying the "difference-in-differences" model are ways that can only lessen, but not eliminate, the basic methodological problem. Some reliance on theoretical reasoning is needed. For example, if a state provides higher benefits and longer time limits for its welfare recipients, its job placements are likely to be lower; if the state offers a more generous child care program, then its job placements are expected to be higher. The state programs may be ranked by the level of their generosity, and even if specific explanations for the differences in outcomes cannot be attributed to particular components of each program, there is a value in knowing the relation between various outcomes and the overall levels of program generosity. I end, therefore, with the modest proposal of evaluation by the traditional means within economics of a theoretically based nonexperimental study.

References

Burtless, Gary. "The Case for Randomized Field Trials in Economic and Policy Research." *Journal of Economic Perspectives* 9, no. 2 (Spring 1995): 63-84.

Fishman, Michael E. and Daniel H. Weinberg. "The Role of Evaluation in State Welfare Reform Waiver Demonstrations." In *Evaluating Welfare and Training Programs,* eds. Charles F. Manski and Irwin Garfinkel. Cambridge, MA: Harvard University Press, 1992, pp. 115-142.

Garfinkel, Irwin, Charles F. Manski, and Charles Michalopoulos. "Micro Experiments and Macro Effects." In *Evaluating Welfare and Training Programs,* eds. Charles F. Manski and Irwin Garfinkel. Cambridge, MA: Harvard University Press, 1992, pp. 253-273.

Greenberg, David and Mark Shroder. *The Digest of Social Experiments.* Washington, DC: The Urban Institute Press, 1997.

Gueron, Judith M. and Edward Pauly. *From Welfare to Work.* New York: Russell Sage Foundation, 1991.

Heckman, James J., and Jeffrey A. Smith. "Assessing the Case for Social Experiments." *Journal of Economic Perspectives* 9, no. 2 (Spring 1995): 85-110.

Hotz, V. Joseph. "Designing an Evaluation of the Job Training Partnership Act." In *Evaluating Welfare and Training Programs*, eds. Charles F. Manski and Irwin Garfinkel. Cambridge, MA: Harvard University Press, 1992, p.. 76-114.

Manski, Charles F. and Irwin Garfinkel. "Introduction." In *Evaluating Welfare and Training Programs*, eds. Charles F. Manski and Irwin Garfinkel. Cambridge, MA: Harvard University Press, 1992, pp. 1-22.

Moffitt, Robert A."The Effect of Employment and Training Programs on Entry and Exit from the Welfare Caseload." *Journal of Policy Analysis and Management* 15, no. 1 (Winter 1996): 32-50.

Endnotes

1   Clearly, if persons assigned to the treatment group that consisted of the old welfare system were permitted to refuse and to enter the new welfare program, then the validity of the controlled experiment would be fatally impaired. The assignment process would no longer be random, but would instead depend on various unobserved factors that would prevent attributing causality to the treatment.

2   The following example is suggested by Kaplan and Meyer in their chapter: a controlled experiment to test the effects of different co-payment schedules for child care. This would not only affect the quantity and quality of child care purchases, but would be expected to affect the employment and earnings of the parent — directly because of the effect of child care on the parent's employment and indirectly because the co-payment schedule affects the net wage and the net earnings of the employed parent in the family. A higher co-payment imposed when earnings rise acts as an effective tax on the rise in earnings.

3   The problem in attributing causality to component parts of a program also exists with controlled experiments, as noted above.

4   Consider that the *levels* of two states' outcomes are likely to reflect not only the differences in the states' programs but also the states' long-standing differences in institutions, population composition, histories, and so forth. Now assume that these long-standing differences determine their pre-program measures of an outcome, such as the proportion of families on welfare. By measuring the *change* in this outcome that accompanies the change in the welfare system, the investigator may be able to attribute the outcome change to the change in the welfare programs. In comparing this change across two or more states we are measuring a difference in differences.

5   A more optimistic view of the scope and coverage of administrative data, with particular reference to the data available in Wisconsin, is given by Kaplan and Meyer in their chapter.

4

Alternative Designs for Evaluating National Welfare Reform

Robert Haveman
Department of Economics
La Follette Institute of Public Affairs
University of Wisconsin — Madison

The Legislation and the Evaluation of Its Effects

T he 1996 federal welfare reform — the Temporary Assistance for Needy Families (TANF) legislation — has important implications for the well-being of the entire low-income population, and in particular for those individuals and families who could have been eligible for assistance under the pre-reform law. Time limits went into effect starting July 1, 1997, the entitlement to support is abandoned, some groups eligible for support under pre-reform law are no longer eligible, and states are required to tailor-make their own systems of support through the block grant provisions of the new law.

While all of these changes have significant implications for the well-being of the low income population, the new law has several features that make a reliable evaluation of its overall impact — and the particular impact of any state's implementation of the law — difficult, and perhaps impossible. These include:

❖ A key provision of the new law is the block granting of funds to individual states, together with the requirement that each state design its own tailor-made system of support largely free of federal requirements regarding benefit eligibility and levels, and administration. As a result, a national welfare system characterized by some degree of coherence and similarity[1] will be replaced by a system in which state-specific policies will show substantially greater disparities. Subsequent to its implementation, the pre-reform system will be replaced by 50 quite different systems, constrained only by the few mandates in the national legislation. As a result, the diversity across the nation of "systems" for the support of the low-income population will be far greater than existed under the old law. This fact has particular relevance for any effort to provide an overall, nationwide assessment of the new law, but it also has important implications for designing an evaluation of any particular state's policy response to the federal legislation.[2]

❖ Because the new law represents a national policy change with state-specific implementation, there are several different levels on which evaluation can focus. The broadest level is that of a national evaluation in which the analyst would seek a picture of the overall impacts of the law, neglecting state or regionally specific effects. Alternatively, one might seek an assessment of the effects on a state's population of the particular version of the policy change implemented in that state. It is the latter form of assessment to which this paper is addressed.[3]

❖ The embedding of a state's policy change within a large-scale national policy shift poses a variety of research challenges for the analyst. On one hand, the analyst may be able to compare the behavior and administrative changes occurring over time in one location (state) — such as the Wisconsin Works (W-2) program — to those occurring in another location. Such a simple comparison, however, is not equivalent to an evaluation of the impacts of the policy change because underlying social and economic conditions in the different states may change in different ways and at different rates. Alternatively, the goal of the evaluation may be to assess the changes in variables of interest attributable to a particular state's policy change (for example, a shift from the pre-W-2 AFDC program to W-2), which is a question of "evaluation." Such an evaluation requires that change in underlying economic and social conditions in the state (apart from changes that are due to the policy shift) be known, and that the research is able to control for these changes. In both cases, research is hindered by the fact that, in a "general equilibrium" world, what happens in a particular state will be affected by the policy changes that are adopted in other states.[4]

❖ The process and speed of the transition from the old welfare system to the new system will not be uniform across the states. Some states installed and implemented a new and radically different program generally consistent with the new law on short notice; others have made changes far more slowly. This has clear implications for identifying the time horizon necessary for an evaluation of the entire national policy change, but it also has important implications for structuring the evaluation of the policy changes occurring in a particular state (e.g., evaluating the effects of W-2). Successful evaluation of the policy change adopted by a particular state is required to take account of the speed of implementation within that state, as well as the speed of implementation in neighboring states.

❖ The extent of policy change that will be undertaken by individual states in response to the new law is potentially enormous. The populations eligible for support under any state's old and new systems will be quite different. While the pre-reform system in all states had the objective of supporting the income of eligible people, the new system will seek to enforce work on a different pool of eligible citizens, and to condition assistance on work. The financial incentives offered by states to their low-income populations under the new law will be quite different from those that existed under the old law.

These considerations pose difficult problems for program evaluators concerned with either evaluating the effects of the new law on the nation, or the effects of those changes in legislation that will be adopted by particular states on the well-being of their citizens. Some of these involve large questions of evaluation design; others involve practical questions regarding which outcomes (variables of interest) are to be studied. In this paper, I will discuss the evaluation design issue (emphasizing the choice of design strategy for evaluation of a particular state's initiative), and comment on the difficulties confronted by *all* feasible designs. All of the available evaluation design options have serious fundamental problems; any overall decision regarding which design is the most effective will depend on considerations of both the cost of undertaking the evaluation, and the relative weights assigned to the various problems associated with each of the designs.

Some Basic Principles for an "Ideal" Evaluation

In this section, I describe the characteristics of an "ideal" evaluation of a state-based welfare reform measure, and outline some of the principles that should guide such an evaluation. These basic principles must be kept in mind in thinking through both the ideal evaluation and any feasible evaluation.

Some Assumptions

In discussing this "ideal" evaluation, I make a number of assumptions, most or all of which will be violated in any feasible evaluation. In a subsequent section, I discuss feasible evaluation strategies in a complicated world in which these assumptions do not hold.

In my view, one question is central in designing a state-based welfare reform evaluation study: What is the impact of the policy change on the economic well-being and the economic activities (e.g., work effort, family structure changes, health and nutrition changes, changes in the care and nurturing of children) of those individuals and families that are the most likely to be affected by the policy change?

A key word in this question is "impact," implying that the study seeks to isolate the changes in particular variables that are attributable to the policy from the changes that may be due to other factors. A second key point is the focus on individual people and their well-being. After all, a public policy is efficient only if the benefits that it conveys to people (its positive impact on their lives, living conditions, and well-being) exceeds the costs that it imposes on them.[5]

If this fundamental question regarding net well-being effects cannot be answered reliably, one should seriously question the wisdom of devoting substantial resources to studying the wide range of other questions that might be asked regarding changes that might follow upon the policy shift. Consistent with this point of view, I presume in the following discussion that a well-designed, longitudinal sample survey of households, and the measurement of outcome variables observable in survey responses, must form the core of a reliable analysis. However, while I emphasize what can be learned about the impacts of a state's policy change from appropriately structured household surveys, I do not ignore the important evaluative information that can be obtained through both administrative data and time series information on aggregate effects. This information can be studied apart from data obtained from the survey of households.[6]

Adopting this state-based evaluation posture avoids some of the problems that would confront an evaluator attempting to measure the impact of the policy change on the entire nation. However, this posture creates other problems. Perhaps the largest is that created by the potential migration of citizens in response to the policy change. In discussing the ideal evaluation, I ignore the difficulty for the evaluator posed by policy-induced migration.

Second, in discussing the characteristics of an "ideal" evaluation, I assume that the policy change from the pre- to the post-reform systems will be discrete, and that the characteristics of the pre-reform system and the post-reform system can be clearly identified and described. This neglects the fact that, in some states, major reforms have been undertaken prior to — and in anticipation of — passage of the new law, so that both defining and measuring the pre-reform (or without policy) system will be problematic. It also ignores the likelihood that real-time policy implementation will be slow and uneven, so that in the years following passage of a state's reform law all that the analyst will be able to observe will be some unknown combination of the pre-reform system and the post-reform system. In this situation, identifying the post-reform system may be impossible; any actual evaluator will have to assess how best to measure the effects of a "policy change process" as opposed to a discrete policy change.

Third, in discussing the ideal evaluation, I assume that the post-reform system will develop in response to the 1996 legislation, and that no major changes in federal law will be made in subsequent years through additional legislation. In any real-time evaluation, this assumption too is problematic.

Fourth, I assume that the policy change undertaken by states in response to the national law will be designed to "change the culture" in the state. That is, I assume that one of the objectives of the policy will be to change citizen perspectives regarding the responsibility of the public sector to provide income support, and of individuals to accept responsibility for their own financial well-being. Hence, virtually all low-income citizens will be affected by the legislation; evaluation should not be limited to the population of current program recipients, or those who would have been eligible for the current program.

Fifth, I assume that each of the designs considered is "feasible" in the sense that there is no prohibition in any state's legislation that would forestall any particular approach, and that securing data necessary for implementing a specific design is possible, even though that might require data collection and household surveys in other states.

Some Basic Principles

Several basic principles are relevant for securing a reliable evaluation of the policy change embodied in the new welfare law. These include the following:

❖ Precise specification of both the "factual" and the "counterfactual" is necessary. The analyst needs to have a clear description of both the nature of the public intervention *without* the new policy, and that existing *with* the new policy in place. More concretely, in considering the design of an evaluation of a particular state's policy change, the analyst needs a clear description of the nature of the state's welfare system as it existed prior to the

new welfare reform law (that is, without the new law),
and as it exists (or will exist) with the new law.

❖ Evaluation of the impact of introducing a new policy involves comparing the observed level of a variable of interest (e.g., the work hours and earnings of benefit
recipients and other low-income individuals) with the
new policy in effect, L^n, minus the observed level of the
variable with the prior policy, L^p.

❖ Having made the assumptions indicated by these two
principles, a sound evaluation of the impact of a replacement policy requires that *both* L^n (the factual) *and*
L^p (the "without policy" counterfactual) be observed
and measured reliably. Only in this way can Δ, the impact of the policy change, be obtained. If the new policy
is imposed as a replacement of the prior policy, the measurement of L^n is, in principle, straightforward; it is the
level of the variable observed over time subsequent to
the imposition of the new policy. Observation of L^p,
however, is not so simple. It requires identification of a
counterfactual which will yield behavioral incentives
and state of the world conditions (and hence, observed
levels of the variable of interest) identical to those that
would have existed with the prior policy in effect.
Hence, in a context in which a new policy replaces an existing policy (e.g., the replacement of the prior welfare
system with the new system that will exist given the
1996 legislation), this basic measure of the impact of the
policy change may be difficult to obtain.

In general, there are three ways of measuring the
counterfactual level of the variable of interest, L^p. They are:[7]

1. Establishing an experimental design, such that a randomly assigned sample of those decision makers affected by the policy
change continue to operate under the rules of the prior policy,
P. In this case, the level of the variable of interest can be measured for this randomly selected control group, used as L^p, and
compared with L^n observed and measured for the treatment
group operating under the rules of the new policy, N.

2. Defining a comparison group of individuals who are not randomly assigned, but who confront behavioral incentives and
state of the world conditions that are identical (or at least

similar) to those of the prior policy, P. Here, the variable of interest can be measured for individuals in this "control site," used as L^P, and compared with L^n observed and measured for the group confronting the rules of the new policy, N. This will be referred to as a "comparison site design."[8]

3. Defining a comparison group of individuals who are not randomly assigned but who, in fact, confront the prior policy, P. Here, the variable of interest is measured as it exists (or existed) for the "control group" (taken to be those confronting the prior policy), used as L^P, and compared with L^n observed and measured for the group confronting the rules of the new policy. This design will be referred to as a "pre-post design."

The Principles, and Choosing an Evaluation Design: The Experimental and Comparison Site Options

These basic principles have implications for the decision regarding the choice of a design strategy for evaluating a state-specific welfare reform, in the context of a national law encouraging a wide variety of state-specific policy changes. In this section, I discuss the experimental and comparison site design options, and indicate the implications of the basic principles for each of them.

An Experimental Design

The "social experimentation" technique has become the method of choice among many evaluators assessing the impact of proposed changes in social policy measures.[9] Using this technique, individuals in the target group (for example, a state's citizens, or a state's lower income citizens) are randomly assigned into a treatment and a control group, with only the former group being subjected to a "treatment" in the form of a policy environment that differs in some well specified way from the "without policy" environment. The standard policy proposal to which this design has been applied is, for example, a new job training program viewed as a replacement for the existing training environment. Simultaneous observation of the two groups over time will reveal a difference between them in the level of a variable of interest; that is, a difference between the level of the variable of the treatment group, L_t, and the level of the variable of the control group, L_c. This difference — $\Delta = (L_t - L_c) = (L^n - L^p)$ — is taken to be the impact of the policy. This procedure assumes that the new (or "treatment") policy does not affect the underlying "state of the world" (or that the new policy is "small"). Stated alternatively, this technique assumes that the level of the variable observed under the prior (or "without") policy reflects the state of the world into which the new policy is introduced, and hence that only the change in the level of the variable from that observed with the prior policy to that observed with the new policy is relevant.

With this latter assumption, the experimentation technique can proceed if the randomly assigned control group can be isolated from the treatment group, such that the control group becomes the counterfactual against which the treatment group is compared. This requires that, in spite of the policy change, it is feasible to secure a control group of individuals who will be confronted with the state of the world represented by that which existed under the prior policy. In general, the experimental studies of training and welfare-to-work programs have met these constraints (See Gueron and Pauly, 1991; Friedlander and Burtless, 1995).

If an experimental design is chosen for studying the impact of the policy on households and individuals, a separate design for using administrative and aggregate data for studying the effect of the policy would have to be developed. By definition, administrative/aggregate information is available 1) only for civil jurisdictions or administrative agencies, and 2) in time series form. Hence, the design of administrative and aggregate data collection for policy evaluation must employ a pre-post design format. The different conceptual bases for the evaluation — contemporaneous observation of samples of control and treatment group members in the experimental design and before-after administrative information for the pre-post design — could pose problems of interpretation.

A Comparison Site Design

With this design, a group of individuals located in an environment with both state of the world and behavioral incentives identical to those existing under the prior policy in a particular state (e.g.,

Wisconsin), P, must be identified. Then, the level of the variable of interest must be measured for this group, and taken to be L^P. From this, and the similar measurement of the variable of interest for the group of individuals confronting the new policy in the state of interest, N, a reliable estimate of $\Delta = (L^n - L^P)$ can be obtained.

As in the case of the experimental design, this counterfactual group facing the state of the world associated with P must both match and be isolated from the group of individuals who are subject to state of the world and the incentives of the new policy, N. However, while the random assignment procedure of the experimental design assures that the control group "matches" the characteristics of the treatment group, there is no such assurance in forming the comparison site group. Hence, in this design, a "statistical match" of individuals in the two groups must be made.[10]

This design must also confront the difficulty of securing comparability of those elements of the state of the world that are *not* associated with the difference in policy between P and N between the treatment and control (comparison site) groups. In the context of welfare reform, statistically matched individuals located in a comparison site must face economic and social conditions identical to those that prevail in the site subject to N (e.g., Wisconsin). In sum, the only aspect of the environment that can differ between individuals in the new program site, N, and those in the comparison site is the incentives and constraints associated with the policy that is in place.

Most important, the incentives and constraints of the policy in place in the comparison site must be identical to those of the prior policy, P, in the site for which the evaluation is being undertaken. The fact that pre-reform policy differences between any two states (or sites) are likely to be substantial is an unavoidable fact, and reduces the ability of an evaluator to secure a comparison state in which existing policy is identical (or even similar) to pre-reform policy in the state for which the evaluation is being made.

Finally, the implications of the comparative site design for the use of administrative and aggregate information in evaluation must be recognized. Because the nature of the data available in the comparative site will inevitably differ in subject matter, coverage, and definition from that available in the evaluation site, serious difficulties will be encountered in securing comparable administrative or aggregate information from two geographic sites required for a reliable evaluation. As with the experimental design option, a separate strategy would have to be developed for securing reliable pre-post administrative and aggregate data from the evaluation site for studying the effect of the policy.

The Principles, and a Pre-Post Design

In both the experimental and the comparison site designs, assessing the impact of the policy change requires contemporaneous measurements taken over the groups representing the with-policy and the without-policy alternatives (respectively, the treatment/control and the comparison site/policy site groups). In the pre-post design, however, this assessment for the without-policy alternative requires measurement while the prior policy, P, is actually in effect (that is, prior to the implementation of the new policy, N, in this site); assessment of the effect of the new policy, N, on relevant variables is made subsequent to implementation of the new policy.

In the pre-post design (as with the experimental and comparison site designs) two groups of individuals must again be designated. In this case, one group must be subject to the prior policy, P, and the other subject to the new policy, N. As with the comparison site design, this will require a statistical matching of individuals in the two groups, and with this an associated loss of comparability.

The problem of securing comparability of those elements of the state of the world — changes in demographic, social, and economic variables apart from any effect of the policy — that are not associated with the difference in policy between P and N is also serious in this design. And, as in the case of the comparative site design, the seriousness of this problem is not under the control of the evaluator. Because an evaluation using the pre-post design is based on measurements at two points in time, the analyst must attempt to secure identical underlying economic and social conditions during both the pre- and post-periods. Securing such identical (or even similar) state of the world circumstances is devilishly difficult. In the absence of such similarity, statistical control for differences in these environmental conditions will be required. The basis for securing such control is not clear.[11]

However, unlike the comparison site design, securing an accurate representation of the prior policy, P, does not pose a problem in the pre-post design. By definition, the incentives and constraints confronting individuals in the without (or pre-reform) period are those of the pre-reform policy.

Finally, adopting this design for evaluating the impact of the policy change on households and individuals has the important advantage of being entirely "within site," and hence consistent with the necessary "within site" design for the use of administrative and aggregate data for evaluation purposes. The impacts of the policy on families within the state (obtained through a longitudinal household survey) could be made consistent in both time and coverage with the impacts measured by administrative and aggregative data.

Trade-Offs Among the Design Options: A Summary

This discussion has revealed problems associated with each of the potential designs, and hence the need for considering trade-offs among the difficulties and the costs of each.

The experimental design has a serious (and, perhaps, fatal) flaw: In the face of a policy change that seeks to change the "culture" of public income support expectations within the state, it will be difficult or impossible to isolate a within-state control group from the incentives of the new policy. Implementing an experimental design also confronts the problem that a state is required to permit some of its citizens to continue to rely on the pre-reform system, and to mandate that program administrators work with these clients in a manner consistent with the operation of the program prior to the policy change. Conversely, the experimental design has the advantage of measuring the outcomes for the control and experimental groups contemporaneously, hence securing a constant state of the world (other than the changed incentives and constraints imposed by the policy change) across the two groups. This design for evaluating the effect of the policy on households and individuals, however, implies the need for a separate design for the use of administrative and aggregate data for program evaluation, given that these data are available within the site on only a pre-post basis.

The comparison site design also encounters serious difficulties. The major difficulty is that of securing a comparison site that has a "current policy" in effect that is identical (or similar to) the pre-reform system in the state whose policy change is being evaluated. Given that all states have to respond to the policy mandate of the 1996 legislation, it is unclear that any state will meet this without-policy-change requirement.[12] A second serious problem is securing comparability in terms of the nonprogram state of the world characteristics (e.g., economic and social conditions) between the comparison state and the state whose policy change is being evaluated. Third, this design strategy requires statistical matching of the households in the comparison state with those in the state whose policy change is being evaluated. Fourth, while this approach avoids the costs and difficulties of implementing a random assignment strategy, it may require the permission of the authorities in the comparison state to undertake a selective household survey for this purpose, and does require data collection in a separate and perhaps distant jurisdiction. Finally, like the experimental design, adoption of this design requires development of a separate pre-post, within-site design for the use of administrative and aggregate data in evaluation.

The pre-post design faces the difficult problem of securing comparability in the state of the world characteristics (e.g., economic and social conditions) between the pre-reform period and the post-reform period. Unlike the experimental design and the comparison site design, this strategy does not measure impacts contemporaneously. Developing techniques for statistically adjusting for the effects of differing underlying economic and social conditions on those household variables and market changes that are central to the evaluation would be necessary. (As indicated in footnote 7, development of models that would enable reliable adjustments is not straightforward.) Unlike the other designs, however, the with-program and without-program groups can be clearly identified. While specifying the policy change in this case seems relatively straightforward, the real-time evolution of state policy may preclude a clear delineation of the with- and without-policy environments (see below). The pre-post design, however, does place the results from it on the same analytical footing as the evaluation results obtained from the use of within-site administrative and aggregate data.

Problems and Prospects for a Pre-Post Evaluation Design for Wisconsin Works (W-2), and Next Steps

To assess the options for designing a pre-post evaluation of W-2, it will be helpful to define the constraints and the environment with which the evaluation will have to cope. The following are some facts and presumptions relevant for considering this issue:

❖ While successful evaluation of W-2 requires that the nature of the policy change be clearly defined, this requirement may not be attainable. Indeed, some of the elements of W-2 are currently being implemented in several counties, with all counties being urged to seek employment for applicants prior to offering income support benefits.[13] This is so even though formal, state-wide implementation of W-2 (though perhaps somewhat changed from the initial proposal) did not occur until the last quarter of 1997. This fact will make evaluation of W-2, by any design, difficult.

❖ It seems unlikely that the state of Wisconsin will be willing to exempt some sites (counties) from the W-2 legislation so as to make an experimental design feasible.

❖ Major welfare reforms in other states will also be pursued over the next few years.

❖ Throughout the nation, but especially in Wisconsin, reform of the welfare system will be the primary instrument for "changing the culture," a phrase meant to convey a major and discrete change in the social expectations regarding work and individual responsibility of low earnings capacity individuals (especially, poor single mothers). This culture change has already begun in Wisconsin.

❖ The economy of the state in subsequent years may not be as robust as it was in 1997, though there is little reason now to assume a major downturn. However, because of W-2, the low-wage labor market will experience an increase in labor supply (and hence downward wage pressure), relative to conditions without W-2.

I conclude that a pre-post evaluation design is the most feasible of the options for securing a reliable assessment of W-2. I reach this conclusion not because of any inherent superiority of this design. Rather, the characteristics and requirements of the experimental and the comparative site designs, together with the constraints imposed by the policy environment (e.g., reforms designed to change citizen expectations and the "culture," simultaneous and differential policy changes in all states in response to the federal legislation), severely limit the feasibility of these designs, relative to that of the pre-post design.[14]

Whatever evaluation of W-2 is undertaken, that assessment should focus on its effects on the well-being — as measured by the income, work, and structure — of low-income families in Wisconsin. While, in my view, this should be the primary focus of any evaluation, there are other important questions that are not addressed by this focus. These questions largely concern the provision and availability of public and private services to Wisconsin citizens, and the accessibility of other sources of income to them (especially employment income). These provision and accessibility issues can be thought of as elements of the economic environment in which low-income citizens live, which elements may be affected by W-2. Prominent examples of these elements could include:[15]

❖ the availability of quality day care services and the price of these services
❖ the availability of alternative sources of income, housing, food, and education/training services from nonwelfare (including private) sources
❖ the availability of family planning and abortion services.

In addition, there are other changes in non-W-2, income-related program services that might reflect the impact of W-2. While some of these may be captured in a comprehensive and carefully designed longitudinal survey, program and administrative data might be better able to reflect the impact of W-2, including:

❖ the level of foster care placements in various parts of the state
❖ food pantry and emergency housing and other service provision by public and private agencies

❖ the incidence of eviction from public or subsidized housing due to inability to meet rental payments

❖ the prevalence of nutrition deficiencies and behavior problems in the local schools.

Finally, it might be of interest to assess the impact on a variety of policy-relevant variables not directly affected by the policy change, and which may not be picked up by the survey data, such as the level of child support collections from absent parents, the incidence of marriage (abortion, nonmarital childbearing) of young women and men, or the level of employment of young married males.

These considerations suggest the importance of simultaneously initiating efforts to design a plan for using administrative and aggregate data for evaluating W-2. As indicated above, adoption of the pre-post design for evaluating the impact of the policy change (from the prior Wisconsin AFDC-based welfare system to W-2) has the important advantage of being conceptually consistent with the necessarily pre-post nature of within-state administrative data. Hence, the design for a pre-post evaluation should be made at the same time as, and in coordination with, the design of a strategy for collecting administrative and aggregate socioeconomic data. A clear delineation of the nature of the findings from the two coordinated, but independent, evaluation efforts should be attempted at the outset, so as to avoid duplication of efforts in gathering pre-post information.[16]

Some Final Thoughts

In this discussion, I have not considered the alternative of a combined comparison site/pre-post design. Such a design would allow both the cross-time and the cross-site effects of the policy change to be discerned. This would enable a "difference-within-differences" analysis framework which, by exploiting both the cross-time and the cross-site effects of the policy change, could provide additional observations and reliability.[17] Designing such an evaluation would be exceedingly complex, and would not eliminate the need to obtain statistical control for the effect of changes in demographic, social, and economic factors apart from the policy change on those variables relevant for evaluation. This combined strategy also has potentially large cost implications that should not be neglected.

If either a combined comparison site/pre-post design — or one of either the comparison site or pre-post approaches — are adopted, the evaluator will confront the difficult problem of distinguishing state of the world changes that are *not* due to the changed incentives and constraints imposed by the policy change, from the effects of the policy itself. The most concrete example of this problem is the need to adjust pre-post results from both the household survey and from administrative/aggregate information for changes in the underlying state of the economy from the period prior to the adoption of the new policy to the period after (see footnote 10). The relevant question here is: How would the work status (or some other relevant variable) of the individuals in the household survey have changed from the before to the after period, if underlying demographic, economic, and social conditions changed without any policy change? If this question could be answered, one could adjust observed changes in the relevant variables for the effects of changes in the state of the world apart from the policy shift.

Apart from the studies cited above, little thought has been given to this issue, in spite of major recent advances in statistical modeling of the determinants of changes in time series data. Given the importance of the question, and the nature of the policy change at issue, additional research efforts designed to develop reliable statistical models for forecasting without-policy changes relevant to evaluating state welfare reform seem worthwhile.

References

Bell, Stephen H., Larry L. Orr, John D. Blomquist, and Glen G. Cain. *Program Applicants as a Comparison Group in Evaluating Training Programs: Theory and a Test*. Kalamazoo, MI: W. E. Upjohn Institute for Employment Research, 1995.

Blank, Rebecca."What Causes Public Assistance Caseloads to Grow?" Chicago: Northwestern University, 1998.

Cancian, Maria and Barbara Wolfe."Outcomes of Interest: The Universe of Outcomes Likely to Interest Different Constituencies,"

Madison: Institute for Research on Poverty, University of Wisconsin–Madison, 1997.

Chernick, Howard. "Fiscal Effects of Block Grants for the Needy: An Interpretation of the Evidence." *International Tax and Public Finance*, 1998.

Cook, Thomas D. and Donald T. Campbell. *Quasi-Experimentation: Design and Analysis Issues for Field Settings*. Boston: Houghton-Mifflin, 1979.

Friedlander, Daniel and Gary Burtless. *Five Years After: The Long-Term Effects of Welfare-to-Work Programs*. New York: Russell Sage Foundation, 1995.

Garasky, Steven. "Analyzing the Effect of Massachusetts' ET Choices Program on the State's AFDC-Basic Caseload." *Evaluation Review* (December, 1990): 701–710.

Garasky, Steven and Burt Barnow."Demonstration Evaluations and Cost Neutrality: Using Caseload Models to Determine the Federal Cost Neutrality of New Jersey's REACH Demonstration." *Journal of Policy Analysis and Management* 11 (1992): 624–36.

Gueron, Judith M. and Edward Pauly. *From Welfare to Work*. New York: Russell Sage Foundation, 1991.

Heckman, James J., Hidehiko Ichimura, and Petra Todd. "Matching as an Econometric Evaluation Estimator: Evidence from Evaluating a Job Training Programme. *Review of Economic Studies* 64 (1997): 605–54.

Heckman, James J. and V. Joseph Hotz. "Choosing Among Alternative Nonexperimental Methods for Estimating the Impact of Social Programs." *Journal of the American Statistical Association* 84, (1989): 862–874.

Hollister, Robinson G. Jr., Peter Kemper, and Rebecca A. Maynard. *The National Supported Work Demonstration*. Madison: University of Wisconsin Press, 1984.

Kaplan, Thomas and Daniel Meyer. "The Structure of a Proposed Impact Evaluation of the Wisconsin Works Program," Madison:

Institute for Research on Poverty, University of Wisconsin — Madison, 1997.

Mohr, Lawrence B. *Impact Analysis for Program Evaluation.* 2nd ed. Thousand Oaks, CA: Sage Publications, 1995.

O'Neill, June. *Work and Welfare in Massachusetts: An Evaluation of the ET Program.* Boston: Pioneer Institute for Public Policy Research, 1990.

O'Neill, June E. and Dave M. O'Neill. *Lessons for Welfare Reform: An Analysis of the AFDC Caseload and Past Welfare-to-Work Programs.* Kalamazoo, MI: W. E. Upjohn Institute for Employment Research, 1997.

Piliavin, Irving and Mark Courtney."Prospects for Comparing Wisconsin Works to Welfare Reform Programs Outside the State." Madison: Institute for Research on Poverty, University of Wisconsin–Madison, 1997.

Rossi, Peter H. and Howard E. Freeman. *Evaluation: A Systematic Approach.* 5th ed. Newbury Park, CA: Sage Publications, 1983.

U.S. Congressional Budget Office. *Forecasting AFDC Caseloads, with an Emphasis on Economic Factors.* Washington, DC: Congressional Budget Office, 1993.

Watts, Harold and Albert Rees. *The New Jersey Income Maintenance Experiment.* (Vol 2.). New York: Academic Press, 1977.

Weinberg, Daniel. "A Survey of Program Dynamics for Assessing Welfare Reform," memo, U.S. Census Bureau, October 29, 1996.

Ziliak, James P., David N. Figlio, Elizabeth E. Davis, and Laura S. Connelly." Accounting for the Decline in AFDC Caseloads: Welfare Reform or Economic Growth?" Unpublished paper. University of Oregon at Eugene, 1997.

Endnotes

1   Prior to the new law, each state had a support system consisting of: a state-specific AFDC program that provided income support to primarily single-parent families, and which had to meet a detailed set of federal requirements and specifications; a federal food stamp program that provided food-based assistance on a national, uniform basis to both families supported by the AFDC program in a state, and to other low-income families; and a state-specific Medicaid program that provided health care support to AFDC-supported families plus other low-income families that met certain criteria, which (like AFDC) had to meet a detailed set of federal requirements and specifications. While this pre-reform set of programs varied by state in terms of benefit levels and accessibility, it retained a semblance of a coherent national system through both the uniform national food stamp program and the uniform, federal requirements for the AFDC and Medicaid programs.

2   See comments in the concluding section regarding the potential of using growing state disparities in policy regimes to provide at least a relative assessment of any particular state's reform program.

3   Assessment of the national impact of the policy change may well be more feasible than assessing the effects of a particular state's new law. At the national level, a number of data sets, such as the Survey of Income and Program Participation (SIPP), the National Longitudinal Surveys (NLS), and the Current Population Survey (CPS), exist to provide the basis for an assessment of the changes that the legislation has had over time on the populations of interest. Moreover, the Bureau of the Census has designed a nationally-representative, longitudinal survey, the Survey of Program Dynamics, that builds on SIPP, and that will have pre-reform period, reform implementation period, and medium-term post-reform period information. A wide variety of program eligibility, access and participation, income and in-kind benefits (by source), economic and demographic variables, as well as a variety of other information relevant to assessing the effect of the reform on family circumstances will be included in the survey. (See Weinberg, 1996.) The Urban Institute project on "Evaluating the New Federalism" makes use of some of these databases in their impact evaluation of the reform, and, in addition, has undertaken special surveys in a selection of states, the National Survey of American Families.

4   Introduction of harsh programs in one state, for example, may encourage the migration of low-income potential recipients in that state to neighboring states with more generous programs. See Chernick (1998) for a discussion of the incentives for jurisdictions to change policy financing arrangements as a result of TANF; such changes in one state are likely to spill over to neighboring states as well.

5   This focus on the well-being of individuals and families does not imply that assessments of the policy change on other variables, such as costs to taxpayers, getting people to work, or availability of child care slots, is not important. Other analysts concerned with the impact of TANF may, indeed, place higher weight on assessing some of these impacts.

6   Indeed, the case for the "pre-post" evaluation design rests heavily on the superiority of the "with" and "without" comparison of administrative and aggregate data that is possible with it.

7   There is an extensive literature that assesses alternative designs for evaluation studies of the impacts of public policy interventions, including Rossi and Freeman (1983); Mohr (1995); and Cook and Campbell (1979).

8   Most discussions of this possibility consider another, appropriately chosen, jurisdiction as the "control group" to which a state's residents would be compared.

9   The earliest experimental evaluation of a social policy intervention is the New Jersey Income Maintenance Experiment (Watts and Rees, 1977). Another prominent experimental design, in this case for evaluating a training program, is the National Supported Work Experiment (Hollister, Kemper, and Maynard, 1984). The Manpower Demonstration Research Corporation (MDRC) has undertaken a large number of experimental evaluations of welfare-to-work programs during the late 1980s and 1990s (Gueron and Pauly, 1991; Friedlander and Burtless, 1995).

10 The loss of comparability associated with a statistical match — as opposed to random assignment of a state's permanently poor residents to a prior policy regime and the new policy regime — is an important limitation on the reliability of results based on the comparison site design. See Rossi and Freeman (1983) for a description of this control method. A great deal of recent work has been done to improve the reliability of statistical matches in constructing control groups. Important contributions include Heckman, Ichimura, and Todd (1997); Heckman and Hotz (1989); and Bell, Orr, Blomquist, and Cain (1995).

11 The problem of statistically controlling for the effect of changed social and economic conditions on variables relevant to evaluating state changes in welfare policy is similar to that faced in studies that have attempted to model or "forecast" the change over time in state welfare caseloads. In these studies, the challenge has been to measure how underlying changes in demographic, social, and economic conditions will affect the number of welfare recipients, as reflected in entry and exit rates of welfare programs. Assessment of the forecasting success of the former studies is decidedly mixed. See U.S. Congressional Budget Office (1993); O'Neill (1990); Garasky (1990); O'Neill and O'Neill (1997); Garasky and Barnow (1992); Ziliak, Figlio, Davis, and Connelly (1997); and Blank (1998).

12 In principle, establishing a within-state comparison group design might be possible. This would require that some part of the state maintain the prior

policy regime, and consciously administer that regime as if no state policy change had occurred. (For example, it has been suggested that, in Wisconsin, counties that border Minnesota, and which are dominated by Minnesota newspaper, radio, and television media, should be administratively mandated to maintain the pre-W-2 AFDC program.) It seems unlikely that a segment of a state could, in fact, be kept immune from a state-based policy change with implications as fundamental and far-reaching as those required by the federal legislation.

13 For example, the Pay for Performance program is effectively in effect in several counties in Wisconsin, resulting in the sanctioning of large numbers of families. This program has more in common with W-2 than it does with the conventional, pre-policy-change AFDC program.

14 In particular, an experimental design seems infeasible because of (1) the absence of state exemption of sites or individuals from the provisions of the W-2 policy (and the maintenance of pre-reform AFDC service provision for these sites or individuals), and (2) the statewide culture change which will affect all low-income citizens, including existing recipients and potential applicants, rendering impossible the establishment of a reliable L^p, even were state exemptions to be granted. A comparative site design seems infeasible because (1) no state with base economic and social (and other state of the world) characteristics similar to Wisconsin will have in place a welfare system similar to the pre-reform Wisconsin system, hence rendering impossible the establishment of a reliable L^p, and (2) the culture change posited for Wisconsin will also influence the behavior of low earnings capacity citizens in other states, even if these states have not implemented a change as drastic as W-2, again eliminating the possibility of establishing a reliable L^p.

15 Cancian and Wolfe in this volume discuss the program and aggregative data relevant to evaluating state welfare reform, and trade-offs that must be confronted in designing an evaluation study using this information.

16 See Kaplan and Meyer (1997) for an evaluation design that rests on the use of administrative and aggregate data.

17 See Piliavin and Courtney (1997).

SECTION III

THE WISCONSIN WORKS PROGRAM

A.
A COMPREHENSIVE DESIGN

5

Toward a Basic Impact Evaluation of the Wisconsin Works Program

Thomas Kaplan
Institute for Research on Poverty
University of Wisconsin — Madison

Daniel R. Meyer
School of Social Work
Institute for Research on Poverty
University of Wisconsin — Madison

Introduction

T he Personal Responsibility and Work Opportunity Reconciliation Act of 1996 overturned 60 years of federal welfare policy, eliminating the federal structure of Aid to Families with Dependent Children (AFDC) and replacing it with the Temporary Assistance for Needy Families (TANF) block grant which states can use to design and operate programs for the poor. In this chapter, we present a proposed impact evaluation of the Wisconsin TANF program, Wisconsin Works (W-2). Because our proposal does not cover all domains and groups potentially affected by W-2, and discusses only a few indicators within some domains, the proposal should be read as a "basic evaluation plan," containing our view of the minimal elements of an impact evaluation of W-2. Additional impact evaluations focusing on other potential consequences of W-2 should supplement this basic evaluation.

As the introduction to this volume indicates, the W-2 program is a highly complex undertaking implemented gradually over a phase-in period. The official start of W-2 occurred on September 1, 1997, but important parts of the program had already begun before that and the program was not fully operational until April 1, 1998. A useful evaluation of such a program will not be easy to perform. Measuring the impact of one discrete change when related policies remain constant is difficult enough in social programs. Measuring the impact of many major changes that occur continuously over a long period — with no easy ability to randomly assign participants to treatment and control groups or determine in other ways how the program would have evolved without the policy changes — is still more difficult.

Overview of the Evaluation Plan

The Scope of the Evaluation

Because W-2 is an attempt to completely replace the previous welfare system, it could influence many dimensions of the everyday life of AFDC recipients, as pointed out in the accompanying paper by Maria Cancian and Barbara Wolfe. Indeed, hopes of influencing several dimensions of the daily lives of AFDC or potential AFDC recipients — ranging from their work life to the way they relate to their children — are a distinguishing feature of emerging versions of comprehensive welfare reform. To reflect the aspirations of program designers and the fears of program critics, evaluations must cover multiple dimensions, but they must also be small enough to be manageable. We view our task here as limited: We propose a "basic" impact evaluation, an evaluation built around selected critical consequences that we believe *must* be evaluated. We have selected six primary impact domains (income, dependency, child care, child welfare, health status, and living arrangements and family structure) based on judgments that they (a) are central to the purposes of the reform and to the well-being of the families affected, and (b) offer a high likelihood of finding a measurable effect with data that are now available or could be available in the future. We also identify a second tier of impact domains that we consider important but not as central.

Just as W-2 could affect many dimensions of everyday life, the program could affect many groups, including W-2 participants, those who would be eligible but do not participate, those not eligible but likely to be affected (primarily adults in the low-wage labor market, including those with no minor children), employers, child care providers, schools, social service agencies, governmental units, and taxpayers. Again, to keep this proposed evaluation manageable, we focus our attention on individuals rather than employers, institutions, or entire markets. We do not propose a benefit-cost analysis, which would require a major and complex effort. Determining direct costs in a benefit-cost analysis is fairly straightforward, although the analysis would have to be encompassing enough to incorporate expenditures on food stamps and the Earned Income Tax Credit as well as child care, cash assistance, and medical assistance. Indirect costs and benefits are quite problematic, particularly a comparison of the indirect costs of W-2 and AFDC. Examples of costs and benefits that would be difficult to estimate include increased (or decreased) costs borne by the educational system if children are less (or more) prepared for school, increased human costs and costs in the social service and criminal justice systems if individuals are afraid to leave situations of domestic violence because they perceive fewer financial resources available to make it on their own, the potential for increased institutionalization of children with disabilities, long-term increases or decreases in juvenile crime, increases or decreases in the general readiness of the labor market, etc.

We propose a *limited* evaluation approach, one that we believe has the potential to answer the most critical questions, even though more complex or comprehensive approaches are possible. We therefore recommend a single counterfactual and a similar approach to evaluating each potential impact. We envision that other evaluations would also be done, perhaps on other impacts, perhaps with other approaches, and we periodically comment on areas that we tentatively view as most promising. We believe that our contribution is not to identify an idealized evaluation, but to think about the difficult decisions one must make if one is to conduct a limited evaluation, with a limited budget. In summary, we view our task as identifying key impacts (but not all impacts) covering key concerns (but not all concerns), with a limited approach.

The Counterfactual

We propose that the primary comparison be between outcomes under W-2 and outcomes in Wisconsin before the implementation of W-2 (a pre-post design). Part of our reasoning stems from the weaknesses or unsuitability in this setting of other options. (For a more comprehensive review of these other options, see the chapters by Haveman and Cain.) One method of evaluating W-2 would be to randomly assign some applicants to W-2 and others to AFDC. But experimental designs work best when four conditions are met: (a) the agencies that would implement random assignment are cooperative (Hotz, 1992); (b) only a few program elements are undergoing change (because it is then administratively feasible to operate an experimental and control program); (c) the control group can easily be isolated from "contamination" introduced by the experiment (Cook and Campbell, 1979); and (d) the intervention is not expected to generate community feedback effects (Garfinkel, Manski and Michalopoulos, 1992).

W-2 meets none of these conditions. First, it is unlikely that agencies implementing W-2 (primarily the Wisconsin Department of Workforce Development, or DWD) would be willing to operate a parallel AFDC system in some locations. Second, even if the DWD wanted to operate a parallel AFDC system, the new client work requirements under TANF would complicate such an effort, and the administrative demands of continuing a parallel AFDC system while simultaneously creating the organizational structures to operate W-2 would be very high. Third, a control group cannot be isolated, in part because the W-2 reform has generated substantial publicity. Fourth, W-2 could well generate large community feedback effects. Garfinkel and colleagues describe (1992) several potential types of community feedback effects: market-equilibrium, information-diffusion, social-interaction, and norm-formation. All potentially apply to W-2. The program could clearly affect the equilibrium of the low-skill labor market by requiring a large number of people to work, and a randomized experiment would mismeasure these effects unless the number of people in the control group not required to work were trivial. Moreover, the designers of W-2 hope that it causes shifts in social interactions and a fundamental restructuring of norms in low-income communities, changes that would be less likely to occur if only a portion of the community were subject to W-2.

124

A second possible counterfactual strategy would be to compare results under W-2 to results from jurisdictions outside the state. This may be particularly useful to policy makers because they are unlikely to consider the pre-W-2 system in Wisconsin as a policy-relevant alternative, whereas another state's approach to assisting low-income families might be more feasible. Nonetheless, a comparison of W-2 to AFDC is of significant scientific interest, and it is also politically relevant in the sense that proponents of welfare reform make the claim that their proposals will be better than AFDC. Comparisons of W-2 to the system in another state would be most helpful if the case can be made that the other jurisdictions would have evolved identically to Wisconsin had it not been for their varying public assistance strategies. Differences in the well-being of low-income households or the status of the low-wage labor force could then reasonably be attributed to the different public assistance strategies. But many other policy and economic variables could influence observed differences among states, and it would be hard to show that the divergence in public assistance programs was the critical variable. Some forces affecting low-income families affect those in different states differently, such as a recession in a particular industry, a natural disaster, or state policy toward related public programs (elimination of General Assistance, removal of public schools from the property tax, etc.), so a cross-state comparison does not ensure that the only relevant difference between two states is whether low-skill parents face W-2 or an alternate public assistance regime. A final difficulty with this approach is that states have very different administrative recordkeeping systems, and, as we outline below, we propose relying heavily on administrative data in the basic evaluation.[1]

A pre-post time series design is not without serious problems of its own. The main problem is the possibility that something else changed at about the same time that AFDC was changed to W-2 (Cook and Campbell, 1979). Clearly, some major factors *did* change: for example, the minimum wage increased from $4.25 to $4.75 per hour in 1996 and again to $5.15 per hour in 1997, making an evaluation of W-2's effect on wages in the low-skill labor market problematic. Similarly, benefits under the Earned Income Tax Credit (EITC) were altered significantly in 1990 and in 1993 through phased increases, so an increase in employment among low-skilled workers may be the effect of EITC changes rather than the replacement of AFDC with W-2. Finally, the ending of AFDC, changes in the food stamp program, and changes in the supplemental security income

(SSI) program — all components of the federal welfare reform passed in 1996 — will take effect contemporaneously with W-2, further complicating the simple comparison of W-2 and AFDC. Below we identify some strategies for dealing with these changes, recognizing that none are perfect. We selected a pre-post design not because it is flawless, but because it is feasible, cost-effective, and seems no more flawed than other designs.

Our reliance on a pre-post design does not negate possibilities for meta-analysis of pre-post studies in several states, and, indeed, this is in some ways a superior strategy if feasible. With its limited evaluation funds, it may be possible for the federal government to encourage enough common variables and definitions so that meta-analysis of pre-post evaluations could investigate the independent effect of selected variables. By comparing the post-reform with the pre-reform in each state, and evaluating the "difference in differences," the evaluator could state with more confidence that observed results were caused by W-2 (or perhaps even by particular features of W-2). While we are intrigued with this approach, we do not propose it here because we are concerned about its feasibility and cost-effectiveness, and because our one-state, pre-post model is consistent with a basic, limited evaluation.

Our reliance on a pre-post design also does not negate possibilities for randomized evaluations of particular program components. For example, the state is evaluating the child support pass-through component of W-2 through a random assignment evaluation in which most W-2 participants will keep all child support paid on their behalf but a small control group faces a different child support policy. Moreover, Wisconsin could decide that families in a few counties would be randomly assigned to different child care co-payment schedules. Such randomized evaluations of particular components would enable policy makers to examine the effects of alternate program elements, while not compromising the main thrust of the reform. In this limited evaluation, however, we are more concerned with determining the overall impacts of W-2 than with determining the program mechanisms responsible for these impacts. Identifying with reasonable certainty the key impacts of W-2 will be a large enough challenge; determining the independent impact of particular features within W-2 seems, in general, too daunting.

Basic Data Source

We propose to depend primarily on administrative data to examine effects. Our preference for pre-post administrative data over surveys stems in part from the expense of obtaining data through surveys over time. Capturing the effects of an intervention on income growth, for example, would require panel studies measuring the same people over a period of years, and panel studies are the most expensive kinds of surveys to operate. In contrast, it is possible to follow the same family's income tax records much more efficiently over time.

Panel surveys are especially difficult to conceptualize as a way of evaluating the impact of W-2 in Wisconsin because the first wave of the survey could at best have been mounted in 1997, when evaluations of W-2 were first considered but well after much of W-2 had already gone into effect. Because so much of W-2 had already been implemented before the formal start of the program, the best way to assess its full impact is somehow to go back in time to capture the situation that existed before W-2 began. Administrative data in both electronic and paper form do extend back into the past and offer some reliability, and our proposal rests heavily on such data. Further, it may take some time before W-2 is operating smoothly, and thus W-2 may have different effects in its first years of operation than in subsequent years. If these effects are of interest, this makes a panel survey even more costly, because either a very large initial sample would have to be selected (in order to ensure that there would be a sufficient number of new W-2 recipients in later years) or a new sample would have to be drawn each year. Drawing new samples each year and following them through administrative data, however, is less expensive. Finally, the implementation analysis may reveal that W-2 is implemented very differently in some counties than others. Using administrative records as a sampling frame would enable researchers to oversample in some counties several years *after* the program differences had been detected. In contrast, a desire to oversample from particular counties not even identified until a substantial period of time after the program has been in operation would be quite difficult in an evaluation relying on survey data.

Although administrative data are clearly less expensive to obtain than survey data, that advantage would be meaningless if the administrative data were not accurate. It is difficult to assess the relative accuracy of survey and administrative data because a reliable independent information source is not easily available. Many low-income people appear to report lower total income in surveys than their reported expenditures would suggest, a finding that has led some researchers to conclude that survey data on income in low-income households is flawed (Mayer and Jencks, 1989). Edin and Lein (1997) found that low-income single mothers reliably recalled all their sources of income only after multiple sessions with an interviewer in whom they had developed some trust, first totaling all expenditures for a month and then being prompted to recall all the income that had supported those expenditures. Such intensive and repeated interviewing is not feasible in large-scale survey efforts. Concerning earnings alone and not other forms of income, Kornfeld and Bloom (1996) found rough agreement between earnings data reported by unemployment insurance administrative agencies and survey data reported by participants in the National Job Training Partnership Act Study. In general, the surveys reported higher average earnings, but because differences between income reported on surveys and through the administrative data remained constant over time, they did not bias measurements of program impact. About half the difference in income reported by the survey and administrative data sources reflected work not reported to unemployment insurance agencies. As we discuss below, other administrative data sources can compensate for some of these reporting gaps in the unemployment insurance system.

Even though we rely on administrative data for the basic evaluation we propose, we believe that surveys of low-income families could provide valuable additional information. Because administrative data typically have very limited demographic information, an intriguing possibility is to conduct a simple survey gathering demographic information on individuals in the administrative databases. Analyses using the Urban Institute's New Federalism Household Survey could also supplement the analyses proposed here; we do not rely on it as a primary data source because we believe annual data on the same families over a period of more than five years is desirable. A comprehensive panel survey of the low-income population, while much more expensive to gather than the administrative data we propose using, could provide a wealth of important data. Furthermore, while we propose primarily quantitative analyses in the basic evaluation, analyses using ethnographic data would also add an important untapped dimension to our knowledge about the effects of W-2.

Time Period

All evaluations face a difficult decision regarding the length of time a program will be evaluated, as discussed by Cancian and Wolfe.[2] If the time period is too long, the evaluation will be expensive, the results may be too late to influence program development, and the counterfactual becomes more difficult (a pre-post evaluation has to face increased likelihood of other significant events occurring during the evaluation period that could create their own effects; similarly, more time increases the likelihood that significant reform will occur in the "control" site in a cross-site design). If the period is too short, however, other difficulties arise: A program evaluated too early for too short a period may not tell us anything about the way the program would work when it is more mature and some of the "debugging" has occurred (e.g., Campbell, 1984); further, programs like W-2 seek to affect community norms, and this process takes some time. Complicating this decision further is the fact that W-2 has time limits built into some of its components: No one can receive subsidized job services for more than five years unless granted an exception, and thus any evaluation that is concerned about the effect of this five-year limit must span a long enough period that some will exhaust their eligibility and outcomes can then be examined. Similarly, participants can only take part in each of the three subsidized components (Transitions, Community Service Jobs [CSJs], and trial jobs) for 24 months. Finally, W-2's proponents recognize that in the short term, income may decline, but the hope is for longer-term increases in income. Again the evaluator needs to allow enough time to elapse that the individual who received valuable work experience in a trial job could be in the unsubsidized workforce long enough to show wage gains resulting from that experience.

Therefore, we propose a two-part evaluation, a three-year examination (focusing on short-term effects), and a seven-year examination (focusing on longer-term effects; in seven years some families will have exhausted benefits and the time period should be long enough to capture longer-term wage increases). Further, we propose that no impact evaluations be done for the first year, only process evaluations, allowing at least some time for the program to change, develop, and reach a steady state.

Impact Domains to Evaluate in a Basic Evaluation

We propose that an evaluation to answer only the most important questions should focus on six impact domains: income, dependency, child care, child welfare, health status, and living arrangements and family structure. We select these six because we believe all are central to the purpose of W-2 and to the well-being of affected families. We also believe that data sources for income, dependency, health status, and family structure are sufficient to offer the prospect of finding a measurable effect. The data sources for child care and child welfare are less certain, but could be improved with minimal future investment.

Primary Potential Impact 1: Income and Poverty

Hypothesis 1.1: W-2 will have an impact on incomes among low-income families with children. Because some factors are likely to result in increased incomes and others in decreased incomes, we do not specify the predicted direction of effect. In this domain, we propose that it is important to identify whether incomes of low-income parents as a whole increase or decrease, as well as identifying the types of families experiencing increases and the types experiencing decreases.

Rationales: Income increases could occur through five primary mechanisms:

1. Some low-income families do not currently have the job skills to compete in the labor force and would receive few unsubsidized job offers if they were to search. Because W-2 provides CSJs and/or trial jobs for these individuals, they may eventually obtain the job skills (and/or the work experience) that will enable them to earn more than they could have earned in the past and also be able to earn more than they would have received on AFDC.

2. Closely related to the first group is a group of recipients who have some job skills and could receive some job offers, but the wage offers they would receive would be too low to make working worthwhile. This could occur either because work expenses like child care and transportation are so high or because the job offers they would get would come without health insurance. For these individuals, W-2's provisions of child care and health insurance, combined with the requirements to be working, may shift the incentives and move them into employment; as a result they will eventually earn more than they would have had the old AFDC system been in existence.

3. Adults in some low-income families do not currently work outside the home because AFDC allowed them to receive benefits with minimal effort. By eliminating the possibility of receiving cash assistance without effort, by limiting the amount of time a family can receive any assistance, and by requiring employment, W-2 may push these individuals into the labor force, which will eventually lead to higher incomes than they would have received under AFDC.

4. Many husband-wife low-income families are not currently eligible for assistance because of well-known limitations in the AFDC-UP (Unemployed Parent) program and severe funding restrictions for child care assistance. Because W-2 opens child care assistance and health assistance to husband-wife families, disposable income will automatically increase for some families. Further, the provision of subsidies for child care may enable some families that were single-earner families to become dual-earner families, increasing their incomes. Finally, if AFDC encouraged family break-up by primarily helping only single-parent families, under W-2 these families may stay together, and family incomes in husband-wife families are generally higher than in single-parent families.

5. Under AFDC, a recipient family was able to keep only $50/month of child support, with the remainder going to offset AFDC costs. W-2 allows families receiving assistance to keep the entire amount of child support, which directly increases incomes. Further, some ethnographic evidence suggests some nonresident parents only paid $50/month of child support because additional amounts did not benefit the family (Edin, 1995). Thus W-2's elimination of this disincentive to pay may

131

increase the total amount of child support paid, which would further increase the resident parent family's income.

On the other hand, W-2 could reduce income. W-2 will not provide any benefits to three groups of families who used to receive AFDC. First, because W-2 has a time limit for receiving benefits, some families will exhaust this time limit and stop receiving benefits. Second, because W-2 is not an entitlement, it is possible that during periods of recession the budget will be exhausted, and then some families who would have been participants will not receive benefits. Third, the sanctions for noncompliance are stricter under W-2 than they were under AFDC before 1996, and thus more families will become ineligible for benefits for not complying with various provisions of W-2. In each of these cases in which a family no longer receives benefits, whether their total income increases or decreases depends on their response to this new regime.

In addition to the families who receive nothing from W-2, for some families W-2 will provide some assistance, but at a level below what they received under AFDC. Because W-2 benefits do not increase with family size, one key group is large families. Those with three children are likely to receive approximately what they would have received under AFDC. For larger families, the disparity between W-2 and AFDC will be substantial, although total income will depend on a family's response to the lowered benefits.

Data, Comparison Group, and Analysis Approach: This is a domain in which we have fairly reasonable data on the AFDC period, with the ability to examine earnings of AFDC recipients before, during, and after receipt (through the quarterly earnings records of the Department of Industry, Labor, and Human Resources, or DILHR, now the Department of Workforce Development) and family income (through an extract from the tax records of the Department of Revenue, or DOR).[3] The chapter in this book by Martin David discusses a related approach in more detail.

Our proposed approach is built around three main comparisons:

❖ comparing income changes of W-2 and AFDC recipients

❖ comparing pre- and post-W-2 income changes of a broader sample of low-income families

❖ comparing pre- and post-W-2 income changes among higher-income families.

For the W-2-AFDC comparison, we propose selecting two samples of W-2 recipients in 1998 (or another year after full implementation of W-2), a sample of those who entered the program during the year and a sample of those who were participating at the beginning of the year. Using the Social Security numbers of the adults, we propose merging tax, earnings, W-2, and food stamp records to calculate the total income of these families in each year from 1999 through 2005. For the comparison AFDC group, we would select two parallel samples of recipients drawn from the administrative AFDC records for 1988. Again we calculate their family incomes in each year from 1989 through 1995 using Social Security numbers, tax records, earnings records, AFDC records, and food stamp records. (Note that the W-2 group would look different from the AFDC group on several dimensions because of policy differences between the programs; for example, the W-2 sample would contain more husband-wife families.) We propose drawing separate samples of entrants and current recipients because many analyses show that these two groups are quite different (e.g., Cancian and Meyer, 1995; Friedlander and Burtless, 1995).

The primary longer-term evaluation is a comparison of the later family incomes (2005 and 1995) for these samples of entrants and recipients. The analysis includes estimating a multivariate equation in which later family income is the dependent variable and the key independent variable is whether this is a family who was an AFDC recipient (the early period) or a W-2 recipient (the later period).[4] A variety of variables will be incorporated as control variables, including features of the local labor market, individuals' educational levels, family size and structure, etc. We will also explore interacting the variable indicating the period with a variety of sociodemographic characteristics to determine if W-2 had different effects for different groups of people.

The main short-term evaluation is a comparison of the 2001 incomes of the 1998 W-2 recipients with the 1991 incomes of the 1988 AFDC recipients, using a similar analysis. The three-year time frame also enables the researcher to examine whether a difference between W-2 and AFDC is a result of the program change or merely the result of long-term time trend.[5] The analyst could calculate income three years later for several samples of AFDC recipients, perhaps drawn from each year between 1988 and 1992. If time trends are detected, it may be possible to then remove this trend from the comparison of W-2 and AFDC.

Another analysis could test whether W-2's effect on incomes differs for those experiencing W-2 when it is first established from when it is a more mature program. By using administrative data, it is relatively simple to draw other W-2 samples, perhaps from 1999 and 2000, to follow them three years after their W-2 experience as well, and to test whether W-2's effect differs as the program develops.

Another analysis could be a test of whether some types of W-2 programs lead to different effects, as suggested by Holden and Reynolds in their paper. Agencies administering W-2 have considerable latitude in several program features, and it is therefore possible that the "intervention" will look very different in different counties. If the implementation evaluation identifies key program differences across sites, we propose using this information to test whether different types of W-2 programs lead to different effects on incomes.[6]

All of the analyses above are tests of whether the later incomes of W-2 families are different from the later incomes of AFDC families. But W-2 may also affect willingness or ability to enter into the program, as well as the economic well-being of low-income people who do not enter the program but must compete against the new job entrants the program is likely to stimulate. We can use administrative data to compare the incomes and public assistance utilization of a broader sample of low-income families with children (those below 200 percent of the federal poverty line) during the AFDC and W-2 periods, although we could not easily distinguish program entry effects on the income of these families from potential effects of job displacement caused by W-2. We could also follow the incomes over time of W-2 applicants who are denied eligibility for the program or who are deemed job-ready and eligible for case management (and perhaps child care) services only, although no comparable caseloads necessarily existed during the AFDC period. To make the comparison between low-income families with children during the AFDC and W-2 periods, we propose drawing two additional samples of low-income families with children, defined as families with income less than twice the poverty line. We propose drawing these samples based on Wisconsin tax records from 1998 and 1988, and then to examine income in 2001 and 1991 (short-term effects) and 2005 and 1995 (longer-term effects). Perhaps the tax data would have to be supplemented with survey data to gain a full sample of low-income nonrecipients. Once the sample was selected, an analysis parallel to the analysis of recipients would be conducted.

One method of increasing our confidence that any observed change in incomes was due to W-2, rather than to other factors, is to include a variety of control variables. Another method is to compare incomes over time of higher-income families with children, defined as having taxable income above 300 percent of poverty (taken from the DOR records of the same years), with analyses parallel to those described above. Because W-2 is likely to have little effect on the incomes of upper-income families, this will provide one estimate of general changes in income over these periods, and this could strengthen our confidence in whether observed changes between AFDC and W-2 were due to W-2 or to other changes in the economy. For example, if the family incomes of the low-income sample in 2001 are higher than in 1991, but the family incomes of the higher-income sample did not change, this could increase our confidence that the effect was the result of W-2 (or other changes affecting only the low-income population) rather than economy-wide changes.[7]

Issues and Limitations: One difficult issue for evaluating the effect of W-2 on income is the definition of "income." The traditional definition employed by the Census Bureau has included only pretax cash income. Many analysts prefer a concept of disposable income, which includes near-cash in-kind benefits and also deducts taxes. While assigning the cash value of food stamps to a household's income is straightforward and generally noncontroversial, there is less consensus over whether and how to value public health insurance, employer-provided health insurance, housing assistance, or the value of home ownership.[8] In the basic evaluation we propose here, which relies only on administrative data, we will not have measures of employer-provided health insurance, housing assistance, or a good measure of home ownership, limiting the measure of income we can construct. For those filing tax returns, we propose to calculate income by summing taxable income, AFDC/W-2 benefits, food stamps, and the federal Earned Income Tax Credit, and subtracting federal and state income taxes and payroll taxes. For those not filing tax returns but with in-state AFDC/W-2 income or in-state earnings, we will estimate income by summing earnings, AFDC/W-2 benefits, and food stamps, and subtracting estimated payroll taxes. We will also explore subtracting estimated out-of-pocket child care expenditures; unfortunately, these will be more available under W-2 than they were under AFDC.

Another issue facing this analysis and the ones that follow is defining who is a W-2 recipient. We propose that individuals receiving trial jobs, CSJs, or W-2 Transitions are clearly recipients. Although families that receive child care subsidies only could be considered recipients, we propose to not count them as W-2 recipients in these analyses because we generally lack information on families that only received child care assistance from the AFDC period. Similarly, if there is accessible information on individuals receiving Medicaid only from the AFDC period, we could include both them and the corresponding group from the W-2 period (those receiving health insurance subsidies only). If the data are available, analyses could be conducted both with and without this group. Another difficult group includes those who come for help, are referred to a private sector unsubsidized job, begin working, and receive only case management services. While W-2 considers these individuals clients, and appropriately will count them as successes, we believe that they cannot be included in the sample of "W-2 clients" because a comparable person was not included as an AFDC client (and some individuals did receive this type of help from AFDC, although presumably a much smaller number). The analysis of income changes using the entire low-income sample may enable us to estimate effects on this "referral-only" population.

A final difficult issue concerns what variables to hold constant in this analysis. This is a well-known problem of quasi-experimental designs; we discuss two examples, family structure and the local unemployment rates, but the issue relates to several other variables as well. In evaluating W-2's effect on income, one perspective is that the analyst should examine effects on single-parent families and husband-wife families separately. The argument for doing so is that because husband-wife families typically have higher incomes than single-parent families, and because a higher proportion of W-2 recipients are husband-wife families, a finding that W-2 participants have higher incomes than AFDC participants may merely reflect the composition of the caseload rather than an effect of W-2. On the other hand, W-2 could affect family structure decisions, and under this perspective, an evaluation of W-2's effect on income should not control for family structure. Similarly, the analyst would want to control for the local unemployment rate, because a change in the unemployment rate could confound an analysis of the effect of W-2. On the other hand, if W-2 affects the local unemployment rate, the analyst should not hold this constant. Both perspectives have limitations; our general proposal would be to conduct both types of analyses.

The proposed evaluation strategy has several limitations related to gaining information on income. First, relying on Wisconsin's administrative records of income misses some individuals; for example, no information is available on those who move out of state. Second, tax records also miss information on those who do not file taxes; individuals with taxable incomes below about $6,000 are not *required* to file forms. This is less of a problem in Wisconsin than it would be in other states because Wisconsin offers a refundable credit for low-income renters and homeowners, increasing the likelihood that a low-income family will file a tax form.[9] Further, incorporating information from the earnings records and welfare records increases the coverage, because individuals who do not file tax forms frequently have income in these other records. Analyses conducted with data from the Wisconsin child support project suggest that income estimates should be available for about 90 percent of a low-income sample and perhaps over 95 percent. Nonetheless, the 5 to 10 percent for whom we lack income information are likely to be the most vulnerable group, and they deserve more attention. One approach in the comparison of W-2 and AFDC recipients would be to identify those who were initially W-2/AFDC recipients who do not appear in later administrative records, attempt to locate them, and survey them.

The measures of family income are also limited. Taxable income does not include various income sources, including transfers and child support.[10] For those not filing tax forms, earnings records from DILHR/DWD are limited in that they only report earnings in *covered* employment, which does not include earnings in the informal sector. Expenses associated with working are not fully available: the amount of federal and state taxes is straightforward, but child care costs may not be, and work-related transportation expenses will definitely not be.

Tax records provide only limited information on family composition, and family composition is needed to determine family income. Tax filing status can tell us whether the taxpayer is married or not on December 31, but cannot tell at what point the marriage or divorce occurred. Second, there is no way to identify other adults in the home (cohabitors, roommates, relatives); to the extent that these individuals contribute to the family's income, we will underestimate income.[11]

A related concern is that administrative records contain very limited information on these families. For families who have never received AFDC or W-2, the tax record includes only the age of the adults, filing status, the number and ages of children, and address. For families who do not file taxes and have never received AFDC or W-2, and appear in the sample only as part of the DILHR/DWD earnings file, we would not even know this information. Thus for many families we will not know basic data such as race and educational level. This information will be available for any families who ever received AFDC or W-2, but even for these families we will not know whether they speak English nor anything about their family of origin, and we will have only sketchy information on work experience. We consider this limitation potentially quite problematic, and believe that the development of a short survey gathering basic data on individuals who are in the administrative records should be explored.

The degree to which we can be certain that W-2 caused differences in income under W-2 and AFDC is limited by other changes that occurred between the AFDC and W-2 regimes, as discussed earlier. One key change is the increase in the minimum wage. There are several ways to try to account for this, none of them entirely satisfactory. One way would be to use the results of other studies on the effect of the increase in the minimum wage on family income. One could then subtract this effect from any observed difference in income, assuming that the remainder was due to W-2. A second approach would be to simulate what income in the AFDC situation would have been like had the new minimum wage been in effect,[12] and to compare income under W-2 and the new minimum wage with simulated income under AFDC and the higher minimum wage. A third approach is to redefine the "treatment" to include not just W-2 but W-2 and a new minimum wage. In this type of issue in which alternative approaches seem justifiable, the basic approach we favor is that the researcher conduct multiple analyses, report the results of different analyses, and make the data available for others who would prefer another approach.[13]

Evaluations of any policy change of this magnitude in a complex and dynamic environment will be imperfect. Although this approach contains several limitations, alternatives also present serious problems, and we believe this approach has the potential to provide reasonably clear information on the impacts of W-2 at a reasonable cost.

Hypothesis 1.2: W-2 will decrease incomes among adults *without* children.

Rationale: Three provisions of W-2 may have a direct impact on the earnings (and therefore income) of adults without children. First, W-2 will force many low-skilled parents into the labor market, so the general supply of low-skilled people wanting jobs will increase. This increased supply will decrease wages for low-skilled jobs. The increased supply will also cause employers to be less likely to retain marginal current employees. Second, W-2's provision of employer subsidies for hiring from a targeted class may make the hiring and retention of nontargeted employees less likely, decreasing their incomes. Finally, W-2 creates many community service jobs in nonprofit organizations and local governments. The possibility of having access to a large number of potential employees at little or no cost may cause these organizations to forego hiring individuals that they would have hired and may make them less likely to retain marginal employees, both of which lead to lower incomes. (Because public employee unions will be paying close attention to employment trends in local government, any potential impact in this direction may be more pronounced in nonprofit organizations than in local government.) Although these changes could affect all individuals and families without children if the increased supply of low-skilled labor changes the general wage structure, we expect the effects to be concentrated in the low-skilled end of the labor market.

Data, Comparison Group, and Analysis Approach: The approach to evaluating this question follows the approach to evaluate the first hypothesis: Draw a sample of low-income families and individuals without children in 1998 and 1988, calculate their incomes in 2001/1991 and 2005/1995; examine whether the level of income in 2005/2001 is lower than in 1995/1991; and examine whether individual changes in income from 1998 to 2005/2001 are lower than they were from 1988 to 1995/1991.

Issues and Limitations: The difficulties of defining income and the data limitations discussed above are also relevant here. An additional difficulty is that the DILHR/DWD data include only information on quarterly earnings, not information on hours worked or weeks worked. Thus an evaluator can identify those with low earnings and determine whether the proportion with low earnings increased, but cannot differentiate those who changed the number of hours they worked to keep total earnings roughly comparable. For example, assume that W-2 causes hourly wages to fall. Some individuals who were working 250 hours quarterly at $10/hour (total quarterly earnings of $2,500) under AFDC may decide under W-2 to keep total earnings constant even though their hourly wage has declined to $5/hour, working 500 hours/quarter. This important effect of W-2 could not be detected under this basic evaluation scheme. A final issue is that we are proposing to limit the analysis to low-income families and individuals. We do this because this is where we expect the effects to be concentrated, although low-wage secondary workers in families that are not low-income may also be affected.

Hypothesis 1.3: W-2 will change the proportion of families with children who are poor, and will change the poverty gap (the aggregate amount needed to bring everyone up to the poverty line). Conventional measures of poverty in the United States are merely measures in which family income is compared to a threshold that varies by family size. Because of this, the rationales, data, comparison group, basic approach, issues, and limitations provided under Hypothesis 1.1 are relevant here. The additional issues are in determining an appropriate poverty threshold and identifying what income is to be compared to this threshold. The official governmental approach has well-known limitations (see Citro and Michael, 1995, and Ruggles, 1990, for recent critiques). We propose to use a variety of measures of poverty, including the official measure and a measure as close to that proposed by the Panel on Poverty and Family Assistance of the National Research Council (Citro and Michael, 1995) as data will allow.

Although the limitations noted above are also relevant for this hypothesis, an assessment of poverty status makes the need for accurate information on family composition more critical, since the number of people in the family affects the poverty threshold. Further, the lack of information on child care and other work expenses is particularly troubling for measures of poverty status that rely heavily on the assumption that the critical concept is disposable income rather than gross cash income. Still, there are no better alternatives in that there is no information on work expenses during the AFDC period.

Primary Potential Impact 2: Dependency

Hypothesis 2.1: W-2 will lead to a decreased reliance on means-tested transfers among low-income families with children. Although there are several possible ways to conceptualize "dependency" and "reliance" (Meyer, 1990; Smiley, 1996; U.S. Department of Health and Human Services, 1997), we focus here on the proportion of income that comes from means-tested transfers (programs specifically for the poor) (Meyer, 1990; Gottschalk and Moffitt, 1994; Meyer and Cancian, 1996; U.S. Department of Health and Human Services, 1997).

Rationale: First, the rationale under Hypothesis 1.1 above suggests several mechanisms through which earnings would eventually increase; because all of these are increases to the denominator (income) without increasing the numerator (means-tested transfers), the share of income from means-tested transfers is predicted to decline automatically. Second, some recipients will immediately move into unsubsidized employment, which obviously decreases their reliance on transfers. Third, some recipients will move immediately into trial jobs; among these people, at least the portion of wages that is not part of the subsidy to the employer is nontransfer income, and they too should thus show decreased reliance on transfers. Fourth, as we noted above, W-2 could lead to increased child support, which, as an addition to income that is not a means-tested transfer, would also decrease the transfer ratio. Finally, recipients who lose transfer income due to time limits, lack of entitlement, or sanctioning will also see their transfer ratio decrease.

Data, Comparison Group, and Analysis Approach: The basic structure of the evaluation of this question parallels that of the evaluation of incomes. We begin with the two basic recipient samples: W-2 recipients in 1998 and AFDC recipients in 1988. For the short-term evaluation, we suggest calculating the "dependency ratio" three years later (2001 and 1991), using a combination of tax records, earnings records, and benefit records. For the longer-term evaluation, we propose calculating dependency ratios for 2005 and 1995. We would estimate a multivariate equation in which the dependency ratio is the dependent variable, the key independent variable is whether this is a person who was an AFDC recipient (the early period) or a W-2 recipient (the later period), and we would incorporate other control variables.

Thus the main evaluation in this domain has to do with whether *recipients* are able to become less dependent. But W-2 may also affect whether low-income families become recipients; in fact, by opening eligibility to two-parent families, more people may receive benefits. To evaluate this possibility, we will use the sample of low-income families with children described above, and conduct an analysis in parallel fashion to the analysis of recipients.

Issues and Limitations: All of the issues about the difficulty of knowing what to include in income mentioned above are also applicable here. But looking at the percentage of income derived from means-tested transfers also highlights some new difficulties in deciding what is a means-tested transfer. Some benefits are clear: food stamps, the AFDC benefit, SSI, and W-2-Transitions are all means-tested transfers. Presumably the Earned Income Tax Credit and public subsidies for child care and health care (both Medicaid and the public portion of the premium under W-2) are also transfers. But within the W-2 program, how should we view trial jobs? From a taxpayer perspective, the subsidy going to the employer is a benefit available only to the poor, and any earnings above the subsidy counts as earnings (nonbenefit). But from the perspective of the recipient, they are *working* for the entire amount, and none of it should count as an "unearned" benefit. Community service jobs create a similar problem, although it is clear that the state treats these as grants, rather than earnings. Finally, what if one effect of W-2 is that private not-for-profit organizations provide more vouchers or cash to some individuals who have exhausted their time limit for benefits or who have been sanctioned under W-2? These "gifts" do not count as transfers from the taxpayers' perspective, but they represent a transfer of dependency from public assistance to private charitable sources. (Note, however, that public administrative records do not keep track of these private sector transfers, so in practice this would not be evaluated in a basic evaluation even if it were thought to be conceptually important.)

Primary Potential Impact 3: Child Care

The quality of child care arrangements for low-income families could be affected by W-2. Folk and Bloch identify in this book several potential effects of W-2 in the domain of child care; we focus here on what we view as the most important, child care quality. We select this outcome because it has the potential to have long-term effects on child development and because questions of the availability of child care for W-2 participants will be addressed in the companion paper on implementation evaluation. Unfortunately, reaching agreement concerning an appropriate measure of child care quality is difficult. We focus on two indirect measures: formal parental complaints lodged against child care providers and substantiations of abuse or neglect by child care providers.

Hypothesis 3.1: W-2 will cause (a) an increase in formal complaints against child care providers made to the office that licenses the providers, and (b) an increase in substantiated cases of child abuse and neglect by child care providers.

Rationale: W-2 requires co-payments and sets the co-payment amount as a percentage of income with adjustments for the level (certified, licensed, etc.) of child care; these provisions may lead families to select lower cost child care options. Further, W-2 establishes a new category of child care providers who have limited training requirements and for whom there is limited regulation, and these providers may provide lower quality care. Finally, by requiring work of all recipients, demand for child care is likely to outstrip supply (at least in the short run), increasing the general cost and causing some to accept child care arrangements of lower quality than they would have liked.

Data, Comparison Group, and Analysis Approach: Complaints can be made to the office that licenses child care providers, but it is not clear whether this office has kept, and will keep, track of complaints, particularly complaints about those providers with provisional licenses. If these data are kept, analyses of the effects of W-2 on substantiated parental complaints might be possible.

The most serious allegations, those for abuse or neglect, however, *are* part of the child welfare recordkeeping system. Standard data processing forms used throughout the state indicate whether perpetrators are child care providers and the type of child care set-ting — center, family child care, or care provided in the child's own home. (It is not always clear, however, whether county staff investi-gating abuse and neglect cases enter these data reliably.)

We propose to examine records in counties that have adequate records to determine the annual number of substantiated abuse/ne-glect reports in which the perpetrator was a child care provider. Pre-sumably the entire child care market is affected by W-2, so we propose looking at incidents of abuse/neglect by child care provid-ers among the entire potential population of child care users, not merely among welfare recipients. Counties are the proposed unit of analysis. The analysis strategy is fairly straightforward: identify the counties in which there are adequate records, count substantiated incidents over a several-year period, and, through a multivariate time series analysis, determine if the number of substantiated inci-dents after the implementation of W-2 is greater than the number prior to W-2.

Both complaints and substantiations of abuse and neglect will have to be expressed as rates. Otherwise, any increase in raw num-bers could be the effect of more children in child care and not an in-dicator of child care quality. Unfortunately, so far as we know, the number of children in Wisconsin in child care is unknown; perhaps the number could be broadly estimated from data on child care use in the Survey of Income and Program Participation (SIPP), although that survey is not designed to be representative of a state.

Issues and Limitations: Even if the rate of substantiated parental complaints could be adequately estimated, this is a quite limited measure of quality. The number of complaints can be affected by the level of information about how to lodge a formal complaint, the per-ceived threshold of dissatisfaction under which one is justified in making a complaint, and the likelihood of corrective action follow-ing complaint, all of which could change substantially over a sev-eral-year period.

The number of substantiated abuse/neglect incidents is also less than perfect. A child care provider could negatively affect a child's development and emotional well-being without creating an incident that parents felt was clear enough to warrant calling it abuse or neglect. In addition, parents with other child care options may remove their child without lodging an abuse/neglect complaint. Parents with few other child care options may not want to risk losing the only arrangement they have been able to find by taking such serious action. Nonetheless, substantiated incidents of abuse and neglect are so serious that we believe they are important to track and to try to evaluate.

It is unfortunate that better measures of child care quality are unavailable. The generally accepted measures of child care quality are child/staff ratios, the size of child groups (regardless of ratios), the child care training and formal education of providers, and the frequency of turnover of child care providers (Gormley, 1995). We know little about these measures in Wisconsin, but it would be appropriate to start to collect this data for licensed, certified, and provisionally certified providers. Even if formal pre-post analysis and causal inference are impossible, a careful start at monitoring these measures is desirable.

Primary Potential Impact 4: Child Welfare

In this section, we refer not to child welfare in the sense of overall child well-being, but to the official concerns of the formal child welfare system in Wisconsin — child abuse and neglect, and the placement of children in substitute care (primarily foster care) when parental care is unavailable or considered inadequate. In another chapter, Mark Courtney considers these issues in greater detail.[14]

The relationship of reports and substantiations of child abuse and neglect to actual abuse and neglect is not well known. Reports can increase because of greater public attention to the issue or because of legal changes concerning who is required to report suspected cases, even if the underlying rate of abuse or neglect remains unchanged. Nevertheless, some relationship presumably exists between the underlying phenomenon and reports and substantiations of it. Because actual abuse and neglect is unambiguously bad, it is useful to try to assess whether major social policies such as welfare reform influence the direction of the imperfect indicators of the problem available to us — reports and substantiations of abuse and neglect. The W-2 program could influence child abuse and neglect reports and substantiations in several ways:

❖ If parents do not participate in the required W-2 programs and are sanctioned, they lose a source of income that would have been available to them under W-2. The loss of income could lead parents to neglect the basic health and physical needs of their children, which could in turn increase the reports and substantiations of neglect. Although Wisconsin statutes officially prohibit findings of neglect solely for reasons of poverty, a finding of neglect because a parent did not take full advantage of all opportunities available in W-2 would be possible.

❖ Parents who would under AFDC have worked in the labor force for few or no hours each week but who participate for 40 hours per week under W-2 may find the pressure of full-time work combined with single parenting to be overwhelming, and they may behave inappropriately to their children as a result.

❖ Reports and substantiations could rise simply because new officials — the Financial and Employment Planner or the Supportive Services Planner in a W-2 agency — are playing close attention to the family.

❖ Child abuse and neglect could fall because parents who formally did not conform to broad social values of independence do so under W-2. The parents may feel better about themselves generally and thus more competently fulfill their parenting roles.

The placement of children in foster care could increase or decrease for largely the same reasons. Parents who do not conform to the requirements of W-2 may, if they have no income to support their child, leave child welfare authorities with no choice but to place their children in alternative arrangements and, eventually, even to terminate parental rights. On the other hand, it is possible that some parents forced by W-2 to take control of their work lives would improve their general functioning enough so that W-2 could reduce the need for out-of-home care.

For reasons identified in the Courtney paper, a panel study following low-income cases starting before and continuing well after the imposition of W-2 would be desirable. However, as that paper points out, the panel size would have to be quite large to detect statistically significant differences over time, because the percentage of any population in the formal child welfare system owing to abuse, neglect, or out-of-home placement is small. In addition, a survey approach is complicated by the fact that some of W-2 had already been imposed before a survey was possible, and retrospective questions eliciting accurate information about abuse, neglect, or out-of-home placement would be hard to construct. We thus turn again to administrative data for the basic evaluation design, although an additional targeted evaluation of child welfare issues, probably using survey data, also has merit.

Data, Comparison Group, and Analysis Approach: This approach would be demanding, but it would be possible to use the basic pre-post samples described above to obtain some information about the direction of change in child welfare indicators. The tax information provides the county of residence and a name or Social Security number, and it would be necessary to ask selected counties if, in the particular year at issue, any child in the family was reported or substantiated as abused or neglected or placed in out-of-home care. Once these matches have been accomplished, the basic comparison could be similar to the income/dependency comparisons described above: Is there a change in the low-income samples before and after W-2, and is that change different than in the middle class sample?

Issues and Limitations: One likely difficulty with this analysis is that only small numbers of families are affected by child welfare programs. As a result, any change may not be statistically significant even if it would have enormous practical significance. Also, we expect that data from the AFDC period would be available in only a limited number of counties, which may or may not be representative of the state. The major difficulty is likely to be separating the impact of W-2 on child welfare from the impact of other changes in the child welfare environment. There has been a strong trend over time toward increased use of out-of-home care and greater reporting and substantiation of child abuse and neglect. Any increase in these phenomena after W-2 is implemented may be greater than the increase under AFDC solely because of these other factors. In this case, comparing increases among low-income samples potentially affected by W-2 with increases among middle-income samples may not be very informative, because the child welfare system predominantly affects low-income people.

Primary Potential Impact 5: Health Status

Although Medicaid benefits will continue to be available to most W-2 recipients, W-2 could have important health care implications, in at least the following ways:

❖ Low income is at least a predictor, and possibly a cause, of poor health among children (Geltman et al., 1996), and family incomes could rise or fall under W-2.

❖ The future administrative relationship between W-2 and Medicaid remains to be fully developed. It is not certain that eligibility for W-2 will confer the same automatic eligibility for Medicaid which existed under AFDC, or that a joint application process will exist. Health status could be affected if the process of achieving eligibility for Medicaid becomes more time consuming and complex.

❖ Parents who would have worked in the labor force for fewer hours under AFDC than they are required to work under W-2 may reduce utilization of routine primary health care, because the parent might not be able to fit routine health care into a busier schedule. On the other hand, it is conceivable that parents who feel better about their less dependent social role could feel empowered with respect to use of the health care system. At any rate, it would be desirable to know if W-2 changes the utilization of routine health care by low-income children.

❖ W-2 could influence the level of prenatal care received by women expecting their first child. Under the Wisconsin AFDC program, women who were pregnant and had no other children and who fell below income and asset thresholds gained eligibility for Medicaid upon confirmation of pregnancy. This remained the case under W-2. Under the AFDC program, however, women with no other children became eligible for AFDC in the seventh month of pregnancy, whereas under W-2 women in this status are not eligible for W-2 benefits until after their child is born. Since some women delayed obtaining their Medicaid card until they become eligible for AFDC benefits in the seventh month, the lack of cash benefits throughout pregnancy under W-2 may reduce the use of prenatal care.

❖ W-2 could also affect the prenatal care of women who are enrolled in W-2 and have other children. Women who have a child and subsequently become pregnant must remain in a W-2 work program; the only time they can obtain benefits without participating in a W-2 job or activity is during the first 12 weeks after birth. Although a medically difficult pregnancy might qualify the mother for the W-2 Transitions program and activity compatible with her medical condition, it may still be the case that the requirement to work through pregnancies could impair the health of some pregnant women and their newborn children, at least in comparison to what would have been the case under AFDC. It is also possible, however, that the greater self-reliance imposed by W-2 could positively influence the care a pregnant woman takes during her pregnancy.

Data, Comparison Group, and Analysis Approach: The chapter by Maria Cancian and Barbara Wolfe offers many useful suggestions for assessing utilization of routine care. Perhaps the most direct indicator would be to measure the percentage of children below age 6 on Medicaid who received Healthcheck screens (the Wisconsin equivalent of the Early and Periodic Screening, Diagnostic, and Treatment program) and standard immunizations. Both indicators are available from Medicaid administrative records, and both should be sensitive gauges of the use of routine health care. We propose limiting the evaluation here to Medicaid recipients before and after implementation of W-2, because we assume that Medicaid eligibility and "take-up" among low-income children will not change as a result of W-2. Medicaid was not tightly linked to AFDC in the early 1990s because of expanded Medicaid eligibility features, and Medicaid is similarly not linked to W-2. Case heads who do not wish to subject themselves to W-2 might conceivably avoid obtaining eligibility for Medicaid because the same agency may confer eligibility for both programs. But any visit to any health care provider is likely to lead to Medicaid enrollment, because providers want to be reimbursed.

Assessing the impact of W-2 on the health status of newborns requires a broader approach, discussed in the chapter by Gary Sandefur and Molly Martin. The most widely accepted indicator of the health of a newborn is birth weight, measured by discrete categories: normal birth weight (5.5 pounds and above); low birth weight (3.3-5.4 pounds); and very low birth weight (under 3.3 pounds). Because both birth weight and the mother's Social Security number appear on birth certificates, it should be possible to match maternal Social Security numbers with income tax records to compare the proportions of births to low-income women (with incomes below 200 percent of the poverty line) in each birth weight category before and after the creation of W-2. If desired, this could be augmented with a measure — either the Kessner or Kotelchuck index (Kotelchuck, 1994) — of the adequacy of prenatal care. (Such an index could be constructed from data available on birth certificates for each birth.)

Issues and Limitations: One significant limitation of a pre-post comparison of health care utilization among Medicaid children is that the state's administrative emphasis on routine health care has been increasing, and health care providers are under more pressure to offer it. W-2 is thus not the only relevant change, and it will be hard to disentangle the effects of W-2 from the new administrative emphases. However, much of that increase in emphasis occurred in the early 1990s and may not affect a pre-post study if the "pre" period is the mid-1990s.

A pre-post comparison of birth weights is reasonably straightforward, although it may be necessary to perform the comparisons separately for the major racial/ethnic groups identified on the birth certificate, since a change in the racial/ethnic composition of mothers in the state could influence birth weights independently of W-2.

Primary Potential Impact 6:
Living Arrangements and Family
Structure of Low-Income Households

As noted in a chapter by Gary Sandefur and Molly Martin, W-2 could conceivably influence marriage and divorce and both nonmarital and marital childbearing patterns in Wisconsin. If AFDC encouraged nonmarital births by providing financial support to parents without requiring any work or work-like activities, W-2-required work activities may decrease nonmarital births. Similarly, if AFDC encouraged divorce or separation or discouraged marriage because eligibility was easier for those who were single parents, W-2's offer of services contingent only on the income and assets of the family, without regard to whether the family contains one or two adults, could decrease divorces and increase the rate of marriage. Moreover, by eliminating the practice of providing benefits based on the number of people in the assistance unit, W-2 could reduce the fertility of welfare recipients. Finally, if W-2 is perceived as offering attractive assistance into the labor force, the program could encourage women to have one child, whether in or out of wedlock, to obtain W-2 eligibility.

Determining the actual influence of W-2 on these and related possibilities will be difficult. W-2 administrative records will need to contain data on the number of people in the household, because child care co-payments and premiums for the W-2 health care program will depend on household income relative to the poverty line. But because these calculations do not require information on the actual composition of the assistance unit (number of adults and their relationship to each other, number of children, and the relationship of the children to the adults), it is not certain that administrative records will contain such data.

In contrast, the likelihood of good administrative data on births is much higher than the likelihood of good administrative data on family composition. About 70,000 babies are born each year in Wisconsin, and the birth order of the child and the marital status, zip code, and Social Security number of the mother are recorded on the birth certificate or a worksheet attached to it. The availability of the Social Security number allows for matches to income tax and wage records. Thus one analysis could be a comparison of the percentage of births to low-income women that were nonmarital in the AFDC and W-2 periods. A second analysis could use the zip code data to identify low-income areas and compare the percentage of nonmarital births in these areas pre- and post-W-2. A third type of analysis could examine the later fertility of recipients of AFDC and W-2. By merging AFDC, W-2, and birth data, the analyst could compare whether recipients had another birth within a given time period.

Because administrative records on marital status are not likely to be available, a brief survey could be done to collect these data. Respondents could be asked about their marriage and divorce histories (to obtain "pre" information for the AFDC period) and their recent and current marital status. Questions for collecting both current and retrospective information could be adopted from national surveys. Alternatively, the Social Security numbers of AFDC and W-2 case heads could be matched against Social Security numbers in divorce records to gain a sense of the relative impact of AFDC and W-2 on divorce.

Because W-2 could affect childbearing and marital decisions by women not on the program, the full impact of W-2 on living arrangements and family structure is discernible only through a consideration of the broader low-income population, not just of those on AFDC or W-2. Whatever type of data is used, the sample would need to consist of families with minor children and with incomes below, for example, 200 percent of the poverty line. Attributing any observed changes to W-2, rather than to broader cultural and environmental factors that influence marital and fertility decisions, will be challenging.

Secondary Potential Impacts

We view several potential consequences of W-2 as of slightly less evaluative significance, generally because they are less central to the purposes of the reform or likely to affect fewer people. These impacts include homelessness, residential mobility, and the living arrangements of children with disabilities.

Secondary Potential Impact 1: Homelessness

W-2 could influence the level of homelessness among low-income families with children. The program could increase homelessness because families that would have received AFDC may not receive W-2 funds, either because they do not want to subject themselves to the work requirement of W-2 or because they exhaust their time-limited benefits. With no other source of income, they may lose the ability to pay rent and thus face eviction. On the other hand, W-2 could conceivably decrease homelessness because, if W-2 succeeds as its advocates hope, income will rise among program participants. Some participants may move to higher-income neighborhoods, perhaps closer to their jobs. Rental prices may decline in their former neighborhoods because of reduced demand.

Both the Milwaukee and Madison homeless shelter programs have one intake point for families seeking shelter. When families reach that intake point, at least if a prospect of providing services exists, a common form is filled out. The form notes family status (single person, children, etc.), Social Security number, and a staff person's selection from a list of possible "events precipitating homelessness." At least in Milwaukee, these forms have remained roughly constant since 1990, so that limited comparisons before and after W-2 are possible. Evaluators could:

❖ Examine the number of families cited as homeless with "loss of benefits" described as the reason for homelessness before and after W-2. This could, however, include families losing SSI or other program benefits, not just AFDC. Evaluators would probably have to examine AFDC administrative data to determine whether someone with that Social Security number was on the program and lost benefits at about the date of the homeless report.

❖ Investigate the extent to which people become homeless not for loss of benefits but because they did not apply for benefits. Some people may, in effect, choose homelessness over what they believe to be the rigors of the W-2 program. No simple approach to discovering this is available. Qualitative research in homeless shelters would probably be the best approach.

Attributing any change in the level of homelessness to W-2 will be difficult for at least two reasons: (a) federal policies have been changed to make it easier for landlords to evict Section 8 tenants, which presumably increases homelessness independent of W-2, and (b) the growth in supply of homeless shelters that has occurred over the last several years presumably increases the number of people served by them, again independent of any changes in W-2. A comparison of the number of people who are homeless (according to the form filled out by homeless program staff, augmented by checks of AFDC administrative data) because of loss of AFDC benefits should be less influenced by the Section 8 change. Still, it will be hard to control for the possibility that more people who lose benefits may present themselves to homeless shelters if they believe that capacity exists to serve them. For families (as opposed to individuals), the alternative to application to a homeless program is probably not so much actual homelessness — living in a parked car or on the street — but rather efforts to move in with relatives or friends. The perceived availability of a homeless shelter for families then could reduce doubling up and increase apparent homelessness among families independent of W-2.

Some define homeless families as including those whose financial emergency causes them to live with others when they would prefer to live separately (Jencks, 1994). We know of no way to determine if W-2 influences the level of this kind of "near-homelessness." It would be possible, however, to follow a sample of people sanctioned from W-2 or who reached the time limit. Although we could not be certain whether any problems observed were greater than what would have been the case under AFDC, carefully documenting the extent of any problems would be important.

Secondary Potential Impact 2: Residential Mobility

Short of homelessness, frequent moves from one household to another may be another response to economic pressure. Frequent moves among families with children (whether for a better job, or a worse job, or to move in with others) can complicate school performance and reduce the ability of parents to draw easily on informal resources in the community that might help them with their parenting tasks, such as friends who can provide occasional child care or help their children obtain summer jobs (McLanahan and Sandefur, 1994).

W-2 could increase or decrease the level of residential mobility for the same reasons it could affect the level of homelessness. Low-income families may lose income because of W-2, causing them to be evicted or to have to move to avoid eviction. W-2 participants may also move to find a job, or they may move to better quarters because W-2 helps them obtain increased income. We would not propose in this part of the evaluation trying to ascertain whether any change in geographic mobility attributable to W-2 stemmed from higher or lower income, but only whether W-2 has had an effect on geographic mobility.

A standard pre-post design could be applied to this issue, relying on tax returns, which indicate place of residence as of December 31. The basic question would address whether the number of moves made by low-income families increased after the implementation of W-2. A corresponding analysis of the number of moves made by middle-income families before and after W-2 may increase confidence that any change among the low-income sample was indeed an effect of W-2. If some reason other than W-2 would lead low-income people to change their housing at a rate different from that of middle-income people, this analysis would overestimate the impact of W-2. We can identify no such factor at this time, but we cannot discount its possible existence. A final complication is that an analysis based on tax data cannot identify multiple moves within a calendar year, only changes from one year to the next, thus underestimating actual mobility.

Secondary Potential Impact 3:
Parents and Children with Disabilities

For parents who do not qualify for SSI but who have a condition that makes an unsubsidized job in the regular labor force unlikely, the W-2 program offers the W-2 Transition category. Some of these adults function at a fairly low level by conventional standards. In cases in which low IQ is the primary test for qualifying for SSI, a person functioning acceptably as a parent must often have an IQ score below 60 to qualify for SSI. The character and quality of the W-2 Transitions placement for those adults who score in the 60s on IQ tests but do not qualify for SSI is perhaps more a concern of implementation than of impact evaluation, although some monitoring of adults who reach their five-year limit may be appropriate. We assume that many will be exempted from the five-year limit and continue in the W-2 Transitions program.

For children with disabilities, as the chapter by George Jesien and others notes, the primary impact of W-2 will be through new demands on their parents. Parents who under AFDC could have stayed home and attended to their children may no longer have that option under W-2, although it is possible that many parents in this situation will be placed in the Transitions program and given the assignment of caring for their disabled child. Again, whether that happens is probably more a concern of implementation than of impact evaluation, although what happens when a parent in this situation reaches the five-year limit is of interest.

From the standpoint of an impact evaluation, the most important concern is probably a potential increase in the placement of children in foster or institutional care because the parent under W-2 cannot stay home with the child. This could occur either because the parent reaches the five-year W-2 limit or because the parent (especially if other children reside in the family) does not wish to restrict herself to the income available under the Transitions program. A parent seeking more income may move to higher levels of the W-2 program that would not allow the parent to remain home with the disabled child. A special, and affordable, child care setting for a child with disabilities — especially after school and during school vacations — would then have to be available. Employers of these parents may also have to allow the parents a more flexible schedule than is usual for employees, so that parents can go to their child's school or child care settings to address occasional crises. If such child care is unavailable or unaffordable, or if employer flexibility is not forthcoming, the result may be a higher number of out-of-home placements.

One evaluation approach would be to select school districts in Wisconsin enrolling large numbers of children with two of the disabilities likely to present the greatest challenge for a working parent — physical and cognitive. (Those with emotional disabilities should probably be omitted because changes in federal SSI provisions especially complicate a pre-post comparison for these children. For the same reason, legal immigrants could be omitted from the sample.) School district records indicate the child's living situation: with a parent, a relative, in a foster home, etc. The basic question would be whether children with physical and cognitive disabilities were more, less, or about equally likely to live with a parent under AFDC than under W-2.

The changes in the federal SSI program that were part of the welfare reform act of 1996 will complicate the ability to attribute changes to W-2 through a pre-post analysis. Children who lose SSI benefits may for that reason alone be more likely to be placed in out-of-home care. We try to control for this change by limiting the comparison to children likely to qualify for SSI both before and after the SSI changes, but this is unlikely to be a perfect control.

Other Potential Domains and Populations

Because W-2 is such a broad intervention, it could potentially affect a wide variety of other domains and populations as well. The following are several other possibilities for careful evaluation:

❖ A potential for increased asset accumulation, because W-2 has different asset provisions.

❖ A potential for decreased employment stability, because employers may be less likely to retain marginal employees.

❖ A potential for increased dependency among low-income families without children, because if their wages and employment stability decline, their food stamp usage might increase.

❖ School readiness among entering kindergartners could be affected.

❖ Tthe educational achievement of older children could be affected.

❖ The rate and severity of juvenile crime could be affected.

References

Campbell, Donald T. "Can We Be Scientific in Applied Social Science?" In *Evaluation Studies Review Annual*, eds., Roos F. Connor, David G. Attman, and Christin Jackson. 9 (1994): 26-48.

Cancian, Maria and Daniel R. Meyer. "A Profile of the AFDC Caseload in Wisconsin: Implications for a Work-Based Welfare Reform Strategy." Institute for Research on Poverty, Special Report no. 67, University of Wisconsin–Madison, 1995.

Citro, Constance F. and Robert T. Michael, eds. *Measuring Poverty: A New Approach*. Washington, DC: National Academy Press, 1995.

Collins, Ann and J. Lawrence Aber. "State Welfare Waiver Evaluations: Will They Increase Our Understanding of the Impact of Welfare Reform on Children?" Working Paper, National Center for Children in Poverty, Columbia University School of Public Health, New York, 1996.

Cook, Thomas D. and Donald T. Campbell. *Quasi-Experimentation: Design and Analysis Issues for Field Settings*. Boston: Houghton Mifflin, 1979.

Edin, Kathryn."Single Mother and Child Support: The Possibilities and Limits of Child Support Policy." *Children and Youth Services Review* 17 (1995): 203-30.

Edin, Kathryn and Laura Lein. *Making Ends Meet: How Single Mothers Survive Welfare and Low-Wage Work.* New York: Russell Sage Foundation, 1997.

Folk, Karen Fox. "Welfare Reform under Construction: Wisconsin Works (W-2)." *Focus* 18, no. 1 (1995): 55-57.

Friedlander, Daniel and Gary Burtless. *Five Years After: The Long-Term Effects of Welfare-to-Work Programs.* New York: Russell Sage Foundation, 1995.

Garfinkel, Irwin, Charles F. Manski, and Charles Michalopoulos. "Micro Experiments and Macro Effects." In *Evaluating Welfare and Training Programs*, eds. Charles F. Manski and Irwin Garfinkel. Cambridge, MA: Harvard University Press, 1992.

Geltman, Paul L., Alan F. Meyers, Joshua Greenberg, and Barry Zuckerman. "Commentary: Welfare Reform and Children's Health." George Washington University Center for Child Health. *Health Policy and Child Health* 3, no. 2 (Special Report,1996): 1–6.

Gormley, William T., Jr. *Everybody's Children: Child Care as a Public Problem.* Washington, DC: Brookings Institution, 1995.

Gottschalk, Peter and Robert A. Moffitt."Welfare Dependence: Concepts, Measures, and Trends." *American Economic Review* 84, no. 2 (1994): 38-42.

Hotz, V. Joseph. "Designing an Evaluation of the Job Training Partnership Act." In *Evaluating Welfare and Training Programs*, eds. Charles F. Manski and Irwin Garfinkel. Cambridge, MA: Harvard University Press, 1992.

Hoynes, Hilary and Thomas MaCurdy. "Has the Decline in Benefits Shortened Welfare Spells?" *American Economic Review* 84, no. 2 (1994): 43-48.

Jencks, Christopher. *The Homeless.* Cambridge, MA: Harvard University Press, 1994.

Kornfeld, Robert and Howard S. Bloom. "Measuring the Impacts of Social Programs on the Earnings and Employment of Low Income Persons: Do UI Wage Records and Surveys Agree?" Paper presented at the Northwestern University/University of Chicago Joint Center for Poverty Research Conference on "Evaluating State Policy: The Effective Use of Administrative Data," Evanston, IL June 1997.

Kotelchuck, Milton. "An Evaluation of the Kessner Adequacy of Prenatal Care Index and a Proposed Adequacy of Prenatal Care Utilization Index." *American Journal of Public Health* 84, no. 9 (1994): 1414-1420.

Mayer, Susan E. and Christopher Jencks. "Poverty and the Distribution of Material Hardship." *Journal of Human Resources* 24 (1989): 88-113.

McLanahan, Sara and Gary Sandefur. *Growing Up with a Single Parent: What Hurts, What Helps.* Cambridge, MA: Harvard University Press, 1994.

Meyer, Daniel R. *Child Support and Welfare Dependency in Wisconsin.* Unpublished doctoral dissertation, School of Social Work, University of Wisconsin-Madison, 1990.

Meyer, Daniel R. "Supporting Children Born Outside of Marriage: Do Child Support Awards Keep Pace with Changes in Fathers' Incomes?" *Social Science Quarterly* 76 (1995): 577-93.

Meyer, Daniel R. and Maria Cancian."Economic Well-Being Following an Exit from AFDC." Paper presented at the Association for Public Policy Analysis and Management Research Conference, Pittsburgh, PA, October 1996.

Phillips, Elizabeth and Irwin Garfinkel. "Income Growth among Nonresident Fathers: Evidence from Wisconsin." *Demography* 30 (1993): 227-41.

Ruggles, Patricia. *Drawing the Line: Alternative Poverty Measures and Their Implications for Public Policy.* Washington, DC: Urban Institute Press, 1990.

Smiley, Marion. "Private Needs and Public Welfare: Rethinking the Idea of Dependency in a Democratic Culture." Manuscript, Department of Political Science, University of Wisconsin-Madison, 1996.

U.S. Department of Health and Human Services. "Indicators of Welfare Dependence: Annual Report to Congress." Department of Health and Human Services, Assistant Secretary for Planning and Evaluation. Washington, DC, 1997.

Endnotes

1   In particular, different states have different levels of income at which taxes must be filed, and the extent to which low-income families file tax returns probably differs substantially across states.

2   The time frame is one of four trade-offs identified by Cancian and Wolfe. The others are targeted vs. broad-based samples, community vs. individual data, and monitoring vs. evaluating.

3   While federal income tax data have historically been very difficult for researchers to access because of confidentiality concerns, researchers in Wisconsin have been given access to these data after appropriate safeguards have been negotiated. For analyses using Wisconsin tax data, see Phillips and Garfinkel (1993) or Meyer (1995).

4   A simple test is whether later incomes during W-2 are higher (or lower) than later incomes under AFDC, ignoring incomes during the year in which the sample was drawn and in all intervening years. This will suffice for most analyses because it compares the incomes of people three (or seven) years after entry into AFDC (or receiving AFDC) with the incomes of people three (or seven) years after entry into W-2 (or receiving W-2). Other tests would incorporate income during other years, enabling the researcher to estimate whether the *trend* in individual incomes had been affected by W-2.

5   Hoynes and MaCurdy (1994) have recently documented that, by some measures, AFDC spells have been getting shorter since the late 1960s and early 1970s. If this time trend is a result of changes in the low-wage labor market, and if these trends continue, incomes in the W-2 period may differ from incomes in the AFDC period without being caused by W-2.

6   Of course it will be difficult in this analysis to determine whether different effects in different counties are due to different program features or different labor market opportunities.

7   Note that this analysis only enables the researcher to control for factors that affect individuals of all income levels; the researcher could still not distinguish between effects of W-2 and effects of other changes that affected only low-income individuals.

8   Still another difficulty is the possibility that the private not-for-profit sector will provide increased benefits to some families, replacing public benefits. If public benefits are valued, probably private ones should be too if we want to know whether total income for low-income families increased or decreased. However, these figures are generally not available administratively, and the accuracy of self-reports is unknown.

9   In 1995, a family with one child with earnings of less than $8250 and rent of $300/month that does not include heat would receive $724 by filling out

the one-page form. If this family owned a home and paid $1,500 in property taxes, they would receive $1,160. Full-year AFDC recipients are not eligible for this credit.

10 Administrative records of child support income for most families will exist for the W-2 period. Unfortunately the child support administrative data system that existed during the AFDC period had several problems, limiting the comparability of these data across the two periods.

11 An additional difficulty is that there is occasionally not an exact correspondence between where children live and where they are claimed as dependents for tax purposes.

12 The approach is conceptually simple but complicated in practice. Presumably there are three effects of an increase in the minimum wage: low-wage individuals gain higher wages, some low-wage individuals lose their jobs, and some nonworking individuals begin working now that work is more worthwhile. By combining empirical estimates of the magnitude of these effects with several plausible scenarios, one can estimate what income might have been had the new minimum wage been in effect.

13 Another potential limitation is that the analysis attempts to compare two policy regimes that are ten years apart, and any attempt to put incomes in constant dollars is limited by variations in prices over regions, over urban versus rural areas, and over time.

14 We consider the health status of children below. Researchers are only beginning to conceptualize impacts of welfare reform on measures of child well-being that go beyond the traditional measures of health status, child abuse and neglect, substitute care, and educational achievement (Collins and Aber, 1996).

B.

PROCESS AND DATA ISSUES

6

Process Analysis —
The Neglected Stepchild
of Evaluations:
The Wisconsin Works
(W-2) Case Study

Elisabeth Boehnen
Institute for Research on Poverty
University of Wisconsin — Madison

Thomas Corbett
Institute for Research on Poverty
School of Social Work
University of Wisconsin — Madison

T his chapter examines methods for assessing the implementation of a new generation of welfare reforms, using Wisconsin Works as a case study. Assessing the quality of program implementation and functioning is a critical component of comprehensive evaluations, particularly given the dramatic changes that are occurring. Donald Kettl of the La Follette Institute of Public Affairs at the University of Wisconsin — Madison notes:

the new block grant proposals create two kinds of impossibilities: Asking states to do things (like creating one-stop shopping and comprehensive strategic planning) that no government has done before; and asking the states to do things that can be done but which cannot be effectively accomplished in the very short time frame the programs provide.[1]

Throughout the earlier chapters, it has been emphasized that the next generation of welfare reforms constitute a sharp contrast with the past and breaks new ground in program design and management. Understanding how these programs are being operated will be crucial. This paper will examine the basic elements of what constitutes a good program evaluation and will tie these elements to a description of W-2 program implementation and elements.

Dimensions of a Comprehensive Evaluation[2]

A comprehensive evaluation goes beyond the question "does X work," the classic summative question. A serious evaluation starts with a thoughtful political and analytic dialogue to determine what constitutes success in the new program. Equally as important, one must establish acceptable methods for determining *whether or not program managers are running a program that reflects original intent* and *whether the experience at the operational level reflects the intentions of program designers.*

Therefore, summative evaluations constitute only one dimension of a comprehensive evaluation. In the short run, determining whether or not an intervention works is not the critical question in a dramatic innovation such as W-2. Since it is virtually impossible to "get it right" the first time around when dealing with the multidimensional changes encompassed in new-generation reforms, it is reasonable to argue that evaluators should initially focus on whether program administrators are actually doing what they said they intended to do. In addition, evaluators might well focus on providing more immediate feedback required to make mid-course corrections — what is normally referred to as a formative evaluation.

Figure 1 captures a portion of the complexity associated with evaluating these comprehensive reforms.[3] Both anticipated and unanticipated variations in the intervention can occur (column 1) because of differences in the way the program is implemented or because of observed or unobserved differences in the sites (local agencies and counties). The middle two columns summarize factors that can influence the way in which the intervention is done, thereby affecting the treatment outcome of interest or the cost-benefit analysis. The efficiency of management and administrative systems and variations in their procedures may or may not directly affect treatment outcomes. Variation in administration approaches and procedures will have different costs and should therefore be included in any cost-benefit analysis.

Comprehensive evaluations typically would encompass the following:

❖ A **discrepancy** analysis would indicate critical differences between intent and operational reality that may exist: Is the program being *implemented* in a way that is consistent with the original intent.

❖ A **process** analysis would capture key indicators of program operations after they have become somewhat stable and institutionalized. Moreover, the analysis would consider selected temporal factors inherent in

Figure 1
Sources of Variation in the Evaluation of Social Programs

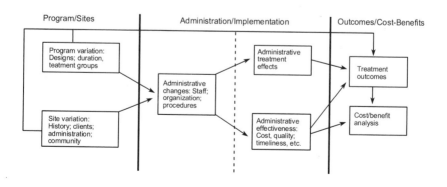

new-generation reforms. For example, the early experience may not reflect how the program will be run over time. Two theoretical possibilities exist. First, there may be a "learning curve," where operations improve as early lessons are incorporated into ongoing processes, staff is better trained or selected, or ill-designed features are corrected. Second, there may be some deterioration of performance as the early energy often associated with a new initiative wanes.

❖ An **outcome** analysis provides data on specific elements associated with the implementation and operation of a new program. These elements may include such things as the observable changes in individuals, families, systems, and communities that are important to the definition of program success. Outcomes are not necessarily process measures, as defined above, nor impacts, as defined below. Outcomes are merely phenomena of interest that observers wish to track and monitor as reforms take place. Where feasible, comparisons still need to be made to make sense of these "outcomes" — perhaps with comparable jurisdictions or with historical data.

❖ An **impact** analysis is an analysis of *net* outcomes. The outcome analysis may provide evidence that things are getting better or worse, but only this analysis can causally link the intervention with key outcomes. It helps sort out false negatives (gross outcomes that are going in the wrong direction, but that would have gotten worse even if the new program did not exist) and false positives (gross outcomes getting better irrespective of the existence of the program). Getting at net outcomes, and being able to make *causal attributions*, requires a more rigorous evaluative design.

These levels of evaluation are not mutually exclusive; they do not represent choices that administrators or program evaluators are required to make. They are best thought of as complementing one another. The first two are formative: The intent is to determine *how well* the program is working from an operations perspective; this involves identifying those components either functioning or not functioning well, and providing the kind of information necessary to improve operations. The latter two are summative: Their intent is to determine whether program objectives are being achieved or not.[4]

Until we know something about the former, however, it is difficult to say much about the latter. If we find outcomes or impacts that are very modest in scale, or whose effects are not measurable, do we assume the intervention failed? Not necessarily. The first question is whether it was tried in the first place or, perhaps more accurately, whether it was tried well. Disappointing impacts can be attributed to an intervention that was tried and found wanting (a "bad" idea that was tried); to an intervention that was never tried (the "good" idea that was never implemented); or to an idea that was so changed in the way it was operationalized that the sponsors would not recognize it (a "good" or "bad" idea that replaced the original "good" or "bad" idea).

This is the dilemma of the black box. Too often there is a belief that we know what is being implemented and evaluated and we then wind up assessing labels rather than realities and drawing totally inappropriate conclusions about the policies under consideration.

Process Analysis —
The Neglected Stepchild of Evaluations

Process or formative-type evaluations typically have been the neglected element of the evaluation industry, subordinate in a policy world that has focused primarily on impacts. That narrow view of evaluation has been changing. In recent years, evaluation requests for proposals (RFPs) have demanded submissions that generally include plans for process, impact, and benefit-cost analyses.

Unlike impact studies, there are no broadly accepted standards for doing implementation or process evaluations. However, a state-of-the-art process evaluation might well encompass the following types of questions and issues:

❖ A *descriptive* analysis, in which the following types of data are presented: *contextual* data on the environment within which the program(s) is operating, including demographic information, labor market information, measures of social disorganization (e.g., economic distress); *population* data on the demographics and circumstances of actual and potential participants; and *agency* data —

general information on organizational structure and personnel.

❖ A *discrepancy* analysis which discusses the *intended* sequence of activities and services in a program model and the *actual* sequence. Program models as articulated in legislation, planning documents, and management interviews are compared with reality as measured through direct observations, case records, and interviews with program operators and participants.

❖ Some form of *participation* analysis which would focus on cross-section pictures that depict the proportion of the target population in various participation statuses in a given month or on a given day. More sophisticated analyses are moving toward longitudinal participation analyses, in which participation is calibrated on the basis of the proportion of the target population that has been engaged in the program over a period of time since initial program contact — for example, the proportion of a given target group participating in X (whatever the innovation calls for) within six months after initial program contact.

❖ Process analyses often include some form of *dosage* or *intensity* analyses. Such analyses attempt to calibrate the extent to which typical or modal participants are engaged in and by the program. The number calculated typically is those who participate over those eligible to participate.

❖ Good process analyses attempt to measure *continuity* of program engagement. This includes measures of "leakage" (falling through the cracks), down time, queuing up for services, etc. Observers might want to know how quickly the system responds to noncompliance by the participant and to significant changes in program status (from a job search component to a community service component). In the most sophisticated of analyses, a description of modal or typical participant experience is undertaken to determine the sequence of activities and events experienced by participants.

❖ Process analyses sometimes attempt to assess program *coherence*. That is, do all key actors view the system as a whole, or key components of the program, in the same way? Do program managers, operations personnel, and participants have similar understandings about pro-

170

gram intent? If a particular message is to be communicated at a particular point, is that what the participant hears; is that what operations people understand respecting their role?

❖ In complex and multi-site initiatives, some process analyses include a *comparative* component presenting cross-site data in ways that highlight similarities or critical differences. This may include comparisons of many of the features noted above: population and agency attributes, program design features, and various performance features. This is particularly helpful when variation in circumstances or approach is likely to be significant.

❖ Finally, some wish to assess overall program *quality*, or the quality of selected program components. This is very difficult to do reliably and well; techniques vary, from relying on observers' judgments, to describing and assessing inputs, or to assessing participants' satisfaction.

Most process analyses are not so comprehensive. What passes for a process analysis is often little more than a perfunctory review of planning documents and a few quasi-structured interviews with key informants. For the new generation of reforms, we need more rigorous methods.

What follows is an attempt to describe W-2 from a ground-level view. The purpose is to disaggregate some of the program components in an effort to understand how the complexities of a program such as W-2 render traditional evaluative methods somewhat ineffective. Examining program elements such as the key actors, the flow of the program, and program time lines is critical to understanding the meaning and reality of a new program.

The Ground-Level View of W-2

W-2 is very complex and is still evolving. Space considerations make it impossible to capture the full scope of the change. We first describe some of the key actors responsible for operating W-2 and then attempt to lay out the critical interactions between the participant and those actors.

Key Institutional Actors

The number of actors and institutional systems involved in W-2 is substantial. There are several populations of interest: the adult caretakers and their children, noncustodial parents, and members of special groups such as minor parents, kinship care providers, etc. Interest also exists in such ancillary systems as child care, health care, child support, child welfare, community supports, the business community, and a host of other institutional contributors to W-2. For the purposes of this paper, however, we will focus only on the institutional actors who operate the system and the program participants with whom they interact.

Understanding the structure and organizational roles in the typical income maintenance agency of a decade ago would have been a relatively simple matter. Since the governing organizational technology was routine and standardized, the participant-agency interface could easily be understood and specified. Personnel could be arranged in a classic hierarchical structure. The character of the participant-worker relationship was specified at the top (sometimes decision rules were built right into the agency's computer system) and organizational communication flows were essentially vertical.

There was little variation (at least theoretically) at the point where participants actually interacted with the agency. The test for the welfare agency of a decade ago was the efficiency and accuracy with which it processed data and made routine calculations. Discretion and professional judgment were discouraged. Role parameters were prescribed. Core technologies were well understood; systems boundaries were clear.

This vision of routine and limited worker-client interactions was never the universal norm, of course. Over time, new and more complex responsibilities were added to the income maintenance worker's duties, among them responsibilities attached to carrying out the requirements associated with new child support and welfare-to-work program initiatives. Welfare agencies also became more organizationally complex, relying upon contracting for certain services or developing team approaches to more effectively complete increasingly demanding operational responsibilities. W-2, however, takes this growing complexity to qualitatively new levels.

The following W-2 roles are grouped by functions that may or may not be performed by the same person. These roles include references to key procedural steps that occur in the process or flow of the program.

- ❖ **Receptionist.** Performs an initial gatekeeping function: receives and processes initial public contacts, determines the initial reason for the visit, and refers visitors to resources within and outside of the W-2 agency.

- ❖ **Resource Specialist.** Performs key gatekeeping and triage functions: assesses needs, performs initial referrals, diverts potential participants away from W-2 to other resources and opportunities as appropriate, assesses job readiness, and conducts preliminary evaluation for additional W-2 services.

- ❖ **Financial and Employment Planner.** Performs case management functions: determines eligibility for work-supporting services, performs job placement screening, develops an Employment Plan, monitors performance, and makes tracking decisions at vital process points.[5]

- ❖ **Supportive Services Planner.** Determines eligibility and provides for the delivery of work-supporting services for W-2 participants who are not placed in W-2 employment positions or receiving case management. This position includes monitoring and reviewing of participant compliance.

- ❖ **Other Agency Personnel.** These positions include the local grievance officer, child support and child care specialists, job developers, motivation trainers, soft-skills trainers, etc.

- ❖ **Selected Community and Service Providers.** Included are child care and health care providers; education and training specialists; counseling, child welfare, law enforcement, and other personnel; housing, food, energy, and others who provide critical supports; employers, job market experts, temporary services agencies; and many more.

A comprehensive process evaluation would include a descriptive analysis of these positions as well as encompass the views and perceptions of nonoperations personnel, those not on the front lines who actually have contact with program participants. This includes program managers and those in the community affected by the program.

Key Procedural Steps

As pointed out earlier, a thorough process analysis would measure the participation, continuity, and coherence of the program. It might also include contextual analyses of environmental and political factors that influenced the way in which a particular innovation emerged and evolved. For our purposes here, however, we focus on a ground-level view — what does the participant experience. If the participant does not experience something different, there exists no new intervention.

Isolating what the participant experiences requires a conceptual framework for identifying key components or modules. The complexity of W-2[6] can be reduced to several macro-activities or modules. These are:

❖ *Signaling*. What participants experience begins before a target group member becomes a participant. What an agency is called, where it is located, how it markets itself determines who seeks out assistance and what prior expectations they bring to their interaction with the program. The W-2 agencies are explicitly designed to send different signals to the low-income community which, in turn, may have strong entry effects.

❖ *Gatekeeping*. This is a simple module relative to others, but quite important, because it encompasses those activities and decisions that the participant first experiences. The character of this experience may say a lot about whether clients continue and about their subsequent behavior and attitudes while in the program.

❖ *Triage/Plan Development*. A very complex set of activities and decisions related to determining participant status at baseline (rough assessment of human capital level, for example), moving the participant into the appropriate track or group, and organizing a set of appropriate activities and experiences.

❖ *Participation/Monitoring*. The basic participant experience in W-2 will be the activities encompassed in one of several tracks — Trial Jobs, Community Service Jobs, and W-2 Transitions. However, tangential involvement with supportive service systems such as child support, child care, health care, and food stamps may also be going on. Monitoring is central, since benefits are tied to work or activity compliance, and other supportive services such as child care and, potentially, health care may depend on continuing co-payments by participants.

❖ *Review/Adjustment*. Everything is time-limited, including exposure to the experiences associated with participating in specific tiers (five-year overall limit, two years in a specific tier; six to nine months in a given subsidized job within a tier). Participants might have their status reviewed a number of times and be retraced through triage (where the participant may be reassigned to a different program track) if they are complying with all the rules. They might face more reviews (and intensive case management) if problems occur or if they do not comply with program rules.

❖ *Exit/Follow-Up*. Actual or potential participants can exit at any time. In fact, diversion from the program is to be encouraged. The kinds of activities that will be developed to minimize recidivism and to otherwise support the family in the labor market (such as access to health care) are still unclear.

Generic W-2 Agency Case Management Flow

The above modules, however useful for a gross analysis, are not discrete enough to develop a detailed implementation or process analysis. Good candidates for closer examination are those points at which critical decisions are made by or about the participant: whether to proceed to another step, which track is to be assigned, and whether or not a participant is in compliance. Although there will be an extraordinary amount of variation in local practices and operations, a generic flow model for W-2 agency case management has been evolving. Figure 2, *W-2 Participant Flow and Access to Services Model*, represents the state depiction of how W-2 should work.

Figure 3, titled *A Generic W-2 Client Flow*, was developed by the authors.

Whatever the final model, the following is an attempt to begin developing an implementation or process analysis plan by identifying key decision points and those points in the sequence of activities at which things can go wrong, or at least can go in directions not intended by program designers and operators. The language used in the subsequent narrative is not intended to faithfully reflect that in the figures. The seminal point is that all program models, no matter how complex, can be broken down into those key decision points or events that inform the character of the participant's relationship with the program.

Screen initial contact. The *receptionist* identifies the reason for potential participant contact (employment or employment service request),[7] determines appropriate referrals to be made, ascertains whether special accommodations need to be made (e.g., whether hearing or physically impaired, non-English-speaking, etc.), collects demographic information, and checks current and prior contacts.

Assess job readiness and family resources. *The Resource Specialist (RS)* determines the current employment situation and assesses basic human capital, determines family composition as it affects work, explores self-sufficiency alternatives,[8] documents the contact, and screens for priority (emergency) service needs. Interviews with the *RS* must be scheduled no later than one business day following the initial inquiry for services.

Identify programs to support employment. At this point, participants encounter a major sorting process. The program expectation is that a majority of clients will "self-sort." The hope is that participants will be able to indicate fairly clearly what their minimum level of need is. Some will then continue on the main W-2 track,[9] others will move to what is called the supportive services track (needing only supplemental work services). The *RS* also develops a preliminary self-sufficiency plan with the participant and refers the participant to child support and other potential sources of benefits such as Social Security and unemployment compensation.

Determine eligibility for FEP and SSP tracks. *The Financial and Employment Planner (FEP)* or the *Supportive Services Planner*

(*SSP*) processes the formal application for assistance. This includes verifying program compliance (child support cooperation, two-week job search, application for other benefits); gathering, recording, and verifying data and making appropriate eligibility decisions; explaining all program requirements and philosophy; and checking for fraud or abuse (including national lifetime time-limit). The *FEP* must meet the applicant within five business days of the date the application is signed. Eligibility for other services such as SSI or food stamps must be determined concurrently with W-2 eligibility. Staff must allow seven calendar days for applicants to acquire validation information, however Medicaid and food stamp eligibility cannot be delayed for lack of information regarding W-2 eligibility.

Develop a participation plan. The *FEP* will identify employment strengths through various assessment tools; negotiate and document a mutually acceptable employability/self-sufficiency plan with the participant to determine the highest appropriate level of work activity for the participant; schedule and assign participants to planned activities (motivational training, employment positions, food stamp employment and training [FSET] programs); and explain all results of the eligibility determination as well as all rights and responsibilities.

Eligibility determination and the initial Employability Plan must be completed within seven business days of the date of the first scheduled *FEP* meeting. The FSET nonexempt individuals who are not participants of W-2 must be enrolled in the FSET program for participation within five business days of determination. Scheduled FSET activities must begin within 30 days of determination.

Deliver employment and training services. The *FEP* now performs a whole range of sophisticated services, including expanding and enhancing the self-sufficiency plan to what is called the "detail" level; assigning the participant ongoing, specific work or training activities (including matching person to openings, negotiating with vendors or employers, establishing feedback mechanisms, and providing or arranging for "soft-skill" services); arranging for rehabilitation services if needed; tracking participant compliance; performing a range of monitoring and documentation services; negotiating all contracts; troubleshooting problems; processing subsidized payments to employers where applicable (Trial Jobs — level 2); processing payments to participants where applicable (Community Service Jobs and Transition Benefits); providing services to advance participants on the self-sufficiency ladder.[10]

Subsidized job activities must be available to the participant within one business day of notification of eligibility.

Provide supportive services to obtain and maintain employment. The *FEP* (*SSP* in some instances) will determine the need for child care and refer as needed for services; reassess need on an ongoing basis and assess noncompliance with rules; identify need for health care and administer the program (issue authorizations, monitor use, process all payments and co-payments, repayments, and overpayments, etc.); provide and administer food stamps, transportation services, job access loans, services under the Employment Skills Access Program (ESAP), and Emergency Assistance (EA) benefits.[11]

Review and management of participant transitions. At a number of points the case must be reviewed and decisions made. Within a track, time limits exist. The *FEP* must determine if another such job should be offered or if the participant should be moved up, or down, the ladder. Time limits in a given track are generally two years. Decisions must be made to extend that time limit, if appropriate. Additionally, there is a five-year lifetime limit. Therefore there are many reviews imposed by state W-2 regulations or required by federal laws.

FEPs must reassess eligibility and employability at least twice each year dating from the date of participant eligibility and at the end of each assigned job placement. In no instance will reassessment dates be more than seven months apart. Food stamp eligibility reviews must occur at three-month intervals.

Provide follow-up services after start of unsubsidized employment. Services continue after the participant has achieved unsubsidized employment. The *FEP* (*SSP* in some cases) will follow up with the participant and/or employer; determine whether continuing services are needed to maintain successful employment; deliver (or arrange) for such services; identify when services may end; close case when activity ceases and document closure.

Many process or flow problems can be identified when program elements are broken down and examined.[12] Following are a few examples:

❖ *Queuing.* As participants flow through the system, do bottlenecks develop at critical points: at eligibility determination, when child care or community service jobs are to be arranged, or when the remediation of a barrier to employment must be addressed? A bottleneck occurs when key events do not take place or important decisions are not made in a prompt and seamless fashion.

❖ *Leakage.* Do participants disappear, get lost in the system, fail to move from one worker to another or one component to the next? This has been a major issue in early welfare-to-work programs and has a greater potential for being a problem here, given the complexity of W-2.

❖ *Misallocation.* Participants are sorted and tracked along different paths at a number of points in the process. Are these allocation decisions made according to accepted policy guidelines? Are participants proceeding along the various program tracks according to a priori expectations?

❖ *Conflict.* All kinds of disputes can arise, given the number of complex decisions to be made and the extent to which discretion is afforded front-line personnel. Are there more disputes than expected? Where are they occurring, and what are the issues?

The simplest tracking devices can be of great assistance in understanding what actually happens to participants compared to what is supposed to happen. Measuring time between significant events and collecting minimal data on the perceptions of key operations personnel and participants can be a useful management tool. Expectations can be compared to reality, problem areas pinpointed, and responses formulated and delivered.

Decentralization and Local Variation

Continuing to use W-2 as an example, it has been difficult for Wisconsin to prescribe a given administrative approach; considerable diversity exists at the local or agency level for several reasons. First, nonroutine, discretionary core activities are not easily managed and controlled by centralized authorities. Second, the state has increasingly wanted to move in the direction of performance-based contracting, in which what an agency accomplishes is viewed as more important than how it accomplishes it. Third, the state has taken some steps to privatize the management of W-2, a step beyond performance contracting.

Both the character of the new reforms and the desire for decentralization increase the prospects for local variation in program design and operations. Some observers believe that several distinguishable models are emerging as counties, welfare agencies, and other potential W-2 providers develop their service delivery approaches.[13] An example of a unique model in at least one county resulted from administrators who believed the FEP role to be so complex that four distinct positions (or roles) were required:

- ❖ *FEP I: Initial Assessment and Referral Specialist.* Conducts the individualized assessment with Job Center customers seeking specialized W-2 assistance. The goal is to explore with the potential applicant the options available to meet personal and employment goals.
- ❖ *FEP II: Applicant Specialist.* Meets with applicants to determine their eligibility for W-2 and non-W-2 programs and services and refers to the appropriate services. This person performs the gatekeeper function.
- ❖ *FEP III: Employability Planning Specialist.* Applicants who have not found employment are referred to FEP III for orientation and enrollment into the appropriate W-2 employment service tier. They are responsible for assigning participants to the appropriate tier or level and for managing their progress through W-2.
- ❖ *FEP IV: Employment Retention Specialist.* For those participants in unsubsidized employment tier, refers participants to employment retention services such child care, W-2 health plan, advanced Earned Income Tax Credits (EITC) payments, child support enforcement activities, transportation services, etc. FEP IV will also provide feedback to the program design and coordination teams within the Job Center that are addressing labor market shortages and retention issues to identify opportunities

for program development and specialized employer retention services.

Other local agency role variations include:

❖ *Job Developers,* responsible for developing relationships and partnerships with area businesses, both public and private, to promote W-2 services and participants and for identifying subsidized and unsubsidized employment opportunities for participants and negotiating contracts with businesses.

❖ *Employment Skills Development Specialists,* responsible for the development and implementation both in the classroom and at the training site.

❖ *Support Service Workers and Child Care Specialists,* responsible for the management and distribution of child care and transportation services for W-2 participants. Their activities include determining eligibility, issuing vouchers, preparing and reviewing payrolls, tracking expenditures, resolving billing issues with providers, serving as a link between participants and community service providers, and analyzing the support needs of W-2 participants.

Such role differentiation reflects the complexity and diversity among W-2 providers. This local diversity argues that there is not a W-2 program, but a host of W-2 programs.[14] Over time there may exist as much structural and procedural variation within Wisconsin as there will exist between Wisconsin and various other jurisdictions. Thus, there is not likely to be a single *implementation* or *process* analysis that will capture the diversity of approaches and strategies. We must think about how to group models over time as agencies find some institutional stability and select those features and arrangements best suited to their philosophy and context.

Addressing the Measurement Challenge

The discussion of measurement issues is kept simple and generic for the purpose of providing a general strategy rather than a detailed plan.

Performing an implementation or process analysis essentially means capturing participants' experience throughout the program. If participants do not encounter an experience qualitatively different than they would have under the old program (counterfactual #1), or different than they would have under alternative policy and program structures (counterfactual #2), then the program has not succeeded in doing anything different and we might be a bit less sanguine about significant impacts. Most new-generation reforms purport to alter the essential *culture* of welfare offices and the way those delivering actual services function.

What are those attributes of the participant's experience that shape the character of their experience in the program, that determine whether the culture of the organization has been transformed? Are there points in the flow of participant-agency contact that should be closely examined? And finally there is the issue of data collection methods.

Salient Attributes of the Participant's Experience

There are a number of attributes that shape the participants' experience with the program and inform their subsequent behaviors. Some of these are:

- ❖ *Clarity.* Altering the culture of offices means communicating a different message to potential applicants and actual participants. Is the message communicated clearly and concisely? Is there ambiguity, or inconsistency, or role confusion among personnel? Recall the number of FEP roles identified above. Are the benefits, obligations, and mechanics of the new system communicated well?
- ❖ *Celerity.* Changing the culture and the message means delivering services quickly and efficiently. If there is excessive "down time," the meaning of the new program may be unclear, the seriousness questioned. This may be particularly true at the front end (contact, gatekeeping, triage, and tracking phases).
- ❖ *Consequences.* There must be consequences for failure to perform on both sides (agency and participant). W-2 would seem to have consequences built in for noncom-

pliance, but administrative failures could still undermine that dimension of the program, particularly in tiers 3 and 4, where the agency issues checks.

❖ *Seamlessness.* A new agency culture would involve the participant in a continuous or seamless experience. Transitions are critical in W-2. When one W-2 placement ends (or is supposed to end), when does the next begin?

❖ *Accuracy.* A number of decisions are made in W-2 about where participants belong and how much they are to pay for child and health care and whether or not they are in compliance with the rules. Some of these decisions are prescribed, others involve discretion. A new culture suggests that decision making conform to the new set of institutional norms — that they be "accurate" relative to the new expectations.

Points of Concern in the Participant Flow

These attributes (clarity, celerity, consequences, etc.) are applied to the key decision points discussed earlier. An in-depth process analysis would explore how these attributes play out at each of the decision points reviewed again below, as well as across decision points when the program is viewed as an interrelated sequence of decisions and events.

Consideration and Contact. What does the agency signal to the community; what signal reaches the community? What does the potential applicant experience when first approaching the program? What is the substance of the initial message (welfare or employment or a broader set of behavioral changes); what is the quality of the message (hostile or supportive)?

Gatekeeping. How is the complex set of services, expectations, data gathering and data verification at the front end carried out? This is an extremely hectic and complex set of procedures, with much information being exchanged and very difficult decisions being made.

Diversion. Diverting potential participants from the program is an important goal but can be abused unintentionally or intentionally (e.g., budget pressures may create perverse incentives). Getting inside this delicate procedure may be critical.

Tracking. Making the decision about where a participant will start in W-2 is another of those seminal decision points with great consequences. Pegging participants too high (tier 2, for example) may lead to failure and employer dissatisfaction. Putting them in too low a track may not set high enough expectations for participants.

Monitoring. Monitoring participant performance and administering benefits and payments is a huge responsibility. Participants can fall by the wayside; disruptions in benefits or co-payments can occur for appropriate or inappropriate reasons. Monitoring may reveal noncompliance, which raises other complex issues, such as how to decide culpability where the facts are unclear.[15]

Transitions. W-2 is full of key transitions: from one subsidized job to another; from one tier to another; from one form of time limit to another. Procedures must be in place regarding how and when these transitions will occur and who will be empowered to make these important decisions.

Exit/recidivism. There are decisions and issues related to exits from the program (though when a person really exits from W-2 is a bit unclear). Some exits may be more desirable than others (employment, as opposed to giving up), and the availability and quality of any work support services delivered may determine recidivism rates or well-being over time.

Integration. Over time, programs such as W-2 and other work-based strategies may well transition from a focus on job placement to a focus on work support and wage progression. That is, what supports can be provided to sustain the individuals' participation in the labor market and improve that participation. Many sensitive decisions can be envisioned here; how does one calibrate the correct amount of help and for how long, balancing legitimate needs against the prospects of introducing a new form of dependency.

Data Sources

Space prevents us from laying out a detailed evaluation plan. There are, however, a number of data sources that can be tapped to examine the issues introduced above. Time, resources, and the evaluator's own preferences and imagination will determine how the various strategies might be woven together. The strategies are:

❖ **Administrative/management data.** A good automated case management system capable of tracking individuals and families over time and across programs will be essential. Few states have such a capability totally developed.[16]

❖ **Special case-tracking efforts**. While automated systems are being developed, generic tracking surveys may have to be developed to track cases over time and keep track of key dates, outcomes, decisions, and service delivery. This may have to be done on a sample basis, for reasons of cost and feasibility.

❖ **Surveys**. Some decision points in the process may be so important that we suggest constructing questionnaires (or some data-gathering device) around those points. If the distribution of new participants across the W-2 tiers radically deviates from prior expectations, we may want to find out why.

❖ **Interviews (structured).** Interviews with operations personnel (those working directly with clients) would seem to be essential to document, among other things, how they view the program, what problems they perceive, and how they see their specific role.

❖ **Interviews (unstructured).** Replicate the above for management, with the unstructured format permitting exploration of problems unforeseen by the evaluators.

The evaluation process of the new reforms builds on tools that have been developed over the past several years, but given the new complexities, takes the enterprise more seriously. At the core, the evaluators must get inside the experience of both the potential and actual participants; identify the key decision points and other points at which things can depart from plans; and capture data that will shed light on what happens as opposed to what is supposed to happen. The evaluators (or program designers) should set expectations about *what* is supposed to happen (e.g., how quickly certain events are supposed to occur, such as finding a child care slot) or *how* it is supposed to happen. This at least creates a set of norms for desired performance against which actual performance can be compared and/or adjusted.

Beyond the Case Study

Wisconsin's welfare reform is merely the laboratory for exploring issues and strategies associated with devolution (waiver-based and law-based) and the consequent emergence of a new generation of policy, program, and management innovation. As devolution plays itself out and the actual practice of running programs for disadvantaged families becomes more diverse, both the need to accurately describe what a program does (and what participants experience) and the challenges of completing such descriptions will increase. The following conclusions are recommended:

❖ General principles and methods must be established for describing administrative and operations models in ways that really communicate what is going on. In part, this means clearly conceptualizing the audience for such evaluations and determining what they really need.

❖ States and evaluators must begin a dialogue over common objectives to guide future work on implementation and process analyses and over common standards for conducting acceptable process analyses.

❖ States must begin to work together toward common definitions of terms and concepts so that communications among states and cross-state comparisons become more feasible.

❖ Evaluators must begin a similar form of communication and exchange in order to develop and improve the practice of doing implementation/process studies.

❖ Program designers and evaluators should begin thinking about how to better integrate formative with summative evaluations. Formative evaluations are designed to alter program parameters or operations. This creates instability that renders causal interpretation of impacts unclear. This tension needs to be resolved.

❖ Administrative outcomes must become a distinct matter of investigation, and systematic (experimental) or natural variations in administrative strategies should be examined to see how they relate to administrative outcomes of interest — measures of satisfaction, efficiency, or accuracy.

Implementing these strategies and methods for program evaluation and analysis will not guarantee a good process evaluation nor will it guarantee that all of the complexities of a program such as W-2 will be able to be captured and described. Many of the program variations are just too subtle and complex to be described accurately and completely. However, implementing these strategies will force states, evaluators, and policy makers to become more cognizant of the importance of these issues and the importance of being able to get inside the black box.

Conclusion and Caveat

This chapter argues for the importance of process or implementation evaluations given the character of the welfare changes being evidenced today. It does not, however, lay out a specific plan for doing a process evaluation of W-2. Rather, it suggests methods for thinking through the reform and identifying the decisions and events that will shape the new program experience to which a participant will be exposed through a retooled institutional culture.

Process evaluations remain an art as well as a science. The protocols and methods are not standardized. Many judgements must be made about appropriate research questions, methodological approaches, and data interpretation that inevitably fall to the analyst's experience and judgment, and intuition. For example, a few short years ago, one Wisconsin county had an AFDC caseload of about 1,200. Pre-W-2 reforms and a booming economy had cut the caseload dramatically. In the spring of 1997, the state and county agreed on budget assumptions that estimated a W-2 caseload of about 600 when W-2 was fully implemented. In a few short months, as the transition to W-2 was about to begin, the caseload had fallen to less than 400 cases. By the time the transition was nearing completion, only about 40 cases were receiving cash assistance through W-2.

This totally unanticipated caseload collapse, which was experienced in counties throughout the state, indicates a true discontinuity in policy making. *But what was it about W-2 that produced such a dramatic effect on caseloads?* A well-designed impact evaluation might be able to tease out how much could be attributed to the economy as opposed to the reforms but cannot get inside the black box to illuminate what participants were experiencing or the processes through which they made critical decisions. For that, we have to plumb the experiences of participants and institutional actors at the ground level.

And we are left with a puzzle. Think of the different pictures of the county program we would have taken were the analysis done when the caseload was 1,200, as opposed to 600, or less than 400, or 40. Undoubtedly, the methods used and the conclusions drawn would have been quite different at each point in time. Moreover, an agency that has seen its caseload fall so rapidly is necessarily thinking about reframing its mission; a picture taken a year hence may yield yet another profile. In an era of transition, the need for many pictures is evident, but our ability to take repeated and reliable snapshots is questionable. It is almost as if we are trying to capture a rapidly evolving drama with the photographic technology of the late 1800s. There is a long way to go.

References

DiNitto, Diana. M. *Social Welfare: Politics and Public Policy*. 4th edition. Boston: Allyn and Bacon, 1999.

Friedlander, Daniel, and Gary Burtless. *Five Years After: The Long Term Effects of Welfare to Work Programs*. New York: Russell Sage Foundation, 1995.

Manski, Charles. F., and Irwin Garfinkel. *Evaluating Welfare and Training Programs*. Cambridge, MA: Harvard University Press, 1992.

Mead, Lawrence M. "The Decline of Welfare in Wisconsin." Institute for Research on Poverty Discussion Paper #1164-98. Madison, WI, 1998.

Rossi, Peter H., and Howard E. Freeman. *Evaluation: A Systematic Approach*. 5th edition. Newbury Park, CA: Sage Publications, 1993.

Scriven, Michael. *Evaluation Thesaurus*. 4th edition. Newbury Park, CA: Sage Publications, 1991.

Wiseman, Michael. "State Strategies for Welfare Reform: The Wisconsin Story." *Journal of Policy Analysis and Management* 15 no. 4 (1996): 515–546.

Endnotes

1   "The Devolution Revolution: Shifting the Politics of Pain," a paper presented at the conference "The New Federalism and the Emerging Role of the States," University of Illinois, Sept. 1996, p. 17.

2   For more in-depth information on evaluating welfare reform see "The Next Generation of Welfare Reforms: An Assessment of the Evaluation Challenge" in this volume.

3   The author is grateful to John Witte for this schematic.

4   We gloss over a contradiction between formative and summative evaluations. To the extent that formative evaluations lead to policy, program, and management changes, additional instability is introduced that makes many summative analyses more problematic.

5   We cannot stress too strongly that this is a simplistic and generic view of W-2. The actual program is likely to be much more complex with an even greater elaboration of these roles. For example, the plan for Dane County (where Madison is located) calls for the development of four distinct FEP roles.

6   We try to capture some of the complexity in the crude flow chart that is attached (Figure 2).

7   W-2 assumes that agency cultures will be radically reoriented at this point. Potential participants will be walking into a Job Center, not a welfare office. They are likely to be greeted by signs and messages that are job-oriented, not income-maintenance-oriented. This is all part of the cultural transformation of welfare that started with the development of the Kenosha Job Center almost a decade ago.

8   Exploring self-sufficiency alternatives essentially is the client-diversion strategy. Key tasks include: identifying extended family resources; identifying transportation and child care resources; exploring health care and nutrition options; exploring various service, training, and employment possibilities. These issues are discussed with the potential participant to determine if an alternative to W-2 participation is feasible and warranted.

9   This track involves preparation for various W-2 employment positions and the delivery of various support services and assistance including child care, the health plan, food stamps, Job Access loans, and emergency assistance. The supportive services track provides all the ancillary services and assistance.

10   Note that complaints and grievances can occur at any time. The initial steps will be handled by a *Local Grievance Officer* (*LGO*) and subsequent steps by the *Division of Hearings and Appeals* (*DHA*). It is not clear how this will really work, since there presumably is no individual entitlement to cash benefits under federal law or W-2.

11 All of these services and benefits, from food stamps to EA, involve a complex set of activities: identifying need, issuing authorizations, monitoring use and assessing any abuse, processing payments or overseeing service delivery, reassessing need or level of benefits and services, and implementing sanctions where appropriate.

12 As a reminder, we are looking only at the participant/worker set of interactions. A number of macro-level or administrative functions and tasks would also be part of any comprehensive process evaluation. For example, key W-2 administrative responsibilities include maintaining all internal operations (e.g., hiring, training, providing management supports, etc.); establishing and maintaining a working relationship with the state, including meeting all contractual agreements; developing and maintaining service partner relationships; establishing and maintaining relationships with the community; and establishing and maintaining positive relationships with employers.

13 According to Dan Kittel, operations manager of the Dane County Jobs center.

14 There are 72 counties and several Indian tribes in Wisconsin. Milwaukee County has been divided into six districts; the W-2 management entity in each was decided by a competitive process that produced an eclectic array of providers, from Goodwill Industries to for-profit firms such as Maximus, Inc.

15 For example, a participant in a community service position may claim sexual or racial harassment while the employer claims negligence and insubordination. How to resolve these matters is difficult.

16 A few states such as California, Indiana, Illinois, Oregon, Massachusetts, Minnesota, and a few others have some components in place.

7

Process Evaluation of W-2: What It Is, Why It Is Useful, and How to Do It

Karen C. Holden
La Follette Institute of Public Affairs
Department of Consumer Science
University of Wisconsin — Madison

Arthur Reynolds
Institute for Research on Poverty
School of Social Work
University of Wisconsin — Madison

A process evaluation attempts to illuminate program administration and client behavior from the start of program implementation to program outcomes. Scriven (1991) describes process evaluation as an activity that "refers to an evaluation of the treatment . . . that focuses entirely on the variables between input and output . . . [and that] refer(s) to the process component of a full evaluation" (pp. 277 ff.). Process evaluation enables evaluators to draw links between program activities and outcomes. It documents delivery of the hypothesized treatment, measuring dosage and duration of that treatment, examining variations in delivery across service agencies and client groups, identifying intervening and confounding activities, and explicitly linking variations in service mobilization, delivery, and duration to variations in measured outcomes.

Policy makers and program administrators need to understand what took place between the initiation of an innovative policy and observed program outcomes and the link between outcomes and that process in order to make decisions about continuing programs over time (e.g., whether, after outcomes are measured, W-2 as a whole or individual components should be continued as is, be modified, or be terminated), and about extending programs to different places (e.g., whether other states should adopt welfare program components similar to those of W-2 in expectation of similar results) or populations (e.g., whether W-2 as a whole or specific components should be extended to families with somewhat higher incomes than the current program cutoff or to noncustodial parents, and whether health benefits should be extended to poor nonparents). To measure only outcomes — simply assuming that the full program was implemented as intended, regarding implementation and process as an unobserved "black box" — provides no guidance on program modification and extensions that might alter outcomes in desired ways.[1] Likewise, measuring process apart from program results may result in practice changes that, even if based on widely accepted "best administrative practice" doctrines, have little impact on program outcomes.

The value of linking process and outcomes is widely accepted though less often put into practice in the evaluation literature. In part because of the challenges of gathering data on organizational expectations and administrative practices across many large program sites (Riggin, 1990) and in part because the effect of different service delivery options is the central evaluation question in some demonstrations, process evaluations linked to outcomes have been found more often in evaluations of relatively small demonstrations of social service programs. Examples include substance abuse education programs (Ellickson and Bell, 1990; Pentz et al., 1989), the spousal abuse response experiments (Sherman et al., 1992; 1984), and juvenile justice experiments (Land, McCall, and Williams, 1990). Despite the widely accepted importance of program implementation evaluations for understanding program causality, Lipsey et al. (1985) observed that only about 10 percent of the large number of evaluations they reviewed provided any documentation on whether programs were implemented as assumed by evaluators and on how program components may have affected observed outcomes. The outcome evaluations of large-scale employment training and adult education programs generally have not been designed with a strongly linked process component, although several important examples are described below (e.g., Cave and Doolittle, 1991; Chadwin et al. 1981; Hamilton, et al., 1997; Mead, 1997; Riccio and Friedlander, 1996; Scrivener et al., 1998).

Key Issues in Process Evaluation

In a process evaluation, a primary task is to assess program coverage and the delivery of program services in such a way as to allow linkage to program outcomes. The main questions addressed are:

❖ Are administrative services and resources that are key to the success of the program in place when implementation begins?

❖ To what extent are program services being delivered to the target population as specified in the program design?

❖ What is the variation in program services and administration across program sites, and how do these relate to differences in the delivery and coverage of services?

❖ How, why, and when did program services and administration change over time?

❖ What are the links between program services and program outcomes?

For at least three reasons, evaluating process is essential to outcome evaluations of social programs:

1. *To validate a fundamental assumption of impact (outcomes) evaluation.* A key prerequisite for conducting an outcome evaluation is that a program has been delivered as intended to the target population, and a process evaluation allows one to test the accuracy of this basic assumption. Much previous research has indicated substantial deviations between the intended and actual implementation of program treatments (Blalock, 1990; Weiss, 1987). The assumption of program implementation must be tested lest the magnitude of program outcomes be

erroneously attributed to diminished program effects rather than accurately attributed to deficient implementation.

Because implementation problems usually result from incomplete delivery of programs or the implementation of the wrong program for the targeted population, outcome evaluations may often and unknowingly underestimate effectiveness. For example, evaluation of the initial Head Start program for preschoolers and their parents greatly overestimated, owing to a lack of process documentation, the extent to which health services, family services, and staff training were available and provided. The outcome evaluation found no effects of the summer program and limited effects of the full-year program, in part because of undelivered services. As Cicirelli et al. (1969) indicated in their report, how the program was implemented "was not a basic question of the study, and the time schedule did not permit intensive investigation of the program." They further explained that "it was impossible to know in detail the actual program that these children experienced" (see also Wu, 1991).

Evaluations of the implementation of Title I educational block grants illustrate a complementary problem — that even if resources are available and services delivered, they may be delivered nonuniformly and fail to reach the target population that is most in need (Doernberger & Zigler, 1993). If services are not available to the population for which program impacts are estimated, impact evaluation findings are misleading, because they are not evaluations of the impact of the intended program but of some other social forces or of some other social programs in place prior to the assumed implementation of the program.

2. *To help explain why a program worked or did not work.* Evaluating program processes helps investigators clarify the precise program elements and features that were implemented well or not so well. This is especially the case for complex, multiple-component programs in which implementation timetables and program components may vary across geographic areas. Consequently, information on the elements that are well implemented can be used to detail the source of the effects of the program.

Alternatively, process information helps explain why the program may not have been as effective as expected or why effects varied across program locations. There are three general reasons why programs do not show their intended effects: inadequate program design or theory, poor program implementation, and inadequacies in the research design or measures. Process evaluations help distinguish among these three reasons for no-effect or small-effect findings.[2] Even if services are delivered, variation in types and targets of service delivery implies that treatment and comparison groups may be imprecisely defined, reducing the ability of the impact evaluation to find effects that may exist. Because many employment training and adult education programs devote little attention to evaluation of program process, it is impossible to assess whether small impacts are ·due to lack of program implementation among the study sample, or to imprecise definition of the "program" variable, or to actual small program effects.

3. *To promote program replication and evaluation utilization.* As noted by Cook and Shadish (1986), evaluators have learned that "analyses of implementation and causal mediation are crucial in evaluation, for they promote explanation, and explanation may be crucial for the transfer of evaluation findings to new settings and populations" (p. 226). By understanding and documenting the workings of a program, its essential operative features can be identified and disseminated for use in other settings, thus promoting program diffusion and replication. Utilization of the results of an outcome evaluation for program expansion or continuation requires that the delivery system(s) be described and the contribution of particular elements assessed.

Examining Process in Wisconsin Works

Wisconsin Works (W-2) is a more complex program in terms of program administration and services than was Wisconsin's AFDC program. (The basic features of the program are outlined in other chapters and are not described here.) In contrast to AFDC, in which eligibility is based on income and assets and leads to entitlement for cash benefits, W-2 eligibility is based as well on noneconomic factors and the program offers a bundle of potential (but not guaranteed) services: the assistance of financial and employment planners (FEPs), referrals to community service agencies, subsidies for paid work, child care, and health insurance.

Wisconsin Works is not an entitlement. The intent of current welfare reform efforts in general, and W-2 in particular, is to change the culture of the welfare population and, as Mead (1996) describes it, to "control the lifestyle of adult participants." W-2 does this by setting conditions for the receipt of aid and imposing strong administrative suasion and sanctions on participant behavior. While initial eligibility includes meeting an income and asset test, continued eligibility also requires, for example, that W-2 clients cooperate in efforts directed at establishing paternity of the dependent child, furnish the W-2 agency with any relevant information the agency determines is necessary, and make a good faith effort, as determined by the agency on a case-by-case basis, to obtain employment. W-2 agencies are likely to operationalize these requirements in different ways, with different consequences for client behavior and program outcomes.

Evaluating Wisconsin Works poses special challenges. One is the innovative nature of the program. Nonuniform implementation timetables across sites will make it more difficult to define the "program" and the components to which individuals entering at different times are subject. Being untried, it may take many years to fully quantify program implementation and document program outcomes for families and children.

The flexibility allowed to area agencies in program administration and service provision will lead to variation across counties in services received by similar participants, even in the fully implemented program; there will not be a single treatment regime introduced at one moment in time, but many different treatments introduced statewide, begun simultaneously and then gradually modified. The type of agencies administering the program and the extent and quality of program implementation will differ by locality and geography. Indeed, the effectiveness of W-2 will depend in large part on decisions made at the local level about program design, administration, and financial support. Agencies may be private or public, and may be those traditionally engaged in job search (e.g., temp agencies) or those traditionally engaged in educational or family services (e.g., Head Start agencies). These different agencies may organize administrative tasks differently, implement program components in different ways and on different schedules over the early months of the program, and have greater expertise in providing certain types of job counseling and placement services. Resource differences across geographic units may include the availability and quality of employment opportunities and training, child care, health benefits, schools, etc. In such treatments, a close tracking of service availability and provision may be especially important.

Evaluations of federal block grant programs, which also were characterized by a high degree of local autonomy in design and administration — including, for example, Title I education programs and community development programs — indicate that global impact evaluations (collapsing across sites) are not only less likely to measure a significant program impact but are often misleading, because the treatment is administered differently across sites. Nonuniform programs are really multiple treatments and should be evaluated as such.

Another special challenge of evaluating W-2 is that even under the optimistic assumptions of successful and full program implementation and appropriate identification of comparison groups, changes in the health, employment, or family status of program participants cannot be attributed to particular program components without some understanding of the organization, coverage, and extent of those components. W-2 is largely a program that mobilizes existing community resources, but may also stimulate their expansion to meet this larger demand. Many of these resources are not under the direct control of program managers. Thus, changes that are attributed to W-2 will be the result in part of local resource availability, the particular resources mobilized for particular client groups, and the success of clients in using those resources to move through the W-2 job tiers toward greater self-sufficiency. Process evaluation can provide insight into whether differential success in moving through the job tiers across sites and client groups and over time among different client cohorts was due to W-2 per se, to particular local resource availability, or to the expansion in local resources provided in response to the program (e.g., training, child care, etc.).

Outcome Evaluation Design
Alternatives and Process

Other chapters in this volume discuss the feasibility of evaluating W-2 using a randomized experimental design (Glen Cain), cross-state comparisons (Robert Haveman), and before-after comparisons (Robert Haveman). Drawing causal conclusions from any of these designs about the link between program components and outcomes implies an understanding of program implementation and process. While the authors do not always explicitly link outcome and process evaluation issues, all recognize the importance of understanding the causal link between specified outcomes and the delivery of W-2 services. Nevertheless, while the authors recognize the importance of understanding program process, none describe how process data are to be collected. This is in part due to the absence of a widely accepted theoretical basis for choosing program components and of standard methods for acquiring process data (but see a recent attempt by Scheirer, 1996).

In the classic randomized experiment, program elements to which individuals are assigned are generally well-defined, individuals are assigned to treatment or control groups at a specific point in time, and their participation is monitored. An experimental design integrates process and outcome evaluation, since the delivery of program services and client selection is designed explicitly to meet evaluation needs. Causal inference is based on measured outcomes and known treatment differences between the randomly assigned groups. Because W-2 is mandated as a statewide program replacing AFDC, assigning individuals randomly to W-2 and to some other non-W-2 treatment would be programmatically difficult, politically unfeasible, and, perhaps most important, not of immediate relevance to policy makers seeking advice on effective W-2 processes. However, program areas or clients within areas (e.g., county, service delivery system) could be assigned to differently administered programs and service options (e.g., by randomly assigning participants to different child care co-payment groups), thereby evaluating the effect of W-2 program components on differential program outcomes. This approach has a precedence in the National Evaluation of Welfare-to-Work strategies (formerly known as the JOBS evaluation) which, adopting an approach that was labeled "unprecedented" in the program's 1997 evaluation report, randomly assigned clients within three program sites to two types of welfare-to-work strategies (Hamilton et al., 1997).

Another W-2 evaluation alternative proposes a cross-state comparison as the counterfactual (see the Haveman chapter). This design seeks to attribute differences in an outcome measure to differences between Wisconsin's W-2 and the counterfactual states' welfare programs. This design requires that cross-state agency data comparably describe substantive program elements and that programmatic differences be distinguishable from other site-specific differences. Several job program evaluations have used cross-site comparisons to examine process effects. The evaluation of the JOBSTART program gathered data on service delivery strategies and characteristics across program sites (Cave and Doolittle, 1991). Though the outcome evaluation used an experimental design, the process evaluation did not and was thus unable to separate the effects across sites of program implementation from other differences in local conditions (e.g., labor market factors). Examination of implementation issues across the 15 sites in the National Supported Work Demonstration (Gueron, 1984) and Mead's evaluation of six county-level JOBS programs in Wisconsin (Mead, 1997) share this problem. Likewise, the comparison of implementation and administrative strategies in Portland, Oregon's Welfare-to-Work Strategy and California's GAIN (Greater Avenues to Independence) program does not fully distinguish the contribution of Portland's particular strategy to measured outcomes (Scrivener, et al., 1998).

Robert Haveman argues for a pre-post (before-after) evaluation design, and Thomas Kaplan and Daniel Meyer describe one possible pre-post evaluation plan. A pre-post evaluation would measure W-2 program effects as differences in the value of selected outcome variables between a period defined as "pre-W-2" and another defined as "post-W-2." The power of this design (i.e., the probability of finding statistically significant effects if they exist) depends on correctly distinguishing the pre- and post-comparison periods, that is, separating the counterfactual "pre-program" (AFDC) years from the "post-program" years during which W-2 is sufficiently operational to have the hypothesized effect on targeted populations and institutions. This design requires accurate information on the implementation process since misclassifying years reduces the power of the statistical tests. When implementation is gradual, it may be that several periods must be defined, including an interim period when the program was only partially in place.

Defining the pre- and post-program years for a W-2 evaluation will not be straightforward. Though officially effective on a legislatively specified date, W-2 cannot be characterized as a discrete point-in-time shift from AFDC to full W-2 implementation. Preliminary demonstration programs altered the "pre-W-2" climate in some counties. Differences across counties in contracting agencies will mean that the "post-W-2" period represents different levels of administrative experience and implementation timing.[3] In a pre-post evaluation design, as is the case in cross-site comparisons, differences in program start-up across counties (e.g., failure to deliver necessary services to some eligible families because services are not yet available) may lead to misleading inferences about program impact akin to those cited earlier in Head Start.

Data for Evaluation

One approach to evaluating the implementation of Wisconsin Works would be to conduct an evaluability assessment, developed by Wholey (1987) as a pre-evaluation effort designed to clarify program intent, the stages and feasibility of implementation, and the likelihood of improving program performance from the point of view of policy makers and interest groups. Although such assessment can be used during any phase of program development, it is especially appropriate at the beginning of new programs, to identify key attributes and the services that managers are most interested in evaluating as well as those that will be provided by the program. Another way to view evaluability assessment is as a delineation of key factors of program administration that may determine program effectiveness.

Some of these key factors and resources will, in part, determine the effects of Wisconsin Works, and are consistent with factors described in background papers for this conference as important to understanding program impacts. Three key points should be considered. First, the social context in which the program and resources are administered will likely affect both implementation and program effectiveness. This argues for site-by-site investigations of program effectiveness. Of course, social context factors may operate differently in each county and may vary by service provider. Second, the identification and coordination of services provided by resource specialists and FEPs are critical to successful program participation. This includes the amount and quality of involvement by the FEP as well as the timing of job placement (e.g., length of service until first job placement). Finally, a focus on the operative resources that will affect short- and long-term outcomes are defined through employment training, child care, health care, and other community supports. Although the extent to which the target population is appropriately referred to services is a key evaluation question, the availability and quality of services and resources will directly influence the effects of program participation.

Gathering data on service delivery differences across program sites and over time is, we assert, both the most central and challenging component of a W-2 evaluation. Data extracted from management information systems (MIS) can provide in-depth information on the characteristics of activities, components, staff and supervisors, as well as on the in-program performance of clients. The evaluation of The National Supported Work Demonstration, for example, used MIS data on administrative/program characteristics over time (e.g., program participation, enrollment, and sanction patterns and rates; participation in nonprogram activities; assignment of clients to various activities or components; client/staff ratios). These data were then used to define administrative variables assignable to each program and merged with participant outcome data (Hollister et al., 1984).

Periodic surveys or supplemental questionnaires given to staff and clients can be used to gather both quantitative and qualitative process data. For example, surveys can collect data from staff and clients on the availability and quality of services, the effects of feedback and managerial monitoring systems, and on the features and effects of delegation of authority systems. In order to understand changes in the perceived and actual roles of administrative staff and the availability and quality of services over time and as the program develops, repeated surveys may need to be undertaken. These data must be identified by time and place in order to match them to clients and services available and received. The WIN program evaluation (Chadwin et al., 1981), for example, gathered data on the organizational characteristics of WIN service delivery units through interviews with national-level program officials and state and regional program administrators, coded these data to characterize each program's organizational and service delivery characteristics, and associated them with performance outcomes. In evaluating process in the relevant sites, the National Evaluation of

Welfare-to-Work strategies gathered data from administrative files to track client services and participation, from client opinion surveys administered two years after random assignment to learn about client experiences and expectations, from a random review of case files, from surveys of case managers and income maintenance workers and their supervisors to gather data on their program experiences and opinions, and from surveys of basic education teachers and administrators to understand linkages with the JOBS sites.

Process data can illuminate unintended program consequences. Wisconsin Works is a time-limited transition-to-work program. Although the threat of loss of program services may better facilitate a client's entry into the labor force than time-unlimited programs, several unintended consequences may occur, as illustrated by the following questions.

❖ Do children receive poor quality child care? The supply of good quality child care providers is very limited. The program incentive for children to enroll in the least expensive care available could place many children at significant risk for developmental problems. Thus, the quality of care that children receive under Wisconsin Works should be extensively investigated.

❖ Does the rapid transition into full-time work discourage parents from enrolling their children in compensatory programs that have proven effectiveness (e.g., Head Start, special education interventions)? Several of these programs are part-day programs.

❖ Does program participation affect the amount and quality of time parents spend with their children? Does participation affect the amount and quality of parent participation in school?

❖ Will employers provide sufficient training for program participants even if the amount of training necessary for an individual employee goes beyond the tax incentives provided to the employer?

A possibility to consider in gathering both outcome and process data is that participants will likely have different rates of compliance. Program success, for example, may depend on an individual's psychological readiness for transition activities and how responsive case workers are to the needs of participants. Level of motivation to participate in the program will probably vary substantially, and this may affect program outcomes. These attributes could be measured in survey questionnaires.

As described here and in other papers, community services such as adult education, health care, and child care may differ across W-2 sites in their availability, coverage, and quality. Since program staff (e.g., FEPs) may be familiar with and will invariably refer participants to these and other services, their ratings may help to reveal the match between participant needs and community resources. Various indicators of interorganization coordination may affect program implementation across communities. Process evaluators may find it necessary to gather information on relationships with other agencies — e.g., the extent to which "agencies share information and resources," on interagency meetings, and on barriers that children and families face in obtaining services elsewhere. Again, such information, which can be provided by program case workers or administrators, helps to define the level of coordination among service agencies that could be utilized in assessing the importance of agency presence and services to the outcomes of welfare reform.

Program administrators, adjusting initially to a completely new welfare system, may be reluctant to fully cooperate with a survey effort outside the normal demands of their administrative duties. For this reason the outcome and process evaluations should be designed to depend heavily on administrative data (as is proposed by Meyer and Kaplan in their chapter) with only periodic and focused site surveys. For this reason, careful thought must be given to process evaluation needs in designing intake and client flow forms. Administrative cooperation in gathering these data can be increased by including evaluation plans (e.g., need for this effort, feedback to administrative staff) in staff training, and by convincing staff of the usefulness to them of these efforts. Contracts written with W-2 service delivery agencies could require periodic reporting of specific site and community resource characteristics.

W-2 administrative data linked to each site would provide information on administrative structure and services in the aggregate. Selecting a cohort of W-2 participants every 6 to 12 months for an outcomes study would provide information on how new cohorts moved through the system and, linked to additional program and periodically updated site-provided data, would allow a comparison of the effects of program implementation and service systems on clients over time.

We should note that if an evaluation of W-2 takes place in a limited number of communities, rather than on a statewide basis, so should the process evaluation. An advantage of site-specific evaluation is the more intensive data collection that is possible. Some mix of methods may be valuable, with a few intensive case studies conducted early in the program in order to discover issues that may be particularly important to highlight in broader survey efforts. In either case, however, the explicit linkage process and outcome data need to be pursued.

Conclusions and Discussion

At the simplest level, stand-alone process data can provide useful descriptive information on W-2 implementation across selected sites. As a mechanism for providing feedback to program managers, this descriptive information should be acquired early in the program, with periodic data collection efforts undertaken as the program matures. Gathering comparable program data across service delivery areas can help answer questions about administrative variation in practices. Programs may change in response to feedback from these initial collection efforts, a process which itself must be measured in order to understand subsequent program outcomes. An early, fairly intensive effort to collect process data in a few program sites would inform program administrators about the management of this innovative program and provide insight to evaluators about the feasibility of collecting the process data for outcome evaluation purposes.

The focus of this paper, however, is on the importance of process data to understanding program outcomes. To link outcomes with program implementation, treatment coverage, and dosage, process data must enable evaluators to assess (1) the extent to which program administrative components are implemented over a treatment period, (2) the coverage and types of services provided to cohorts of clients, and (3) differential effects (as measured by outcomes) of treatment options.

With few exceptions, process evaluation has tended to be treated as separate from impact evaluations of welfare programs. While these separate evaluations have undoubtedly assisted program operators in identifying administrative procedures, activities, and components in need of improvement, the absence of examples that tightly tie implementation to program outcomes has hindered the usefulness of process analysis to policy makers who must make decisions about the continuation, cessation, or modification of programs. At the same time, welfare reform allows considerable latitude in program design and operation, increasing the necessity that policy makers understand how implementation and process contribute to variation in outcomes across programs and across program sites. Evaluations of W-2, including those proposed in these papers, explicitly or implicitly presume knowledge of program implementation practices and timing. As the characteristics of and outcomes for its clients vary across W-2 sites and as other states look to W-2 as an instructive model for their own welfare policies, the importance of program practices to outcome variations will be asked.

The consensus in these papers appears to be the greater feasibility of a pre-post program impact evaluation design, assuming that the primary question to be addressed concerns changes in outcomes under W-2 as compared to the AFDC era. This design requires correctly identifying the period before W-2 went into effect and a period after it took effect. Pre-post designs can most accurately link outcomes to programs when programs are quickly implemented. When implementation is gradual, as was W-2, the period of implementation, which may be long, may have to be treated separately, but even then it is necessary to clearly identify the without-program and with-program periods.

Service delivery across W-2 agencies as contracted by the counties is likely to vary, both temporarily during implementation, but also in the long run. Public and private contract agencies may operate quite differently and mobilize resources differently. Clients may flow through these agencies at different rates. Effects of these cross-program variations in W-2 can be evaluated using the several evaluation designs described in other papers. An experimental design that assigns clients to different administrative regimes can be used to assess the effects of different program provisions within W-2. Cross-county comparisons can examine effects of different organization of services by different agencies, even though it cannot clearly separate local area differences from program differences.

Pre-post design can capture how changing the W-2 program in some substantive way alters program effects. Each of these designs, however, require good process data to causally relate outcome to program input.

Gradual implementation raises questions about evaluation design. Should the emphasis be on process evaluation alone, impact evaluation alone, or some combination of the two? On the one hand, program administrators would like quick and early feedback on program implementation and service delivery in order to alter program services as soon as possible to address unexpected results and unwanted side effects. On the other hand, particular interest groups would like evaluation resources devoted to a "true" test of a fully implemented program in order to discover the effect of the full delivery of the program as intended. We propose a middle-ground position combining these two views: to conduct a long-term outcome evaluation and give attention to documenting program implementation and program services over the period in order to properly specify the timing and type of treatment services received by program clients.

References

Blalock, A. B., ed. *Evaluating Social Programs at the State and Local Level.* Kalamazoo, MI: W. E. Upjohn Institute, 1990.

Cave, George and Fred Doolittle. *Assessing JOBSTART: Interim Impacts of a Program for School Dropouts.* New York: Manpower Demonstration Research Corporation, 1991.

Chadwin, Mark Lincoln, John J. Mitchell, and Demetra Smith Nightingale."Reforming Welfare: Lessons from the WIN Experience." *Public Administration Review* 41 no. 3 (1981): 372-380.

Cicirelli, V. G., et al. *The Impact of Head Start.* Athens, OH: Westinghouse Learning Corporation and Ohio University, 1969.

Cook, T. D. and W. R. Shadish. "Program Evaluation: The Worldly Science." *Annual Review of Psychology* 37 (1986): 193-232.

Doernberger, C. and E. Zigler. "America's Title I/Chapter I Programs: Why the Promise Has Not Been Met." In *Head Start and Beyond*, eds. E. Zigler and S. J. Styfco. New Haven, CT: Yale University Press, 1993.

Ellickson, Phyllis, and R. M. Bell."Drug Prevention in Junior High: A Multi-Site Longitudinal Test." *Science* 247 (1990): 1299-1305.

Gueron, Judith. "Lessons from Managing the Supported Work Demonstration." In *The National Supported Work Demonstration*, eds. Robinson G. Hollister, Peter Kemper, and Rebecca A. Maynard. Madison, WI: The University of Wisconsin Press, 1984.

Hamilton, Gayle et al., *National Evaluation of Welfare-to-Work Strategies: Evaluation of Two Welfare-to-Work Program Approaches: Two-Year Findings on the Labor Force Attachment and Human Capital Development Programs in Three Sites*. Washington, DC: U. S. Department of Health and Human Services and U. S. Department of Education, 1997.

Hollister, Robinson G. et. al., eds. *The National Supported Work Demonstration*. Madison, WI: The University of Wisconsin Press, 1984.

Hollister, Robinson, P. Kemper, and J. Woolridge. "Linking Process and Impact Analysis: The Case of Supported Work." In *Qualitative and Quantitative Methods in Evaluation Research*, eds. T. Cook and C. Reichardt. Thousand Oaks, CA: Sage Publications, 1979.

Land, K. C., P. L. McCall, and J. R. Williams. "Something That Works in Juvenile Justice: An Evaluation of the North Carolina Court Counselors' Intensive Protective Supervision Randomized Experimental Project, 1987-1989." *Evaluation Review* 14 no. 6 (1990).

Lipsey, M. W., et al. "Evaluation: The State of the Art and the Sorry State of the Science." *New Directions for Program Evaluation* 27 (1985): 7-28.

Mead, Lawrence M. "Optimizing JOBS: Evaluation versus Administration." *Public Administration Review* 57 no. 2 (1997).

Mead, Lawrence. "The Potential for Work Performance: A Study of WIN." *Journal of Policy Analysis and Management* 7 no. 2 (1988): 264-288

Mead, L. M. "Welfare Policy: The Administrative Frontier." *Journal of Policy Analysis and Management* 15, no. 4 (1996).

Pentz, M. A., et al. "Multicommunity Trial for Primary Prevention of Adolescent Drug Abuse." *Journal of the American Medical Association* 261 no. 22 (1989).

Riccio, James A. and D. Friedlander. "Understanding Best Practices of Operating Welfare-to-Work Programs." *Evaluation Review* 20 no. 1 (1996): 3-28.

Riggin, L. J. C. "Linking Program Theory and Social Science Theory." In *Advances in Program Theory*, ed. L. Bickman. New Directions in Program Evaluation, No. 47. San Francisco, CA: Jossey-Bass, 1990.

Scheirer, M. A., ed. *A User's Guide to Program Templates: A New Tool for Evaluating Program Content.* New Directions for Evaluations, No. 72. Newbury Park, CA: Sage Publications, 1990.

Scriven, M. *Evaluation Thesaurus.* 4th ed. Newbury Park, CA: Sage Publications, 1991.

Scrivener, Susan et al. *National Evaluation of Welfare-to-Work Strategies: Implementation, Participation Patterns, Costs and Two-Year Impacts of the Portland (Oregon) Welfare-to-Work Program.* Washington, DC: U. S. Department of Health and Human Services and U. S. Department of Education, 1998.

Sherman, L. W., et al. "Crime, Punishment, and Stake in Conformity: Legal and Informal Control of Domestic Violence." *American Sociological Review* 57 (October 1992): 680-690.

Sherman, L. W., et al. "The Specific Deterrent Effects of Arrest for Domestic Assault." *American Sociological Review* 49 (April 1984): 261-272.

Weiss, C. H. "Evaluating Social Programs: What Have We Learned?" *Society* (November/December 1987), 40-45.

Wholey, J. S. "Evaluability Assessment: Developing Program Theory." *New Directions for Program Evaluation* 33 (Spring 1987): 77-92.

Wu, P. "Structural Equation Models in the Analysis of Data from a Nonequivalent Group Design: A Reanalysis of the Westinghouse Head Start Evaluation." Department of Social Relations, Lehigh University, 1991.

Endnotes

1 "Process" and "implementation" are distinct terms as used in this paper, though often used interchangeably in the evaluation literature. Implementation as used here refers to the putting in place of a program and may refer to the period between program legislation and a time when the program is operational with full staff and clients beginning to be served. Process refers to the way in which a program is administered and clients are served throughout the program. A process evaluation will examine the implementation of a program but will also track how the program changes even after full implementation and how clients are served in a fully mature program.

2 It is also the case the program effects can be overestimated if process is not tracked. For example, other services may develop to serve clients removed from a program because of noncompliance. Though this is an indirect result of the new program, absence of process information may attribute higher earnings of these clients to program services rather than to subsidiary services.

3 If implementation is nonuniform across areas, the two time periods may be composed of different calendar years for different areas.

8

Monitoring Income for Social and Economic Development

Martin H. David*
Institute for Research on Poverty
Department of Economics
University of Wisconsin–Madison

Understanding the Impact of 1996 Welfare Reforms

The Personal Responsibility and Work Opportunity Reconciliation Act of 1996 (PRWORA) brings large changes in social assistance. Each state must respond, and more than fifty institutional structures characterize social assistance in the United States. Understanding the change in family well-being and labor market outcomes for individuals induced by this complex change in social policy requires assembly of dynamic data on families and

*   Assistance from staff of the Wisconsin Department of Revenue and Department of Work Force Development is greatly appreciated. Dr. James Eisner retrieved many elusive documents. The document reflects my views; errors are my responsibility.

The permission of Campus Verlag to reprint Martin David's "Monitoring Income for Social and Economic Development" from *Empirische Forschung und wirtschaftspolitische Beratung*, copyright 1998, is gratefully acknowledged.

individuals. Furthermore, understanding requires samples in each administering unit (probably as small as a labor market consisting of a small group of counties). Samples with that level of geographical detail will permit comparisons of social services and subsidized work opportunities across administrative units; some comparisons can also be made with the social welfare system prior to 1997.

These requirements for data are monumental. To some extent they are mandated by the Act, which requires an entirely new administrative recordkeeping system in which the lifetime use of TANF can be monitored for the U.S. population. Individuals' eligibility for TANF benefits will depend on their past use of the program and the benefits received by other family members at households where they live. This system is more extensive than the current systems for tracking unemployment insurance eligibility and social insurance eligibility for the U.S. population.

The massive institutional change triggered by the Act posed a question: How can existing administrative record systems be enhanced to produce data required to understand the outcomes of new social welfare policies? A partial answer for the State of Wisconsin is offered below.

Two dimensions of W-2 require data: Rules that determine who is eligible to benefit from W-2 differ from the rules governing the welfare programs that W-2 supplants. The future short- and long-term outcomes for the population that would have used welfare programs in the past provide evidence of the performance of the W-2 program. W-2 participants will have one distribution of outcomes; non-participants will have another. Understanding the outcomes of W-2 entails a data collection that can produce information identifying who is at risk to require assistance, tracking the experience of those who take up W-2 and its related benefits, and following the group of persons who are no longer receiving benefits from State of Wisconsin programs.

The discussion below argues that continuing integration of administrative data from W-2 and the Wisconsin income tax system can generate a profile of short- and long-term outcomes of the W-2 system.

Background

The State of Wisconsin has a long history of anticipating problems of economic and social development by forward-looking administration and fact-finding. For three decades the Department of Revenue (DOR) has collected samples of tax returns for revenue estimation. The Department of Health and Family Services (DHFS, formerly the Department of Health and Social Services) pioneered in the creation of CRN, now CARES, to integrate program information on income and services provided to families and individuals eligible for Medicaid and the Food Stamp Program. That agency has also funded the Wisconsin Health Survey that collects data on use of medical services and health of the Wisconsin population. The Department of Workforce Development (DWD, formerly the Department of Labor, Industry, and Human Relations), in conjunction with the University of Wisconsin Center of Community Economic Development, pioneered the use of employer unemployment tax returns to generate information about local labor markets that can be used to spur development and redevelopment.

Change in technology and change in the environment to which government services respond require new ways of informing policy makers and citizens about the health of our economy and the well-being of our citizens. A potential exists to combine past efforts of these three agencies into an administrative record database. Such a database would be dedicated to statistical use and would provide information that is needed for understanding the consequences of Wisconsin job development programs, programs supporting small businesses, and programs that reach out to bring potentially dependent adults into the world of work. The database would simultaneously increase understanding of the economic environment in which these programs operate.

Concepts

Five concepts are required to enhance the use of administrative records for monitoring income and setting policy for social and economic development:

❖ *Longitudinal data* that follow a representative sample of individuals and business entities

❖ *Refreshing samples* that represent new residents of the state and new business enterprises

❖ *Program beneficiary* samples that identify users of safety-net and work-oriented programs

❖ *Dual-frame samples* that integrate the approach to the above

❖ *Relational database technology* that makes it possible to combine and extract information from these samples over time.

These concepts will create information that is not now available to administrators, policy makers, and the public from any source. Good data for distributing Title I funds for school districts with high poverty rates are unavailable. Information that demonstrates the success of many beneficiaries of welfare is unavailable. Information that documents the high level of tax compliance and good tax administration in the state is meager, and poorly distributed.

The mission of several agencies — DOR, DWD, and DHFS — can be enhanced by better use of administrative data. Policy makers, legislators, and citizens can be better informed about:

❖ How government activities in several agencies relate to each other.

❖ What government services cost.

❖ What groups are covered by benefits. And

❖ What groups are excluded from benefits.

Implementing these concepts builds on a foundation of administrative information systems that is already in place. For example, the DOR already samples individual tax returns every two years to assist in estimating revenue. The DHFS maintains a database on its population of beneficiaries that integrates information on Medicaid, food stamps, supplemental security income (SSI), AFDC, and some additional social services. The DWD already keeps an on-line system of job applicants and a real-time capability for employers to announce vacancies. Additional effort required to implement the five concepts can be judged from an understanding of present record systems. This discussion seeks to understand how well present administrative records count the Wisconsin population, and how record systems currently in use relate to each other. It seeks to understand how ongoing administrative records can be linked over time. The discussion proceeds by addressing four questions:

1. How do existing administrative records of the DOR, DWD, and the DHFS relate to the Wisconsin population and each other?

2. How can DOR records on individuals be linked over time?

3. How can DHFS and DWD records be linked over time?

4. How can DOR records be used to understand entry and exit from the W-2 program?

Applying Concepts to Wisconsin

Population Counted by DOR and Records on the Safety Net

The population of Wisconsin is partially represented in the records of the DOR. We have persons who file tax returns and persons who do not. Similarly, we have persons who are beneficiaries of the safety-net programs, including W-2, who will be represented in administrative records of DWD and DHFS. Other persons, including some who are in need of assistance, do not benefit from state programs and will not appear in state administrative records. The extent to which administrative records reflect the population of Wisconsin is displayed conceptually in Table 1. Only the group q is not reflected in administrative records. The proportion of the population covered by tax returns, $x + y$, is extremely high because Wisconsin has a refundable Homestead Tax Credit and an earned income tax credit. Those credits are paid to many whose total income is too small to entail tax liability and whose shelter expenses are relatively large. Filing returns by many who owe no tax is what makes a sample of tax returns useful in studying the state's population. Most of the nonfiling population will be beneficiaries of the safety net and will be identifiable because of their use of SSI, food stamps, Medicaid, W-2, WIC, or other means-tested programs. It is particularly significant that the DOR uses information returns to

Table 1 Tax Filing and Beneficiary Status for the Wisconsin Population in a Particular Year			
	Beneficiaries of safety net?		Total
Tax return filers?	Yes	No	
Yes	x	y	x + y
No	p	q	p + q
Total	x + p	y + q	x + y + p + q

locate persons who could benefit from refundable credits as well as persons who are legally required to file because of a gross income above the filing threshold. Both the State Earned Income Tax Credit and the Homestead Credit will be refundable for filers with little income. At any point in time, q will exclude families with dependent children, some earnings, and little unearned income. The principal group in q will be single persons with irregular sources of income that are not reportable on information returns.

Historically the DOR has sampled at least one-quarter of one percent of the forms relating to individual returns (1 and 1N) every two years. The forms are then matched to the corresponding federal income tax returns through the data exchange program of the Internal Revenue Service (IRS). Among other things, this match yields information on use of the Federal Earned Income Tax Credit (EITC). The sample is stratified to yield information on aspects of tax return filing that are important for estimating revenue and analyzing the consequences of proposed legislation. Therefore, returns with lower amounts of taxable income are sampled at lower rates than returns with more significance for the state's tax policy and revenues. This feature is essential to good revenue estimating.

Longitudinal Data

Tax Returns. Panel data for tax returns were pioneered for the State of Wisconsin in the 1960s by Harold Groves, Roger Miller, and Martin David (David, Gates, and Miller, 1974). This panel established the feasibility of tax return panels and provides unique historical information about the Wisconsin population for the years 1947 through 1964.

216

Longitudinal data require two capabilities:

❖ Each individual involved in a return must be followed.
❖ Individuals must be allowed to enter the sample universe. Exits must be accounted for.

The first capability requires:

(a) Individuals must have unique identifiers that persist despite changes in names.

(b) All the identifiers that are associated with a return, either as filers or as dependents, must be captured so that members of the filing unit can be followed.[1]

These capabilities are assured in present returns by the requirements of the *U.S. Tax Reform Act of 1986*. All taxpayers and their dependents are now assigned taxpayer identification numbers.

The second capability relates to the concept of refreshing the sample, discussed below.

Safety-Net Programs. CRN established unique identifiers for each case. CRN also identified eligible units that left the welfare rolls and returned at a later point in time. Robbin and Hedstrom (1981) recommended that CRN implement a panel and maintain a dynamic database of the caseload. These recommendations were not adopted. The successor to CRN, CARES, still does not routinely maintain individual case histories.[2] The PRWORA will require that Wisconsin agencies administering food stamps and W-2 create this capability.

Refreshing Samples

The DOR biennial sample assures a representative selection of taxpayers at two-year intervals. Similarly, a monthly readout from the CARES database assures a representation of beneficiaries at any point in time. Neither the DOR nor CARES samples automatically generate histories of individuals. Those histories can be attained by panel samples based on fixed identifiers, such as the Social Security number. The histories can be readily summarized by updating tables that show "spells" of pertinent activity. For example, DWD will be

	Table 2		
	Tax Filing for the U.S. Population in Two Years		
	Tax Return Filers, Year 2?		*Total*
Tax return filers, Year 1?	Yes	No	
Yes	a	b	a + b
No	c	d	c + d
Total	a + c	b + d	a + b + c + d

interested in the number and length of spells of TANF. The DOR will be interested in the spells of filing proprietor income (Schedule C).

When individuals are followed, e.g., when a panel of data is collected, care must be taken to represent the population at each point in time. Newcomers must be added to the panel sample. Disappearances must be reconciled with known deaths and persons leaving the state. The extent to which nonfilers are eligible nonparticipants in safety-net and work programs must also be ascertained.

Representativeness for two years is illustrated by Table 2, which ignores immigrants and emigrants. Most individuals fall into group *a*, filers of tax returns in both years. Extremely few fall into group *b*, nonfilers in year 2. Work with Canadian income tax records indicates that nearly all of group *b* can be accounted for. Persons who die can be found by matching the sample to vital records; most of the remaining living persons filed tax returns in one of the three years prior to year 1 (Robin-Bleuer, 1996). (Ability to identify the proportion of individuals who do not file in consecutive years (groups *b* and *c*) is a valuable administrative tool for designing audit procedures.)

For Wisconsin tax records, *b* is larger than for the U.S., because some persons move out of state and are not obligated to file nonresident returns. Similarly *c* is greater because more people move into the state. To see this more clearly, a row and column are added Table 3 for nonresidents of Wisconsin who are not required to file Wisconsin returns.

Table 3 Tax Filing for the Wisconsin Population, Distinguishing Missing Nonresidents in Two Years				
	Tax Return Filers, Year 2?			*Total*
Tax return filers, Year 1?	Yes	No, WI resident	Nonresident nonfiler	
Yes	a	b	e	a + b + e
No	c	d	f	c + d + f
Nonresident, nonfiler	g	h	i	g + h + i

The population groups g, h, and i are not at risk for Wisconsin safety-net programs in year 1; the population groups e, f, and i are not at risk in year 2.

To assure that groups c and g are represented in each successive year of a panel, tax returns of individuals who did not file in the prior year must be sampled and added to the returns of individuals being followed. These returns can be identified in administrative processing, as filing status in the prior year is on the return. The identities of some of these people will already be known, because they were claimed as dependents on returns filed previously by others.

To assess the importance of groups b and e and determine that they are no longer taxable or eligible for refundable credits, the DOR can submit these cases for matching to the federal income tax return.

At periodic intervals it will be desirable to supplement information from the tax files as matched and linked with information from other sources. This strategy will be discussed below.

Program Beneficiary Samples

Relationship to the Population. The procedures that generate a panel of tax returns are pertinent to generate a panel of beneficiaries of safety-net and work-oriented programs. Two additional considerations are important: (i) Citizens of the state have a concern for the poor and homeless; (ii) Safety-net and work-oriented programs

Table 4 Family Poverty Status of Individuals and Their Beneficiary Status in Some Period (month or year)			
	Beneficiaries of Safety Net?		*Total*
Family poor?	Yes	No	
Yes	I	II	I + II
No	III	IV	III + IV
Total	I + III	II + IV	sum I - IV

may not reach their target populations. To visualize these problems, we adapt Table 1 into Table 4.

The first row of the table identifies a group that is presumed, by an officially sanctioned criterion, to have unmet economic needs. Group II includes persons who are presumed to need assistance and who are not reached by safety-net and work-oriented programs. They can not always be identified from tax return data because they may not file a return. Probability samples of Wisconsin families must be used. Several sources are available: the "long-form" sample of the *U.S. Decennial Census*, the *Survey of Income and Program Participation*, and the *Wisconsin Family Health Survey*. None of these sources provide high-quality, continuous, annual measures of the distribution of family income by county in Wisconsin. That deficiency justifies the expansion of panel data collected from administrative records.

The *Decennial Census* is the only source of information that describes poverty families by county in Wisconsin. Census data are collected once a decade. (Results are not available until three to four years after the census day).[3] Annual samples of families in Wisconsin either do not represent the state's population, fail to provide a precise measure of poverty status, or fail to give estimates at the county level where many programs are administered. For example, the *Survey of Income and Program Participation* represents only the Milwaukee metropolitan area, where precise measures of poverty by month are obtained for small samples that include few poor persons. The *Wisconsin Family Health Survey* collects information on annual income from a single question that is less inclusive than income measured in the *Survey of Income and Program Participation*. The *Health Survey* gives estimates of the number of households below the poverty line, above twice the poverty line, or in between, for five Wisconsin regions.

Value of a Tax Return Panel. Some of the poor will file tax returns to receive Earned Income Tax Credits or Homestead Credits. They can be located in the continuing panel of tax returns. The number of poor who do not apply for these credits can be estimated by forecasts from the panel data for prior years. The panel provides historical information from which the number of persons moving into and out of poverty in successive years can be estimated. The number of poor migrating into or out of the state can also be estimated. Once a decade, these estimates can be checked against county estimates of the poor from the Census. Once a year, these estimates can be checked against other survey data for Milwaukee or the regions of the state.

Preparing estimates of the poor requires that the tax return panel be organized into family units. Until 1993, combining returns into families and households could not be done precisely (Cilke and Wyscarver, 1990). Multiple tax returns from a given household (including students away at college, spouses filing separate returns) can now be aggregated to approximate a family. Sailer and Weber (1996) have demonstrated that this aggregation comes sufficiently close to Census Bureau counting of families that the difference may be dominated by the failure of the Census Bureau to identify cohabiting adults as distinct from legally married persons. The ability to aggregate tax returns to an approximation of families enhances use of tax data for understanding the well-being of the entire Wisconsin population. It creates the foundation for forecasts of family income distribution in the state.

Beneficiary Samples. Mandates for efficient administration and measures of program performance make it likely that safety-net programs will continue to keep data on their beneficiaries. The PRWORA mandates a record of food stamp and welfare assistance use sufficient to limit lifetime receipt of benefits to five years. Following recipients of SSI, food stamps, and W-2 in Wisconsin entails tracking about half a million persons, some 10 percent of the state population. The continuing entry of persons into these programs and the exit of others implies that a ten-year history of beneficiaries could include three and a half times as many persons [Duncan, 1984, Table 2.1].

Apart from the federal mandate, a history of past program use is important to develop an understanding of the success of programs as measured by time elapsed since the last program benefit was received. History is also necessary to devise appropriate interventions for persons who return to safety-net programs. Both of these uses of beneficiary data dictate a continuing "vital record" of program use, the parity of the current episode of use, and the years since the last use. Such records would need to be kept for a long period following program use, ten or twenty years, perhaps a lifetime.

Taken alone, a panel of beneficiaries tells us little about the success of those who exit. When the beneficiary panel is matched to tax record information, a continuing picture of the economic activity of past beneficiaries can be generated. Data on "life after welfare" (Meyer and Cancian, 1996) can be produced to show some who cross the threshold of median family incomes, and their numbers in comparison to others who never achieve income greater than the poverty threshold.

Dual Frame Samples

Matching of tax return and beneficiary panels cannot be achieved without an integrated sample design that crosses the record systems of all agencies involved. A few examples indicate why:

❖ Persons most likely to be at risk for safety-net programs are sampled at a rate of about one quarter of one percent by the DOR. If all safety-net programs keep records for the entire panel of persons who enter, perhaps 0.05 percent of the income experience of the population will eventually be reflected in matched records. This 2,500 person sample will be insufficient to give information about income for many counties outside the metropolitan statistical areas defined by Green Bay, Kenosha, Madison, Milwaukee, and Racine.

❖ Persons currently benefitting from the W-2 program or food stamps probably constitute no more than 3 percent of the Wisconsin population. The match to the DOR sample will reveal substantially less than 0.008 percent of the population, about 400 persons, since many of these persons will not be required to file tax returns.

A common sampling plan that meets the mission of DWD, DHFS, and DOR can produce matches across a high proportion of records maintained in each agency (Czajka and Schirm, 1990; Czajka and Walker 1989). This can be achieved because the DOR can choose a sample from the poverty population that includes the families who receive DWD or DHFS benefits. Those persons can be traced in future years by the continuing panel of tax returns. On the other side, persons in a DWD or DHFS sample who do not file tax returns alert the DOR to the extent to which a nonfiling population exists, and its importance for enforcement.

Periodic Supplementation of the Administrative Panels

Because some persons (families) do not participate in any safety-net programs and do not file tax returns, it is necessary to supplement the administrative sample with other data. For example, individuals known to shelters, private welfare organizations, and providers of pro bono medical care might be in the population *II* of Table 4. A periodic check to determine what proportion of such persons are known to the administrative record sample provides some understanding of the limitations of the panel procedure suggested.

Relational Database Technology

Relational database technology assures several capabilities that are essential for panel samples. Individuals can be located in long lists at minimal cost. Sampling can be integrated into the administrative processing of cases, without adding additional steps or routines for the case workers and return processors. Matches of records can be made across agencies that provide a basis for integrated sampling, without revealing any other information about the sample. The relational principle assures that data from different months or years will have a unique name. Similarly, individuals must have a unique identity, making it possible to link an individual's records over time. The systems afford logical checking that can identify inconsistencies at the point of data capture and save resources that are wasted in incorrect payments, or separate data entry and verification procedures. Routine reports can be created for monthly and annual reporting. Aggregates can be created for administrative units (counties, school districts), for W-2 service regions, and for state-wide reports.

Most importantly, relational databases can be distributed over a number of locations and a number of types of data sources on different kinds of computers *without losing any capability for linking data.*

Implementation

A Matched Beneficiary-Tax Return Sample

Phase 1. The DOR tax record sample lends itself to an expansion that incorporates the beneficiaries of safety-net programs. The last sample drawn contains tax records for 1995. The next sample will be drawn in 1997. Identifiers of all beneficiaries of safety-net programs in November 1996 can be provided to the DOR in time to permit a sampling of the 1996 income tax returns for all beneficiaries.

The sample of 1996 tax returns will yield less than 100 percent match to beneficiaries in a single month. Some beneficiaries do not file returns. Nonetheless, this procedure has many advantages.

❖ The problems entailed in capturing returns by identifiers can be exposed by an activity that will not impact the quality of the cross-section that DOR requires for 1997.

❖ Sampling by identifier serves two functions: It is the technique that the DOR must follow if it is to convert its cross-sections into a taxpayer panel; it is also the technique that must be followed if DOR data are to be linked to data on current or past beneficiaries of the safety net.

❖ The yield of the sample will serve as a basis for estimating the cost of a continuing effort to match DOR and beneficiary samples.

❖ The match will create a better understanding of the nonfiling population, including the extent of noncompliance and failure of eligibles to benefit from Homestead Tax Credits and Earned Income Tax Credits in that population.

❖ Beneficiaries in 1996 can be matched to tax returns in later years to track persons who are no longer beneficiaries.

Phase 2. When procedures for sampling by identifiers are in place, new beneficiaries from December 1996 to May 1997 can be added to the sample, refreshing the population of past beneficiaries that are being sampled. Completion of phase 2 creates the capability for continuous refreshing of the beneficiary-tax record match.

Phase 2 is also the first step towards a capability for refreshing tax return samples. Each year persons who did not file in the prior year must be identified and sampled. This group will include a high proportion of young people who were dependents on other returns in prior years.

A Tax Return Panel

Phase 3. The mechanism used to create a matched sample of beneficiaries and tax returns can also be used to follow tax returns, creating a panel from the 1995 cross-section sample that already has been collected. Several options exist:

❖ A small sample of 1996 tax returns could be collected in order to develop mechanisms for capturing tax returns on the basis of a list of taxpayer numbers.
❖ Return processing in 1996 can be examined to identify first-time filers, needed to refresh the panel sample.
❖ Panel data can be collected in 1997 as a supplement to the 1997 cross-section

In all cases, the panel sample needs to be designed differently than existing cross-sections. Because income varies substantially from year to year, it is not efficient to follow all the persons in the 1995 sample (Czajka and Schirm, 1990). A logical way to begin the panel is to select from the existing cross-section at the lowest sampling rate used in 1995, 1 out of 244. Higher sampling rates can be used for populations whose characteristics in 1995 indicate that a record of continuing income experience is of special interest to the DOR. For example, returns filed in 1995 that received Homestead Credits could be followed. Returns that show Schedule C or F (proprietors) or returns that show Schedule D or E (capital gains and partnership, royalty, or fiduciary income) could be selected for study, to understand year-to-year variability in those income sources, consistency of industry and employer identifications from year to year, or the proportion of returns that no longer show these sources in succeeding years. Each of these subjects is of interest to tax policy.

When the list sample of 1996 returns has been compiled, DOR will be able to understand the cost of incorporating a panel element in its tax return sample. DOR will also have quantitative data on which it can base decisions on the proportions of returns that should be picked cross-sectionally in each year, and the proportions that should be generated by following a panel.

Phase 4. Phase 3 establishes a panel of taxpayers beginning in 1995. Phase 2 established the continuing beneficiary panel. Because the mission of DWD and DHFS requires that they demonstrate the "success" of the services they render, both agencies would have an interest in tracking the earnings of past beneficiaries. Monthly earnings reports can be developed from unemployment tax returns, but those data offer no insight into family arrangements. DWD and DHFS have an interest in total income and family arrangements that can be gleaned from tax returns. Since DWD and DHFS wish to trace histories, their interest lies in a panel of tax returns linked to past beneficiary records.

A panel of relatively poor taxpayers complements the cross-section of predominately higher income taxpayers that DOR now samples. Were the DOR to collect panel data for higher income persons, it could revise its samples to include a larger representation for lower income families, because following those families is mandated by recordkeeping requirements of PRWORA and desirable for managing the services rendered under W-2 for greatest probabilities of success with W-2 clients.

A panel will enhance the reliability of estimates from the tax record sample. At the same time the increase in scale of the DOR samples and focus on family, rather than tax units, will enhance policy uses of DOR statistics for other agencies. The outcome will be a capability that is able to represent counties, as well as regions of the state.

226

Phase 5. To represent well-being of people in the state, tax returns will need to be aggregated into "families." It will be necessary to obtain the list of all who are related by marriage or dependency status to the filer. Tax returns for each of these people will need to be located. Locating returns of dependents, separate filers, and other persons who file from the same address is more complex and expensive than sampling from a known list. Relational database technology assures that it is feasible. New developments in matching algorithms reduce the number of records that must be studied because of variation in the spelling of street names and other characteristics used in matching. Again, this activity is best begun during a period in which the outcome does not impact the data from which revenue estimates are to be generated.

The creation of families will establish a basis for measuring the rate at which existing family units spawn new tax returns. It can also give insight into the entry of dependents in prior years into safety-net programs.

Benefits of Administrative Panels

Success with Safety-Net Programs

The DWD needs a long-term panel of data on the population of the state for three reasons: It requires knowledge that some clients have successfully overcome problems that lead to dependence. DWD requires knowledge that it is reaching a population that is of social concern. And lastly, it must have data on all former clients to assure that the lifetime limitations on program use are met. Another way of stating these information requirements is to say that the program needs to know how applicants are generated from the population at large and what impact services have on clients at later times. The benefit of a record of *all* experiences with W-2 services is necessary to judge the quality of the program and understand how to make improvements.

DWD needs to reach out to continuing sources of data on the Wisconsin population to achieve those objectives. The DOR file of tax returns is a low-cost source of data, far less than panel surveys. Lacunae in the tax records can be identified, and special purpose studies can be mounted on non-filing persons.

Charting Tax Policy in the Next Century

The DOR can benefit from panel data. Panel data are required to understand more about the nonfiling population; they are required to discover equity and efficiency of taxation on noncorporate businesses; panel data are useful in judging the value of inflation adjustments, and other devices that link history to current returns. The DOR likely would hone the quality of its tax models if it were able to sample using taxpayer identifiers.

Using DOR data capabilities in connection with safety-net programs integrates information on Earned Income Tax Credits with transfer program income that is not collated from statistical records at the present time.

The need to "know ourselves" calls for an integrated panel of administrative data about individuals and families that can be used for statistical studies of tax and welfare policies.

References

Cilke, James, and Roy A. Wyscarver. *The Treasury Individual Income Tax Model*. Washington, DC: U. S. Department of the Treasury, Office of Tax Analysis, 1990.

Czajka, John, and Allen L. Schirm. "Overlapping Membership in Annual Samples of Individual Tax Returns." *Proceedings of the Survey Methods Section of the American Statistical Association*, 1990: 413-418.

Czajka, John, and Bonnye Walker. "Combining Panel and Cross-sectional Selection in an Annual Sample of Tax Returns." *Proceedings of the Survey Methods Section of the American Statistical Association*, 1989: 463-468.

David, Martin H., William A. Gates, Roger F. Miller. *Linkage and Retrieval of Micro-economic Data*. Lexington, MA: D. C. Heath, 1974.

Duncan, Greg. *Years of Poverty, Years of Plenty*. Ann Arbor, MI: Institute for Social Research, University of Michigan, 1984.

Meyer, Daniel R., and Maria Cancian. "Life After Welfare: The Economic Well-Being of Women and Children Following an Exit from AFDC." Discussion Paper 1101-96. Madison, WI: Institute for Research on Poverty, 1996.

Robbin, Alice, and Margaret Hedstrom. *A Report on Data Processing and Machine Readable Records in the Department of Health and Social Services*. (Wisconsin Survey of Machine Readable Public Records). Madison, WI: University of Wisconsin and State Historical Society, 1981.

Rubin-Bleuer, Susana. "Gross Flows from Administrative Data with Missing Waves." *Proceedings of the Survey Methods Section of the American Statistical Association*, 1996.

Sailer, Peter, and Mike Weber. "Creating Household Data from Individual Tax Returns." *Proceedings of the Social Statistics Section of the American Statistical Association*, 1996.

Seigel, Paul M., and John Coder. "Use of Administrative Records to Produce Post-Censal (1993) Income and Poverty Estimates for All US Counties." *Proceedings of the Social Statistics Section of the American Statistical Association*, 1996.

Endnotes

1   The U.S. IRS has demonstrated this capability in its individual tax return panel. (See Czajka and Schirm, 1990 and Sailer and Weber, 1996.)
2   Almost no additional cost is entailed in this historical record, but the capability must be designed into the management information system for safety-net programs.
3   Congress has mandated that the Census produce poverty estimates for small areas. Initial work indicates that it is extremely difficult to estimate poverty counts for counties (Sailer and Weber, 1996).

C.

SPECIFIC OUTCOMES

9

Evaluating the Impacts of W-2 on Family Structure and Maternal and Child Health

Gary Sandefur
Institute for Research on Poverty
Department of Sociology
University of Wisconsin — Madison

Molly Martin
Department of Sociology
University of Wisconsin–Madison

This paper examines some alternatives for collecting and analyzing data on family structure, maternal health, and child health in the context of evaluating the impacts of W-2. Although there is some overlap between the domains of family structure and health, in most respects they are two quite different areas. Consequently, this

Acknowledgments: An earlier version of this paper was prepared for a conference on evaluating comprehensive state welfare reforms at the University of Wisconsin–Madison, November 21–22, 1996. Work on this paper was supported by grants to the Institute for Research on Poverty from the Joyce Foundation and the Charles Stewart Mott Foundation. We thank Burt Barnow, Tom Kaplan, and Robert Moffitt for their helpful comments and suggestions.

paper has two distinct foci. First, the paper explores options for examining the relationship between the shift from AFDC to W-2 on family structure, including marriage, divorce, and out-of-wedlock childbearing. The association between welfare programs and family structure has been a critical element in the national debate over welfare reform, and in the public discussion of W-2. The official documents that describe W-2, however, make no claims about its potential impact on family formation and dissolution. Nonetheless, W-2 contains within it several changes in the benefit structure that many have argued will influence family decisions. These include treating two-parent and single-parent families in the same way and imposing an implicit "family cap," i.e., no increase in benefits associated with an increase in the number of children.

The second focus of the paper is on options for examining the relationship between the shift from AFDC to W-2 on maternal and child health. W-2, as planned by the State of Wisconsin, made major changes in the provision of health care for participants relative to Medicaid. Further, the application processes for Medicaid and W-2 would have overlapped in a manner very similar to the way in which the application processes for Medicaid and AFDC did. The federal government did not grant the waivers needed to make these changes. This makes the process of applying for W-2 and Medicaid more complicated than the old process of applying for AFDC and Medicaid.

The paper discusses three sets of issues regarding the domains of family structure and health: (1) We discuss the hypothetical impacts of W-2 on family structure and child and maternal health. We take seriously the claims of the designers of the program about what it is intended and not intended to accomplish. We do, however, try to think broadly about some possible unintended consequences. (2) We examine sources of data that might be tapped to look at these impacts, concentrating primarily on administrative data and on data collected through surveys. (3) We discuss some of the issues that must be addressed in designing an evaluation of these issues. More specifically, we discuss the merits of combining administrative data, retrospective survey questions, and prospective survey questions.

The Hypothetical Impacts of W-2 on Family Structure and Child and Maternal Health

Family Structure

Although most of the attention given W-2 has addressed its attempt to increase the work effort of people who apply for public assistance, an appeal to family values is one of the eight philosophical principles guiding the development of W-2. More specifically, Attachment 1 to the Program Narrative states the following principle: "Families are society's way of nurturing and protecting children. Both parents, whether or not living with their children, are assumed to be equally responsible for their care. All policies must be judged by how well they strengthen the responsibility of parents to care for their children."

This invocation of family values is somewhat different from that in the federal Personal Responsibility and Work Opportunity Reconciliation Act. In the conference report on this legislation, the Findings section concludes with "Therefore in light of this demonstration of the crisis in our Nation, it is the sense that out-of-wedlock pregnancy and reduction in out-of-wedlock birth are very important government interests and the policy contained in part A of title IV of the Social Security Act (as amended by section 103(1) of this Act) is intended to address this crisis." If one takes these differences in tone and content seriously, one would conclude that W-2 is less explicitly concerned with illegitimacy and single parenthood than is the national welfare reform legislation. Rather, W-2 tries to insure that both parents and the grandparents of children born to minor mothers contribute economically to the care of their children. In later discussion of this principle, the authors state that "W-2 focuses on parents in order to help them succeed in their roles as economic providers."

Nonetheless, W-2 differs from AFDC in the way that two-parent and one-parent families are treated, and in the way that noncustodial parents are treated. First, both two-parent and one-parent families are eligible for assistance. The basic criterion for participation is an economic one based on income and assets. This is a major difference from AFDC, which had more restrictive criteria for participation for two-parent families than for one-parent

235

families. Second, single noncustodial parents with child support orders whose family members meet the W-2 income and asset limit may qualify for limited W-2 services, including self-sufficiency planning, work readiness training, and unpaid community work experience.

W-2 also differs from AFDC in the way that it treats minor mothers. W-2 requires the parents of teenage mothers who participate in W-2 to play a larger role than they did in AFDC. In determining the eligibility of a minor with children to qualify for child care, transportation, and health care, the income and assets of the parents as well as the teen are taken into account. In addition, W-2 asks the parents of the teen to help provide child care in most cases while the teen completes school. The hope of the architects of W-2 is that more teen parents will live with their parents than under AFDC, and that these grandparents will bear more of the financial burdens of caring for their child and grandchild than they do under AFDC.

Given the emphasis of W-2 on improving the efforts of parents to support their children, one potential impact of W-2 on family structure that should be examined is its effect on the role of noncustodial parents in the lives of the children. That is, an evaluation should assess whether or not W-2 increases the economic involvement of noncustodial parents relative to the AFDC program, and it should examine whether other aspects of the involvement of noncustodial parents improve relative to what happened under AFDC. Similarly, an evaluation should study the economic and social support provided by grandparents to minor parents and their children under W-2 relative to the levels of participation in AFDC.

In sum, W-2 provides an opportunity to assess whether treating two-parent and one-parent families in a similar fashion will reduce illegitimacy and single parenthood, and whether the implicit family cap in W-2 reduces out-of-wedlock childbearing among participants in the program.

Child and Maternal Health

The authors of W-2 viewed the provision of health care to low-income families as an important component of the new system. They envisioned a dramatic revision of the provision of health care compared to Medicaid; but Wisconsin did not receive the waivers necessary to implement this feature of W-2.

The authors of W-2 proposed a replacement for Medicaid based on the following principles: (1) W-2 will provide benefits to workers who do not have employer coverage and will try to prevent employers from dropping coverage for employees who might be covered by W-2; (2) families will share in the costs of health care coverage and their contribution will increase with their income; (3) W-2 will endeavor to cover as many people as possible while keeping coverage affordable; and, (4) W-2 will rely on managed care.

These principles would have led to substantial changes in the health care provided to participants relative to AFDC and Medicaid. An income and asset test would have been used to determine if families with dependent children and pregnant women were eligible for the program. The income test allowed higher incomes than required for participation in some other parts of W-2; families could have continued to participate until their income exceeded 200 percent of the federal poverty line. HMOs would have provided slightly less comprehensive coverage than available through Medicaid. Participants would have paid a premium based on a sliding scale structure. A major change would have been that W-2 participants must accept employer-provided coverage if it were available, whereas Medicaid recipients can reject employer coverage in favor of Medicaid if they desire.

These changes may have had an impact on the access to health care and maternal health, infant health, and the health of children. Given the expansion of the potential participant pool, a greater percentage of the low-income population might have received health care coverage. On the other hand, the required co-payments might have proved difficult for some potential participants.

The failure to receive the necessary federal waivers to implement this program made these changes impossible. Under the form of W-2 that was adopted, Medicaid eligibility will continue for children, pregnant women, and families whether or not they choose to participate in the W-2 work or child care programs. W-2 participants will have to meet July 16, 1996 AFDC criteria in order to be eligible for Medicaid. These differences between the rules for determining Medicaid and W-2 eligibility will make it more difficult for the state to determine if W-2 participants are eligible for Medicaid.

Sources of Data

We concentrate on two major sources of data on family structure and child and maternal health: administrative data and surveys. The major sources of administrative data include the Client Assistance for Reemployment and Economic Support (CARES) data and the Child Support Relational Database System (KIDS). CARES data are available for all participants in W-2, and the KIDS data are available for all paternity establishment and child support cases. Identifiers on the records allow researchers to merge records on the same individuals in the two data sets. In addition, other forms of administrative data, such as the unemployment insurance data and the Wisconsin Department of Revenue data, can be used to measure some of the domains of interest in evaluating W-2.

Several national surveys include questions that collect information on family structure and health. None of these surveys have sufficiently large samples in Wisconsin to permit their use in evaluating W-2. Further, these surveys are clearly not designed to meet the needs of evaluators of programs such as W-2. They contain, however, questions that could be modified and incorporated into a survey instrument designed for evaluation purposes. In our discussion of examples of questions that might be useful, we focus on the National Longitudinal Survey of Youth (NLSY) and the NLSY Mother/Child Supplement to illustrate some potential uses of existing survey questions. We also discuss some of the questions in Wisconsin's Family Health Survey.

Involvement of Noncustodial Parents in the Lives of Their Children

Noncustodial parents can be involved in the lives of their children in a number of ways. One of the most obvious ways is by providing financial support to the custodial parent and the children. This financial support can be formal child support, which would be recorded in administrative data, or informal child support, which would not appear in administrative data. Noncustodial parents could also spend time with their children either through formal custody and visitation arrangements or through informal arrangements with the custodial parent. Ideally, we would want to know about both formal and informal financial and social support.

Administrative data will permit the examination of the economic support provided to participants by noncustodial parents with child support orders. This will require merging data from CARES and KIDS. Further, noncustodial parents whose children are eligible for W-2 will have access to certain services, but not paid employment, that might improve their ability to meet their child support obligations. So, some noncustodial parents will actually have information in the CARES data. Once the CARES and KIDS data are matched, investigators will be able to determine the following information about child support obligations and payments: the child support obligation for each month, the child support paid for each month, financial information about the noncustodial parent, the locations of the custodial and noncustodial parents, the current marital status of the parents, and the dates of the beginning and end of cohabitation, the date of marriage, the date of separation, and/or the date of divorce of the custodial and noncustodial parents. The KIDS data do not contain information on informal financial support or social support of any kind.

If evaluators want to examine the informal financial aspects of the involvement of noncustodial parents or the social support provided by noncustodial parents, they will have to collect data directly from individuals through a survey. The NLSY Mother-Child Supplement asks questions regarding the financial support and social involvement of noncustodial parents. The information about financial support is limited and other surveys probably do a more complete job of collecting information on financial support. With respect to the social involvement of the noncustodial parent, some of the information relates to child care for the youngest child. The survey asks who or what type of institution serves as the principal and secondary child care providers for the youngest child. One of the choices the respondent can select is "child's other parent/stepparent." The respondent is also asked where each of their children usually lives: in the respondent's household, with the other parent, with other relatives, etc.

Involvement of Grandparents in the
Lives of Teen Parents and Their Children

The CARES data on participants in W-2 include information on living arrangements. Consequently, evaluators will know with whom minor parents are living. Administrative records do not include information on child care and other support provided by grandparents, so any analyses of this would require collecting data directly from the teen parents and/or the grandparents.

The NLSY Mother-Child Supplement has a series of questions on the living arrangements of the mothers and whether their parents help with child care for the youngest child. The survey also has specific questions as to whether the mother/step/grandmother of the respondent and whether the father/step/grandfather of the respondent is present in the respondent's household. This household composition data combined with the age and marital status information for the respondent can be used to determine who in the survey are unmarried teen mothers currently living with their parents.

In addition, the NLSY Mother-Child Supplement asks questions about whether the parents of the mother provide primary or secondary child care for the youngest child. If the grandmother is the principal or secondary child care provider, the survey collects information about the grandmother's work patterns for the last four weeks. Also, the data record whether anyone outside of the household helps pay for the principal child care services for the youngest child and what relationship to the mother this person has. In this manner, one could determine the nonresidential support grandparents give to young mothers.

A final indicator of grandparents' involvement with the mother and child is whether they provide financial assistance. If another person pays for half of the respondent's living expenses, data is collected about this person's relationship to the respondent and the total income this person gives the respondent. The respondent can identify their mother, father, or parents as the source of this income. Though the respondent is asked if they received any income from a friend or relative in the past year, this assistance can not be attributed to a particular person or relation to the respondent.

Marriage and Divorce

As we noted above, the combined CARES and KIDS data contain information on the current marital status of the custodial parent, other members of his or her household, and if paternity has been established or there is a child support award, and the dates of the beginning and the end of the union between the custodial and noncustodial parent.

Another potential source of administrative data on marriage and divorce is the vital statistics system in Wisconsin. This system collects marriage and divorce certificates and issues regular reports on marriage and divorce. The data that are collected, however, would not be very useful for examining marriage and divorce among participants or potential participants in W-2 since these data do not include Social Security numbers, economic status, residence below the city, village, or township level. This suggests that if an evaluation is to monitor the effects of W-2 on marriage and divorce, it will have to collect data on marriage and divorce directly.

The NLSY gathers retrospective marriage and divorce histories through a series of questions. During the first interview, the respondent is questioned about his or her current marital status and the number of marriages she has had by the time of the first interview. Then, the month and year of the first marriage are recorded, as are the month and year that the marriage ended, if it has terminated. Then, the month and year of the most recent marriage are reported. In the following waves of interviews, the survey obtains data about the first, second, and third changes in marital status since the last interview and the month and year of each change.

Out-of-Wedlock Childbearing

The data collected by the State of Wisconsin on births is much more extensive than the data collected on marriages and divorces. Wisconsin, along with other states, participates in a national effort to collect selected information on every birth that occurs in the United States each year. Much of this information is made publicly available in the National Natality Detail File for each year. The state of Wisconsin reports yearly on out-of-wedlock childbearing by city, village, and township. Further, the addresses collected on the birth certificate worksheet include zip codes, which makes it possible (if the data are of sufficient quality and permission can be obtained) to look at out-of-wedlock childbearing in more detailed geographical areas. In addition, the collection of Social Security numbers on the worksheet makes it possible (again assuming quality and permission) to match birth records with other administrative records. Staff at the Center for Health Statistics have informed us that most birth certificate worksheets do include the complete addresses and Social Security numbers of the mothers. They state that these data are of good quality since it is in the interest of the mother to provide the information in order to receive her child's Social Security card.

An evaluator could also collect original retrospective data on births using fertility history questions that are available in several major national surveys. Birth and marital histories are recorded in the NLSY. The day, month, and year of the birth of the first through fifth child are catalogued. One could compare these dates with those obtained in the marital history section (described above) to determine whether each child was born in or out of wedlock.

Maternal Health

Medicaid will continue to cover pregnant women as it has in the past. The eligibility rules for Medicaid will not be tied to the eligibility rules for W-2. All pregnant women who receive Medicaid will appear in the CARES data, regardless of whether or not they participate in W-2.

In addition, data on the birth certificate worksheets could be used to create a system for monitoring the health of W-2 mothers, other low-income mothers who use Medicaid, and other low-income mothers who use neither Medicaid nor W-2. The National Natality Detail Data Set collects and reports for each birth the date at which prenatal care began, the number of prenatal visits, and the length of gestation. This information is used to compute the Kessner index, a widely used measure of the adequacy of prenatal care. The Kessner Index has three general categories: adequate, inadequate, and intermediate. Adequate care is that which began in the first trimester with an appropriate number of prenatal care visits consistent with the length of gestation. Inadequate care is that which began in the third trimester or that which included four or fewer visits depending on the length of gestation. Intermediate care involves care with other combinations of the month care began, the number of visits, and the duration of the pregnancy (Ventura, 1995). According to the American College of Obstetricians and Gynecologists guidelines, a mother is to receive one visit per month through 28 weeks' gestation, one visit every two weeks through 36 weeks' gestation, and one visit per week after 36 weeks' gestation (Kotelchuck, 1994).

Some researchers have raised objections to the use of the Kessner Index. These criticisms are primarily based on concerns about the index's accuracy and the uniformity with which it is calculated (Kotelchuck, 1994). In addition, the Kessner Index does not evaluate the quality of the prenatal care a woman receives. Nonetheless, the Kessner Index and the information on which it is based are valuable indicators of the health care a pregnant woman receives prior to the birth of her child.

One could also collect original data on prenatal care and other aspects of maternal health by adopting questions from existing surveys. A wealth of information concerning the prenatal health and care a woman receives during pregnancy is contained in the NLSY Mother-Child Supplement. Data are gathered as to the number and month of prenatal visits, whether sonograms and amniocentesis were conducted, the results of these tests, the maternal weight gain during pregnancy, the gestation duration, and the use of vitamin supplements, alcohol, or cigarettes during the pregnancy. Questions such as these could be adopted to determine the mother's health during pregnancy.

Wisconsin collects information on individuals' health status in the Wisconsin Family Health Survey. The best prenatal care information available in this survey is whether anyone in the household is currently participating or has participated during the last twelve months in the Healthy Start program. Healthy Start provides health care for pregnant women and young children who might have problems paying for health care. If someone is participating or has participated in the program, they are identified from among the household list. There is a possibility that data about prenatal doctor appointments may be contained in the question about the person's reason for the last doctor's visit. The category "other" would apply for prenatal care and the respondent is supposed to specify the reason for the visit.

Infant Health

An evaluation of W-2, and the separation of Medicaid from cash assistance, should also examine the health of infants and children. The administrative data system, CARES and KIDS, in W-2 collects no information on the health of infants. Again, an evaluator could use data from the birth certificate worksheet to monitor some aspects of the health of infants born to low-income mothers participating in W-2 and/or in Medicaid. The National Natality Detail Data Set collects and reports for each birth the birth weight of the baby. In addition, the worksheet contains information on the APGAR score, an overall measure of newborn health, and information on abnormal conditions and congenital anomalies of the baby.

One could also adopt existing survey questions to collect information on infant health. Infant health measures are included in the NLSY Mother-Child Supplement. Data relating to the birth of the child include the duration of hospital stay at birth for the infant, the length and weight of the newborn, and whether the child was born early or late and if so, by how many weeks. The survey obtains the infant's health status in the first year of life through questions concerning immunization, well-care check-ups, and health care for illnesses. For well-care and illness treatment, data collected includes the months in which these visits occurred, the type of place at which the infant received the care (i.e., HMO, community health center, private clinic, etc.), and with regard to illnesses, what the major symptoms were.

The Wisconsin Family Health Survey asks questions about the general health status of every person in the household, and therefore all infants. Other health questions include the time since the last general physical examination, the reason for the last doctor visit, and the number of times in the past year the infant has seen a doctor for some health care. A few questions involve hospitalization and emergency care. These include whether the child was hospitalized overnight in the past year, whether the infant has needed emergency room care in the past year, and the nature of the health problem requiring this medical attention. There are not specific questions relating to infant care needs.

A survey could also examine the extent to which infants in W-2 families, Medicaid-covered families, and other low-income families received the benefits that are part of the Early and Periodic Screening, Diagnosis, and Treatment (EPSDT) package of benefits in Medicaid. This package includes immunizations, eye care, dental care, annual check-ups, and school- and community-based care.

Child Health

The W-2 administrative data system contains no information on child health. The major source of administrative data on child health would have to come from individuals and units that were providing health care to participants in W-2. In addition, one could adopt existing survey questions on child health.

The Mother-Child Supplement of the NLSY contains a wide array of information regarding the child's health, including physical, social, psychological, and developmental health. We are only concerned with the physical health of the child. First, NLSY collects data about the extent and nature of any accidents the child has experienced in the past year. Illnesses requiring medical attention experienced in the last year are also duly investigated. Well-care information for children is obtained by asking when was the last time the child saw the doctor for a routine health check-up.

The survey gathers extensive information about possible physical limitations the child experiences. Parents are asked if their child has a condition that limits school attendance, school work, and/or usual childhood activities. The parents also give information as to whether these conditions require treatment by a medical professional, medicine or drugs, and/or special equipment. The Mother-Child Supplement classifies the nature of the condition through specific questioning from a long list of health limitations. Possible conditions include the following: learning disability, asthma, heart condition, serious hearing difficulty, and orthopedic handicap. The length of time that the child has had this limitation is coded in years, and there is an option to code the response as "all his/her life." The NLSY Mother-Child Supplement offers an abundance of information concerning child health.

The Wisconsin Family Health Survey asks similar questions with respect to child health, but without as much detail. The survey asks about the overall health status of the child, the last time the child has seen the doctor, the reason for the last doctor visit, and the

245

number of times in the last year the child has seen the doctor for some health care. Questions concerning hospitalization and emergency room care include whether the child was in the hospital overnight in the last year, and if so for what reason, whether the child was treated in an emergency room in the last year, and if so for what problem. If the child could not attend school or their usual activities were limited during the last two weeks due to illness or other health-related problem, questions cover the length of time of this limitation, the nature of the health problem, and whether a doctor was seen for this problem.

Alternative Designs for Collecting and Analyzing Data

The two major alternatives for collecting data appear to be reliance on administrative records or collecting original data from a sample of families. It is clear that if one is to conduct a comprehensive evaluation of the effects of W-2 on family structure and health, one would have to collect original data from participants and some comparison group.

A more limited evaluation of selected domains with administrative data might, however, be informative. The administrative data that are most promising are probably those that involve out-of-wedlock childbearing, infant health, and maternal health, especially if the more detailed information available on the birth certificate worksheet can be accessed by an evaluator, and matched with state tax records to identify low-income individuals and matched with CARES records to identify W-2 participants. One could also go back in time and construct similar matches for AFDC recipients and low-income individuals who were not participating in AFDC.

One option would be to construct a history of the rate of out-of-wedlock childbearing, birth weights, and prenatal care for the low-income population of Wisconsin for several years back. This history would include all low-income mothers, whether or not they were participating in AFDC at the time their child was born. One could then construct similar records for the years after W-2 began. One could also record other characteristics of the mothers from their CARES and KIDS data, their Department of Revenue records, and their children's birth certificates. Such a data set creates the potential for examining some of the effects of AFDC/Medicaid and W-2/Medicaid on out-of-wedlock childbearing, maternal health, and infant health.

Perhaps the most appropriate way to think of the possibilities for using administrative data is that they could be used to monitor changes or the lack of change in out-of-wedlock childbearing, maternal health, and infant health among subpopulations over time. But it would be difficult to use them to try to assess convincingly the impact of W-2.

This suggests that evaluating W-2 requires moving beyond administrative data to the use of methods that collect high quality information on family structure, maternal health, infant health, and child health, and that allow one to rule out some of the other possible alternative explanations of any changes over time.

References

Kotelchuck, Milton. "An Evaluation of the Kessner Adequacy of Prenatal Care Index and Proposed Adequacy of Prenatal Care Utilization Index." *American Journal of Public Health* 84, no. 9 (September 1994): 1414-1420.

Ventura, Stephanie J. "Births to Unmarried Mothers: United States, 1980-92." Vital and Health Statistics Report, Series 21, No. 53. Hyattsville, MD: U. S. Department of Health and Human Services, 1995.

10

Evaluation of Child Care Services Under the Wisconsin Works Program (W-2)

Karen Fox Folk
Marianne Bloch
Department of Curriculum & Instruction
University of Wisconsin — Madison

$\mathbf{A}$dequate provision of child care services is crucial to the successful transition of welfare participants to employment. According to most research, mothers' child care responsibility, particularly the cost of child care, is the single greatest barrier to employment of mothers of young children (Maynard, 1995; Oliker, 1995). Among single Wisconsin mothers receiving Aid to Families with Dependent Children (AFDC) in 1993, two-thirds had at least one preschool child. In addition, 40 percent had estimated market child care costs of more than half their earnings if they worked full time at $6 per hour (Cancian and Meyer, 1995). Economic labor supply models have documented the strong positive effects of providing child care

The authors would like to thank the following for providing current information on W-2 as implemented: David Edie, Director, Office of Child Care, Department of Workforce Development, State of Wisconsin; Diane Adams, Consultant to the Wisconsin Child Care Task Force; and Nikki Jackson, Dane County Job Center.

subsidies on labor force participation of single AFDC mothers (Connelly, 1990; Kimmel, 1995). In addition to cost, convenience (e.g., hours available, proximity, willingness to take children of different ages) and reliability (e.g., quality of care delivered, low turnover, willingness to take sick children) of child care arrangements have been related to AFDC recipients' ability to remain employed and off welfare (Siegel and Loman, 1991; Weber, 1987; Wolf and Sonenstein, 1991).

On March 1, 1998, AFDC officially ended in Wisconsin and the majority of families previously on AFDC were either off welfare or participating in the Wisconsin Works or W-2 program. This paper reviews the current system of W-2 child care services and presents hypothesized impacts of these services on families and the child care market. Since W-2 has been phased in over the past several years in Wisconsin, preliminary information on the impact of changes in child care provisions under W-2 is also presented. At the end of the chapter, we focus on various evaluation strategies in the context of a comprehensive evaluation of W-2.

Child Care Services as Proposed and as Enacted Under W-2

The provision of child care services to all who are willing to work is an integral part of the W-2 welfare reform program. Program policies include offering individuals "the necessary support services, including child care, and health care to enable them to move into a work setting" (Department of Workforce Development, 1996, p. 19). Under W-2, child care subsidies are available to all families with incomes below 165 percent of the federal poverty line (FPL) who also meet the W-2 assets test.[1] Once families are receiving a subsidy, they continue to be eligible until income equals or exceeds 200 percent of the poverty line. It is important to note that the pool of families eligible to participate in a W-2 employment position is a subset of a larger pool of low-income families eligible for health care and child care assistance. W-2 employment participants must have family incomes below 115 percent of the FPL and meet the assets test, while subsidies are available for all families with incomes below 165 percent of the FPL who meet the assets test.

Families must have one or more children younger than 13 years in need of care so that the parent(s) may be employed. In addition, child care assistance can be used only for employment purposes, but for W-2 participants employment can include up to 10 hours per week of employment-related training. Child care subsidies are no longer allowed for other schooling (e.g., GED, vocational, college or university coursework).[2] In addition, in a two-parent family, a new 1998 regulation requires a minimum combined total of 55 hours of employment per week for the two parents (e.g., 30 hours for one parent and 25 for the other) to receive federally-funded (administered by the state) child care assistance. This is to encourage "economic self-sufficiency" for both parents.[3]

Families are free to choose any state regulated (certified or licensed) child care arrangement for subsidized care, including relatives if the relative becomes at least provisionally certified and is not a co-resident. Parents who use unregulated child care (not licensed, certified, or provisionally certified care), however, are not eligible for any child care subsidies from the state.

To meet increased demand for care and to give parents a wider range of choices in subsidized care, the rules for a provisionally certified category of providers were changed. Currently, all licensed and certified providers in the state (all of whom are considered "regulated" by one standard or another) are required to have varying amounts of training and continuing education. The changed category of provisionally certified providers are no longer required to obtain the child care training that other certified providers are required to have. However, provisionally certified providers are subject to health and safety standards, a criminal background check, and an initial health and safety site visit.

In the past, provisionally certified providers were required to become trained (minimum 15 hours of training) within six months of starting to deliver child care services. These training standards were better than those of many states, some of which require no training for child care providers. The elimination of training in the revised provisional certification category has been considered by many within the state to be an important diminishment of the state's regulations designed to support quality child care.

Provisionally certified providers are reimbursed at 50 percent of the maximum W-2 child care rate for licensed family child care, whereas regularly certified family providers are reimbursed at 75 percent of the maximum rate for licensed care centers within a county. This rate differential was intended to provide an incentive for provisionally certified providers to obtain training and become certified providers.

As proposed in the original W-2 legislation, all families were required to pay some of their child care costs — 7.5 percent for families below 75 percent of the FPL, 10 percent for families from 75 to 95 percent of the FPL, and increasing 1.3 percent for each 1 percent increase in income as a percentage of the FPL above 95 percent of the FPL. In the original legislation, the percentage of cost paid by parents rose rapidly for incomes above the poverty line. However, on this point, debates about the original legislation produced change. Currently families receiving child care subsidies (those with incomes less than 200 percent of the FPL) are required to pay no more than 16 percent of their family's gross monthly income, a sum substantially less than the originally proposed co-payments required of families. However, the difference between the low pre-W-2 co-payment of 1996 and the new co-payment in 1998 can be dramatic for some families.

In the newest proposal in use, co-payments vary with income as a percentage of FPL and the number of children in care. Currently, a single parent with two children at 100 percent of the FPL with gross monthly income of $1,092 (hourly wage $6.49) would pay $114 (11 percent of gross income) as a co-payment for child care in a licensed facility and an $80 co-pay for care in a certified setting. A single parent with two children at 150 percent of the FPL with gross monthly income of $1,623 ($9.44 hourly wage) would pay a $240 co-payment (15 percent of gross family income) for licensed care and $168 for certified care (Source: chart produced by the Wisconsin Council on Children and Families based on original figures from the Wisconsin Department of Workforce Development).

The changes from the original legislation reduced the increase in co-payments for families with more children in care, and reduced the rapid increase in co-payments as family incomes rose above 100 percent of the FPL. These changes greatly decreased the former high marginal effect on net income of rapidly increasing child care and health care co-payments that could have proved a disincentive to families who increased self-sufficiency through increased hours of employment or wage increases.

In the original regulations, co-pay fees figured as a percentage of the cost of care were higher for more expensive care. This provided an incentive for parents to switch to potentially lower quality care (e.g. provisionally certified or family care instead of licensed center care). In the current regulation, co-payments for any type of certified care are 70 percent of co-payments for any type of licensed care. Therefore, accredited licensed child care, considered by the state as the highest quality child care, would cost 30 percent more for a parent than certified child care of any type; there is, therefore, a disincentive for families to seek or keep children in licensed child care compared to certified care. However, with identical co-payments for certified group, certified family, and provisionally certified child care, there is also no obvious economic incentive for parents to choose a provisionally certified child caregiver over a more highly trained certified caregiver.

While these regulations are complex, preliminary anecdotal information suggests that the lower co-payments required in certified child care may be influencing some parents to shift from licensed to certified caregivers, but that provisionally certified child care is not being selected by parents to a greater extent. Current State Office of Child Care information reports that approximately 7 percent of all subsidy funds are spent on provisionally certified care, 21 percent on certified care, and the balance on licensed care. Somewhat greater proportions of providers are provisionally certified in urban Milwaukee County than elsewhere in the state (Personal communication, Office of Child Care, Department of Workforce Development, February, 1998). However, it is far too early to draw conclusions on this question without further research.

The Administration of Child Care Services

W-2 agencies may be private contractors or county social services departments. W-2 agencies primarily do case management to guide participants toward increasingly self-sufficient employment. W-2 agencies will also determine eligibility for child care services, but in many cases separate county human/social service departments administer child care services. County departments often help eligible parents find child care providers and determine child care co-payments. The state computer system issues biweekly checks to providers based on county reports. In addition, the county or a contracted agency such as a child care resource and referral agency is responsible for conducting criminal background checks and certifying child care providers. Counties set maximum reimbursement rates, based on local market surveys.

The Impact of W-2 on Child Care Services

Adequate and timely provision of child care services is necessary for W-2 programs to achieve their goal of moving families to higher levels of self-sufficiency through employment. The broadening of full-time work requirements to all except mothers with a child less than 12 weeks was expected to create a demand for child care services unprecedented in any previous welfare-to-work demonstration projects. Early demonstration projects tried in many states were voluntary for mothers with children under age six, and volunteers with small children may have been those with lower-cost child care options available. The existing research documents the need for child care services to promote self-sufficiency, but gives few clues as to the likely pattern of child care choices when all former welfare recipients are mandated to work full time (Bane and Ellwood, 1994).[4]

It was expected that provision of child care services under the W-2 program would have short- and long-term impacts on parents, on children, and on the child care market for all employed parents. Possible impacts, based on low-income child care research and what is known about the current child care market, are summarized below.

Demand vs. Supply

The demand for child care services under W-2 is likely to exceed supply, especially in the short run. The existing supply of regulated child care is a small proportion of the estimated demand for care as W-2 work requirements are fully instituted. Since W-2 mandatory work requirements are waived if child care is not available, an adequate supply of child care is critical to the success of W-2's welfare-to-work focus.

The W-2 planners expected the new category of provisionally certified providers to help increase supply, but the economic incentives to become a provisionally certified caregiver are not large. In

1994, certified family care providers (who are the same as provisional providers, except for the 15 hours of training required) had annual net incomes of $5,132 for a 58-hour work week (Burton et al., 1995). Provisionally certified and certified family care providers may care for a maximum of three children other than their own. They must submit biweekly attendance reports to counties to obtain state reimbursement and collect the co-payment amount from parents.

The full-time work requirements of W-2 also make the use of relative care less feasible than it was for former AFDC recipients. More than half of poor families rely on relatives to provide child care, but that care is most often provided part time and is less reliable than formal market child care (Kisker et al., 1989; Siegel and Loman, 1991). In addition, many relatives who might have cared for children while at home on AFDC also will now be subject to W-2 work requirements (See, for example, footnote 3).

Another problem is convenient location of child care. Rural facilities are geographically sparse; urban residents often must use buses to transport children to and from care and also for travel to and from employment. This has been cited as a problem in two previous studies of employed Wisconsin AFDC recipients (Cochran, 1989; Weber, 1987).

Shortages of certain types of child care already exist for all families, not just low-income families, and, therefore, it was expected that these shortages would increase under W-2. The areas where shortages were expected to be worst included infant care, before and after school care, care for special needs children, and night and weekend shift care (Hofferth and Phillips, 1991; Maynard et al., 1990). Night and weekend shift care is a particular problem since one-third of poor mothers work weekends and one-half of working poor parents have rotating or changing work schedules (Hofferth, 1995).

While reliable research data are not yet available, preliminary information based on anecdotal field reports is both as expected and somewhat contrary to expectations (Personal communication with Office of Child Care in Wisconsin Department of Workforce Development and Dane County Human Services Department, March, 1998). The available child care funding for subsidies has not been used fully by parents and families eligible to use the funds, indicating lower demand for care than had been anticipated. Approximately 19,500 children were served in December, 1997 at a cost of $7 million that month; the projections had been to serve 55,000 children at cost of $13 million/month (Office of Child Care UPDATE report, 1997).

In some areas and for some kinds of child care, there are more open regulated child care spaces than shortages. However, increased demand for child care due to W-2 work requirements is likely being met by unsubsidized, unregulated care arrangements. As expected, there are reported shortages of infant care and care for children with special needs or disabilities. As in prior studies of employed Wisconsin AFDC recipients, obtaining a family's choice in child care convenient to home has been reported as a problem. Finding adequate evening and weekend care, too, appears to be a problem, as expected, although many may be using unregulated child care for these time periods since regulated care is generally not available evenings and weekends. Before- and after-school care is a problem although child care providers are emerging to respond to this need. These are preliminary anecdotal reports and research is needed to firmly establish effects of W-2 on parents' child care choices.

Effect on Net Income

The proposed schedule of W-2 child care co-payments may lower net family incomes for some families. Child care co-payments under W-2 are much larger than co-payments under the former child care subsidies available to families with incomes below 215 percent of the FPL. Thus, families in the former system who continued to receive child care assistance had net incomes reduced with the change to W-2 co-payments. All families who increase their wages above the poverty level face rising child care co-payments that offset increased earnings. In the original legislation, these marginal offsets were greater than increased earnings, providing little incentive to participants to increase self-sufficiency by working more hours or advancing to a higher wage. While the modified W-2 regulations with a cap on child care co-payments at 16 percent of family income have corrected this problem, there is now a "cliff" at 200 percent of the FPL that greatly reduces net family incomes for those who raise their incomes above the 200 percent FPL level and then become ineligible for child care subsidies.

For example, under the current system, a single mother with two children in licensed care who earned $2,210 per month (199 percent of FPL) would be eligible for child care assistance and make a co-payment of $335, giving her a gross income after child care costs of $1,875. If her income increased to $2,220 per month (200 percent of FPL), she would no longer qualify for assistance and would pay $800 per month for child care,[5] reducing her gross income after child care costs to $1,420, a 24 percent drop in net income. If the same mother had her two children in certified care, increasing her gross income from 199 percent to 200 percent of the FPL would increase her child care costs from $245 to $492, producing a 12 percent drop in gross income after child care.

While this "cliff" effect is relevant for many fewer families than the original co-payment schedule, preliminary reports support the idea that co-payments have remained a problem under W-2. Child care providers receiving state subsidies have reported difficulties collecting co-payments from parents (Wisconsin State Journal, 1998). The effect of co-payments on parents' choices for child care, decision to apply for child care subsidies, or decision to be in the W-2 program is not yet known.[6]

Effect on Quality

The quality of child care for children of W-2 participants may be lower, the same, or higher than it was for families under AFDC; these qualitative changes may have both short- and long-term consequences on families and on child development. Higher co-payments may cause parents to move children from higher quality, licensed care to lower cost certified providers, some of whom may be provisionally certified providers with no child care training. In addition, families may choose nonregulated care for some of their child care needs and not use subsidies. Alternatively, some families, especially those who were not on AFDC and who are now eligible for child care subsidies, may choose higher quality child care for their children than they could afford previously. Many studies have found training of providers as well as a higher caregiver to child ratio to be related to increased quality of care (Galinsky, Howes, Kontos, and Shinn, 1994; Helburn et al., 1995; Maynard et al., 1990). State of Wisconsin regulations and national accreditation standards (more common in licensed child care than certified child care) require more training for licensed family child care and licensed center care than for some types of certified group and family care, especially the new provisionally certified care category. Thus, if parents have incentives to choose certified over licensed care because of co-payment regulations or for other reasons (e.g., proximity, or ability to also care for infants and older children in the family), child care quality may be lowered with possible negative outcomes for children.

Alternatively, the pattern of child care parents "choose"[7] must be compared with prior care; thus, we might expect to find equivalent or even positive outcomes for some children who were able to keep or move to better quality child care under the new rules for child care subsidies. Early anecdotal reports indicate that many parents who had their children at home under AFDC are dissatisfied or uneasy about out-of-home child care alternatives. In contrast, parents among the "working poor" who had no access to child care subsidies under AFDC are happy with new possibilities for purchasing child care due to the expanded availability of child care subsidies.

Many AFDC recipients relied on informal care by relatives or friends and many are likely to continue to use this form of lower cost care under W-2, whether it is regulated subsidized care or unsubsidized and likely unregulated care. Galinsky et al. (1994) found that care by relatives is of lower quality than that in regulated child care homes and this is especially true for those relatives caring for children out of necessity rather than by choice. Less formal care is also more subject to breakdowns that jeopardize employment (Kisker et al., 1989; Siegel and Loman, 1991).

The economic incentives under W-2 for parents to shift children from licensed child care (any type) to a certified (including provisional) child care provider undermine the original intention of child care subsidies for at-risk children, that is, to foster child development and improve school readiness. Under W-2, parents are required to participate in employment and training activities when their youngest child is 12 weeks old; therefore, increased numbers of children are entering different forms of care from an early age. Note that most other states are requiring employment only for mothers of children one year or older. Short-term consequences for children depend upon a variety of factors, including the type of child care they are in compared with home child care, or what alternative care they might have had without W-2 and child care subsidies. Among the possible long-term consequences when children enter school after having had poor child care are increased tax costs to enable schools to provide remedial education and deal with behavioral problems (Vandell,1997). Alternatively, the expanded availability of child care subsidies that enables parents to afford better quality child care settings may result in long-term positive consequences for at least some groups of children.

Effect on Supply

W-2 child care provisions may decrease the supply of licensed and certified regulated child care for all families. There is disagreement about the possible effects of W-2 child care on the general child care market (Davidoff, 1996; *Wisconsin State Journal*, 1996). W-2 planners envisioned greater freedom of choice of care for welfare recipients and an increased supply of both formal and informal child care. Child care advocates expected and anecdotal reports support a current shift by selected groups of parents from regulated child care providers to less expensive, unregulated care. This may be because of co-payments, transportation requirements to child care centers, work hours, or other reasons. There is a possibility of a decline in the number of licensed centers available for all children. Under the former voucher system in place from 1985 to 1997, parents were able to choose either regulated centers or regulated family child care with the same low co-payment. While availability of vouchers was limited, the majority of parents who received vouchers used licensed center child care. This pattern may be changing with the change to higher co-payments for licensed center care. Early research from California and anecdotal reports in Wisconsin suggest these changes may have an adverse impact on the supply of licensed center care (Meyers, 1997).

Evaluating Child Care Services Under W-2

Evaluating the child care services component of W-2 using a pre-post or experimental-control design faces similar problems to those inherent in a comprehensive evaluation of the entire W-2 program. In the pre-welfare-reform world, in which few families were affected by work requirements under AFDC/JOBS (although many were employed part time), the provision of child care services did not have the same importance as it does in the post-reform world, where full-time work is mandated for most W-2 recipients. Establishing a counterfactual, i.e., what the nature of public intervention would have been without the change in place (see the chapter by Robert Haveman), is again complicated by this changed nature of the need for child care services under a mandatory work requirements program. In addition, following its philosophy of providing support for self-sufficiency through employment, the W-2 program extends child care (and health care) services to a pool of low-income families that is larger than the pool of potential W-2 eligibles with mandated employment. Focusing an evaluation only on participants in W-2 employment positions will not capture the impact of child care subsidies on the larger pool of eligible low-income working families.

Evaluating child care services under W-2 requires an assessment of how well these services meet the two goals inherent in providing subsidized child care to low-income families. The goal of W-2 and of the former child care subsidy program is to enable parents to be employed and to move toward economic self-sufficiency. The second goal of child care subsidies in general is to provide care for disadvantaged children that will result in school readiness and, in the future, healthy and productive workers. Evaluation designed to assess the extent to which W-2 child care services facilitate those goals would examine the effects of the program on parents' employment and on children's well-being. An intermediate evaluation goal would be to assess the process of providing child care services, i.e., does the system provide the needed help without administrative delays or bottlenecks, and does it do so equally well in various communities across the state with differing child care markets and employment opportunities?

Important evaluation questions include:

❖ Do W-2 participants receive the help they need when they need it to obtain child care (process evaluation)?

❖ How do the characteristics of child care (i.e., cost, convenience, reliability) and characteristics of subsidies (amount, timing, match with provider cost) affect the ability of W-2 participants to obtain and retain employment (process and outcome evaluation)?

❖ How do child care arrangements affect children's well-being; are arrangements stable and of adequate quality (outcome and impact analysis) compared to the care they were receiving?

❖ How do W-2 child care subsidy provisions affect the ability of the child care market to provide quality child care for low-income children (impact analysis) compared to earlier provision capabilities?

The first two questions are of the greatest importance in evaluating the success of W-2 in meeting its goal of increasing self-sufficiency through employment. The third question is a broader research question assessing both the role of child care and the possible effects on children of W-2 work requirements, reduced time with their own parents, and increased time in out-of-home care. The answer would have implications for the long-term effects on the youngest generation of potential welfare recipients and for future welfare policy reforms. The fourth question attempts to assess the possible unintended consequences of W-2 and the changes in the current child care subsidy system on the entire child care market. This question is related to the broader goal of appropriate child development and improved school readiness for all children, but especially those from low-income families.

Answering some of the above questions could be integrated into a process evaluation of the administrative efficiency of W-2, or an evaluation of the movement of W-2 participants up the job self-sufficiency ladder. This paper considers two possibilities: (1) what could be learned from existing administrative and other child care system data, and (2) what a longitudinal panel study of a sample of low-income households would add to a comprehensive evaluation.

Using Administrative and Other Existing Child Care Data

Administrative Data. The only reliable pre-W-2 administrative data on low-income subsidized child care simply track the number of children served, number of families, and total dollars expended within each category of child care funding by counties and the state. These data provide no information on the relationship between child care subsidies and parent's employment, the focus of the first two and most important evaluation questions. Under W-2, a reporting system which creates a longitudinal record for each individual to monitor time limits within each employment tier and overall will be necessary. The current state administrative system for tracking W-2 participants, monitoring time limits, and applying sanctions does not include information on child care arrangements, cost, or subsidies. However, an automated system for issuing child care vouchers and recording individual usage data from each county is currently operating. Data on individual households receiving subsidies could theoretically be linked to W-2 employment tracking data, but both systems are new, and initial debugging may muddy data collected in the early stages of operation.

Federal reporting requirements of the Personal Responsibility and Work Opportunity Reconciliation Act of 1996 may provide useful evaluation data to track both child care subsidies and use of child care.[8] These federal reporting requirements place a much larger burden on the state than the present system can report and it is as yet unclear how strictly they will be enforced. In addition, the monthly collection requirement is difficult, since many families in unsubsidized employment, receiving only child care and/or health care benefits, would not meet regularly with the W-2 agency staff. Thus there would be no data on the family and employment characteristics of those low-income families in unsubsidized employment to match with data on child care use from the child care subsidy reporting system.

Using administrative data collected by the state would be the least expensive evaluation strategy for child care services, if data from the two newly created computerized tracking systems for W-2 and for child care can be merged. This would require the full cooperation of state agencies and full compliance with federal reporting requirements. If those requirements are met, and data are structured as longitudinal records for individuals, changes in the type of care used, its cost, and other features could be evaluated. The reliability of data that are not vital for issuing payments or tracking time limits could also be questionable if county-level workers inputting the data have little motivation to maintain accuracy; this has been true with previous administrative reporting systems (see the chapter by Haveman).

The missing element in an evaluation using administrative data would be the link between child care arrangements and employment changes. It would not be possible to determine if child care difficulties caused employment loss or if changes in employment caused child care changes without intensive tracking and multiple interviews. In addition, the stability of child care arrangements could be tracked, but no evaluation of their quality would be possible using these data; and without quality measures, only the crudest analyses of the potential effects of child care on child well-being could be done. Another limitation is that administrative data would contain information only on active W-2 participants, not on those who left the program because of child care or employment difficulties. But one strength of using these data is that they could supply information for all counties of the state, allowing comparisons of local variation in the effectiveness of W-2 agencies and answering the question of whether participants receive the child care help they need when they need it.

Child Care Resource and Referral Data. The child care resource and referral system (CCR&R) has data on the supply of licensed and certified care and on parent requests for help in finding child care. These data would be most useful in examining the fourth question, that of possible adverse effects on the child care market arising from W-2 subsidies and co-payment schedules. These data are currently available to parents and employers, and any access to them by the state or research/evaluation projects would have to be arranged with regard to confidentiality constraints. Currently, 17 CCR&Rs serve all 72 Wisconsin counties. To track historical and current data, funding would be needed to download and merge data from the 17 CCR&R data sets into a statewide data set. Statewide data are available for all 17 CCR&Rs beginning in 1995; these would provide one to three years of pre-W-2 baseline data for the state. The State's Bureau of Regulation and Licensing collects data on licensed child care facilities, but no data on certified providers is available statewide except through the CCR&Rs.

CCR&R data on the child care market include information on estimated or actual enrollments and open slots, new facilities and closures for regulated care in licensed centers, licensed family centers, certified family child care homes, and licensed school-age programs. A weakness is that CCR&R data are limited to the regulated child care market, providing no information on changes in use of child care by nonsubsidized relatives or other informal care, and no data on the supply of unregulated providers.

Data on individual parent requests could also provide some indication of changes in demand for particular types of care. CCR&R data on parent requests include the number of requests for each type of child care, and special considerations such as need for evening care or care for special needs children. For each request, the characteristics of the family are also requested on a voluntary basis: age of the child for whom care is requested, ethnic background, family income level, and whether family receives public assistance. The CCR&R data and services are not, however, limited to or targeted to W-2 participants. Thus, not all W-2 participants receive referrals or consultations about child care from a CCR&R. CCR&Rs do serve many low-income families; 60 percent of all parents served by CCR&Rs in 1997 had family incomes below $25,000. Although not all W-2 recipients receive CCR&R assistance, information on AFDC and W-2 receipt could allow some analysis of pre- and post-W-2 child care demand.

Longitudinal Panel Study Before and During W-2

To adequately answer the four questions posed above, a longitudinal panel study of W-2 recipients and nonparticipants who receive child care subsidies, tracking their child care and employment history, is needed. The analysis of administrative data is unlikely to provide sufficient detail to adequately evaluate the role of child care and child care subsidies in low-income families' employment history. A repeated cross-sectional survey of a sample of low-income families as W-2 progresses could provide the greater detail needed on connections among child care cost and availability, child care choices and employment choices. Such surveys could gather retrospective histories for the prior six months or a year from respondents. However, with the new focus of welfare reform on changing long-term behaviors of the welfare-dependent (see the chapter by Corbett), only a multiyear longitudinal design can assess the complex factors influencing individual life course events. Such a design would also have the potential for longer term assessment of child outcomes for children and families living in poverty (see Cancian and Wolfe chapter; NICHD Early Child Care Research Network, 1997a).

Ideally, data collection should have started before the full W-2 program began, to provide information on the effect of W-2 requirements and child care subsidies on changing employment and child care patterns of recipients of both W-2 and of child care subsidies. The sample should be large enough to include low-income families with children of varying ages. As suggested above, it should not be restricted to W-2 participants, since child care subsidies are available to all families who meet income and assets requirements.

Sampling from the population of all families with incomes less than 165 percent of the FPL is important for several reasons. It is important to track the effects of W-2 for current AFDC recipients who exit the system because of the work mandates or their inability to comply with work requirements. Including low-income families also captures young mothers who choose to work part time, an option not allowed under W-2 work participation requirements. Finally, low-income families who do not receive subsidies provide a comparison group for assessing the positive effects of subsidies on employment and quality of care.

The majority of studies of quality child care now indicate a small, but significant relationship between quality of child care and child outcomes (e.g., NICHD Early Child Care Research Network, 1997b; Vandell, 1997); therefore, it is important to follow parents' patterns of child care when parents leave the welfare system, in or out of W-2, with and without child care subsidies. A number of studies have shown improvements in child care quality among those receiving child care subsidies under the existing system (Berger and Black, 1992; Hofferth and Wissoker, 1992). In an evaluation, one might expect that children of parents who can access higher quality child care (e.g., care with lower staff turnover, lower teacher to child ratios, more positive interactions with children, more teacher training) with subsidies will have somewhat better "well-being" or child outcomes than children in lower quality care settings. Current research also supports the possibility that parents may be positively affected by having their children in more stable, higher quality settings and that parent satisfaction also relates to more positive interaction with children at home. Thus, a long-term panel evaluation of family and child outcomes related to W-2 and child care subsidies would be complex, but feasible, and important to assess current policies, and to understand the effect of policies on poor families and their young children. A number of current studies provide models for research and evaluation in these areas (e.g., See Galinsky et al., 1994; Vandell, 1997 and the *Merrill Palmer Quarterly* 1997 special issue for a review of current day care and child outcome studies).

The proposed study would gather information on receipt of child care subsidies, any child care problems that affect employment, and the cost and other characteristics of care used. A longitudinal history of employment, income, and child care changes, and direct questions about the reasons for these changes would allow analyses of the link between child care and ability to improve economic self-sufficiency through employment. Rough measures of the quality of care could be gathered from parents' reports of staff/child ratios and warmth of caregiver's relationship to the child. These are measures that have been correlated with more objective direct observations of child care quality (Galinsky et al., 1994).[9]

The strengths of this evaluation approach are that the study could be designed to adequately answer major evaluation questions related to W-2 child care services. The necessary data could also be gathered in conjunction with other evaluations of the W-2 program. The most obvious limitation is the cost of gathering such data from a hard to reach and highly mobile population. Cost would also prohibit sampling all counties in the state; instead, representative urban and rural samples would be needed.

There are several reasons that investing in a comprehensive evaluation of W-2 child care services is important. First, the proposed W-2 full-time work requirements for low-income mothers of young children are historic and unprecedented. W-2 work requirements exceed federal block grant requirements and will place strong demands on the child care market. Under these conditions, the impact of the cost and availability of child care on mothers' ability to become self-sufficient through employment should become much clearer, but only with adequate evaluation. Second, the change in training requirements for provisionally certified providers reverses the previous state philosophy in Wisconsin that publicly funded child care should be both regulated and provided by trained caregivers to provide a minimum quality of care for low-income children. Including measures of the impact of W-2 on the quality of care is necessary both to assess the short-term effects on children and to estimate the long-term effects on school readiness and other child outcomes (e.g. see preliminary design in NICHD Early Child Care Research Network, 1996; Reynolds, Mann, Miedel, and Smokowski, 1997; Schweinhart, Barnes, and Weikart, 1993). An adequate evaluation of the impact of W-2 child care services will provide crucial information for improving Wisconsin welfare reform and for the design of welfare reform by policy makers in other states.

References

APWA, NCSL, NGA (American Public Welfare Association, National Governors' Association, and the National Conference of State Legislatures). "The Personal Responsibility and Work Opportunity Reconciliation Act of 1996 (Conference agreement for H.R. 3734) Analysis." Available on the World Wide Web at http://www.apwa.org/ reform/analysis.htm, August 9, 1996.

Bane, Mary Jo, and David T. Ellwood. *Welfare Realities: From Rhetoric to Reform.* Cambridge, MA: Harvard University Press, 1994.

Berger, Mark C., and Dan A. Black. "Child Care Subsidies, Quality of Care, and the Labor Supply of Low-Income, Single Mothers." *Review of Economics and Statistics* 74 (1992): 635–642.

Burton, A., M. Whitebook, and L. Sakai. *Valuable Work; Minimal Rewards. A Report on the Wisconsin Child Care Work Force.* Washington, DC: The National Center for the Early Childhood Workforce and the Wisconsin Early Childhood Association (WECA), 1995.

Cancian, Maria, and Daniel R. Meyer. *A Profile of the AFDC Caseload in Wisconsin: Implications for a Work-Based Welfare Reform Strategy.* IRP Special Report 67, Madison, WI: University of Wisconsin–Madison, September 1995.

Cochran, Susan. *Post-AFDC Child Care Assistance Report*, Madison, WI: Wisconsin Department of Health and Social Services, Office of Policy and Budget, Evaluation Section, June 1989.

Connelly, Rachel. "The Effect of Child Care Costs on the Labor Force Participation and AFDC Recipiency of Single Mothers." Institute for Research on Poverty, Discussion Paper no. 920-90, Madison, WI: University of Wisconsin–Madison, 1990.

Cost, Quality and Outcomes Study Team. "Cost, Quality and Child Outcomes in Child Care Centers: Key Findings and Recommendations." *Young Children* (1995): 40-44.

Davidoff, Judith. "Will W-2 Hurt Your Children?" *Isthmus*, April 5-11, 1996.

Department of Workforce Development (DWD), State of Wisconsin. Draft Request for Proposals for Wisconsin Works, Memo from Richard Wegner, Acting Secretary, June 18, 1996.

Galinsky, Ellen, Carollee Howes, Susan Kontos, and Marybeth Shinn. *The Study of Children in Family Child Care and Relative Care.* New York: Families and Work Institute, 1994.

Helburn, Suzanne, M. L. Culkin, J. Morris, and N. Mocan. "Cost, Quality, and Child Outcomes in Child Care Centers." Executive Summary. University of Colorado at Denver, Economics Department, 1995.

Hofferth, Sandra L. "Caring for Children at the Poverty Line." *Children and Youth Services Review* 17 no. ½ (1995): 61-90.

Hofferth, Sandra L. and Deborah A. Phillips. "Child Care Policy Research." *Journal of Social Issues* 47 no. 2 (1995): 1-13.

Hofferth, Sandra L., and Douglas A. Wissoker. "Price, Quality and Income in Child Care Choice." *Journal of Human Resources* 27 no. 1 (1992): 70-111.

Kimmel, Jean. "The Effectiveness of Child-Care Subsidies in Encouraging the Welfare-to-Work Transition of Low-Income Single Mothers." *American Economic Review* 85 no. 2 (1995): 271-275.

Kisker, Ellen E., Rebecca Maynard, Anne Gordon, and Margaret Strain. *The Child Care Challenge: What Parents Need and What Is Available in Three Metropolitan Areas.* Report to Department of Health and Human Services. Princeton, NJ: Mathematica Policy Research, 1989.

Maynard, Rebecca A. "Subsidized Employment and Non-Labor-Market Alternatives for Welfare Recipients." In *The Work Alternative: Welfare Reform and the Realities of the Job Market,* eds. Demetra Smith Nightingale and Robert H. Haveman. Washington, DC: Urban Institute Press, 1990.

Maynard, Rebecca, Ellen E. Kisker, and Stuart Kerachsky. 1990. *Child Care Challenges for Low-Income Families: The Minority Female Single Parent Demonstration.* New York: Rockefeller Foundation, 1990.

Meyers, Marcia K."Cracks in the Seam: Durability of Child Care in JOBS Welfare-to-Work Programs." *Journal of Family and Economic Issues* 18 (1997): 379-406.

Merrill Palmer Quarterly 43, no. 3 (1997), Review Issue.

The NICHD Early Child Care Research Network."Child Care and the Family: An Opportunity to Study Development in Context." *SRCD Newsletter* (Spring 1996): 4-7.

The NICHD Early Child Care Research Network. "Poverty and Patterns of Child Care." In *Consequences of Growing Up Poor*, eds. S.J. Duncan, J. Brooks-Gunn. New York: Russell Sage Foundation, 1997a.

The NICHD Early Child Care Research Network. "Mother-Child Interaction and Cognitive Outcomes Associated with Early Child Care: Results of the NICHD Study." Poster symposium presented at the Biennial Meeting of the Society for Research in Child Development, Washington, DC, April 1997b.

Office of Child Care, State of Wisconsin. Update Report, 1997.

Oliker, Stacey J. "Work Commitment and Constraint among Mothers on Workfare." *Journal of Contemporary Ethnography* 24 (1995): 165-194.

Reynolds, A. J., E. Mann, W. Miedel, and P. Smokowski. "The State of Early Childhood Intervention: Effectiveness, Myths and Realities, New Directions." *Focus* 19 (1). University of Wisconsin–Madison: The Institute for Research on Poverty, 1997.

Schweinhart, L. J., H. V. Barnes, and D. P. Weikart. *Significant Benefits: The High/Scope Perry Preschool Study through Age 27*. Ypsilanti, MI: High/Scope Educational Research Foundation, 1993.

Siegel, Gary L., and L. Anthony Loman. *Child Care and AFDC Recipients in Illinois: Patterns, Problems and Needs*. Report prepared for Division of Family Support Services, Illinois Department of Public Aid. St. Louis: Institute of Applied Research, 1991.

Vandell, D. "Introduction: Child Care as a Developmental Context." *Merrill Palmer Quarterly* 43, no. 3 (1997): 333-339.

Weber, Joan. *Child Care in Wisconsin: Provision of Care, Supervision, and Education for All Children Including Those from AFDC Families.* Madison, WI: Wisconsin Department of Health and Social Services, Bureau of Planning, Division of Policy and Budget, March 1987.

Wisconsin Department of Health and Social Services. 1979. *Child Care in Wisconsin*, WRWP#9. Madison, WI: Wisconsin Department of Health and Social Services, Welfare Reform Study Staff, February 1979.

Wisconsin State Journal. "Wisconsin Day Care Bind Could Pinch Welfare Reform Plans." February 19, 1996.

Wolf, Douglas A., and Freya L. Sonenstein. "Child-Care Use among Welfare Mothers: A Dynamic Analysis." *Journal of Family Issues* 12, no. 4 (1991): 519-539.

Endnotes

1   Prior to W-2, the income level below which families qualified for child care assistance was 215 percent of the federal poverty line. However, although the eligibility level was higher, there were waiting lists for assistance in many counties. Under W-2, child care assistance is now available from the state to support all eligible children in child care.

2   This was a disputed point in the original March 1996 Wisconsin Works legislation that some legislators attempted to change in 1997. They argued that work and child care subsidies should be given to former AFDC recipients who were trying to finish degree programs (GED, community college, or university). Others argued that such a provision would undermine the primary objective of W-2 which is to encourage employment and economic self-sufficiency. The governor supported the latter argument and the 1996 wording in the legislation was not changed.

3   One Hmong case worker in Dane County's Job Center who works with Southeast Asian refugees suggested that this new regulation will be very difficult for Hmong families. Typically, Hmong families are quite large (5-7 children) and Hmong wives speak little English and have done traditional domestic and economic work (e.g., farming, sewing, embroidery) while their husbands took jobs, if possible. Hmong families transitioning from AFDC to W-2 have typically followed this pattern of having the wife stay home to provide child care. With the new employment requirement of 55 hours for both parents, wives will also have to obtain employment.

4   The State of Wisconsin and county offices formerly responsible for AFDC social services planned for this increased need over several years. Federal block grant monies for child care and other state child care funds were used to support child care subsidies for the early demonstration projects. From 1994 to 1996, mothers with children at successively younger ages were mandated to employment in demonstration projects. In March 1996, a mandatory program, "Pay for Performance," was instituted that required adults in families with children one year old or over to work in exchange for wages and child care subsidies. In March 1997, "Pay for Performance" was extended to all families in the state who had received AFDC benefits and who had children 12 weeks of age or older. Wisconsin Works or W-2 with its increased employment and training requirements began for all eligible families in September of 1997, with AFDC officially phased out for all families in March, 1998. The last AFDC checks were issued on March 1, 1998, and the state of Wisconsin announced that AFDC rolls had fallen below 30 families. The dramatic drop in the number of poor families receiving welfare in Wisconsin leads to the obvious question: What has happened to these poor families?

5   The $800 per month is a statewide average for two children in licensed care, and would most likely be higher in urban areas such as Milwaukee.

6   In the first wave of a panel study in Dane County, Irving Piliavin reports that several factors, including co-payments, have created problems for parents' ability to pay for child care. Longer-term research may sort out which factors are most important.

7   "Choice" is also dependent upon availability, affordability, etc. and should be noted not as "free" choice.

8   States must collect information monthly and submit reports quarterly to the U.S. Department of Health and Human Services (DHHS) on those receiving child care subsidies, including: "family income; county of residence; the gender and age of children receiving assistance; whether the family includes only one parent; sources of family income, including employment, IV-A cash assistance, housing assistance, food stamp assistance, and other assistance programs; the number of months the family has received benefits; the type of child care in which the child is enrolled; whether the child care provider is a relative; the cost of child care for families; and the average hours per week of care." Information on child care subsidies must also be reported to HHS every six months. These reports must include: "the number of child care providers that received funding; the monthly cost of child care services and the subsidy cost portion; the number of payments made to providers through vouchers, contracts, cash, and disregards under public benefit programs, listed by the type of child care services provided; the manner in which consumer education information was provided to parents, and the total number, without duplication, of children and families served." (APWA, NCSL, NGA, 1996, p. 23.) These requirements in the original legislation were reduced in the Budget Reconciliation Act of 1997 (H.R. 2015), and a 2/18/98 letter to the Administration for Children and Families from APWA and the National Governor's Association requests that type of child care, total monthly cost of child care, and total monthly hours of child care not be required to be collected.

9   The research design should not make assumptions about quality of child care (e.g., licensed family centers are superior to certified family child care) without carefully considering actual regulatory reports, such as licensing violations and high quality measures such as accreditation. Additional direct observational studies of families and children at home as well as in child care settings is also recommended for a more comprehensive evaluation of the impact of child care subsidies and W-2 related child care requirements on families' and children's opportunities for different types of care and well-being.

11

Evaluating the Child Support Reforms in the Wisconsin Works Program

Daniel R. Meyer
School of Social Work
Institute for Research on Poverty
University of Wisconsin — Madison

Maria Cancian
La Follette Institute of Public Affairs
Institute for Research on Poverty
School of Social Work
University of Wisconsin — Madison

Emma Caspar
Institute for Research on Poverty
University of Wisconsin–Madison

With Judi Bartfeld, Patricia Brown, Thomas Corbett, Robert Haveman,

Thomas Kaplan, Arthur Reynolds, Gary Sandefur, Nora Cate Schaeffer,

Judith A. Seltzer, Barbara Wolfe

Introduction

In the last twenty-five years, child support has increasingly come to the attention of policy makers. Part of the impetus for this has been the rapid growth in the number of single-parent families: Whereas only one child in 12 lived in a mother-only family in 1960, by 1998 the proportion had increased to nearly one in four (U.S. Bureau of the Census, 1998a). More than half of children born in the 1980s were expected to live apart from their fathers before reaching adulthood (Bumpass and Sweet, 1989). This means that the child support system could affect more than half of today's children.

Another factor increasing the importance of child support policy is the economic vulnerability of single-parent families. About two-fifths of all mother-only families are poor (U.S. Bureau of the Census, 1998b), and even father-only families are twice as likely to be poor as husband-wife families (Meyer and Garasky, 1993). While some separated and divorced parents were poor prior to separation, in many others the children and resident parent experience a significant drop in economic well-being, while the non-resident parent experiences a gain in economic well-being. The child support system has been increasingly scrutinized to see if appropriate amounts are being transferred to children who are economically vulnerable.

The public welfare system can be seen as a complement to private child support. Because some children remain poor even when the nonresident parent pays child support, and because some non-resident parents do not pay, public assistance is inextricably linked to the private child support system. As the number of single-parent families grew, and as the private child support system increasingly failed to ensure economic adequacy for the children, the public system burgeoned. Increasing costs in the welfare system combined with increasing concern about potential negative effects of welfare have led to dramatic changes in the public welfare system, culminating in the Personal Responsibility and Work Opportunity Reconciliation Act (PRWORA) of 1996. PRWORA replaced Aid to Families with Dependent Children (AFDC) with the Temporary Assistance for Needy Families (TANF) block grant, which gives the states great freedom in designing their own system of assistance to poor families. Under TANF, Wisconsin has taken the lead in developing a radically different system, the Wisconsin Works (or W-2) program.

Under AFDC, all child support paid on behalf of welfare recipients in excess of $50 per month was used to reimburse the government for welfare expenses. TANF allows states substantial flexibility regarding the handling of child support paid on behalf of families receiving assistance. Most states now retain all child support, or continue to have a $50 per month pass-through. However, in Wisconsin implementation of the W-2 program coincides with a dramatic shift in the interface between the private child support system and the provision of public assistance. Under a new demonstration policy all child support paid is distributed to resident-parent families.[1] This paper describes the strategy that is being used to assess the impact of this change on a variety of outcomes.[2]

Child Support and Public Assistance: Alternative Approaches

At least three approaches to the interface between the private child support system and policies surrounding public support to families with children are possible. First, the policy could be to provide public support and to collect any private support paid on behalf of the family, using this private support to offset public costs. This was the policy prior to 1984. This policy may, however, discourage nonresident parents from paying private support, because none of their payments go directly to their children. Moreover, resident parents and nonresident parents would have an incentive to cooperate with each other and *not* to cooperate with the formal system: By hiding any support from nonresident parents, all support paid by nonresident parents would benefit their children, and resident-parent families could keep both public and private support.

These negative consequences might be alleviated by passing through some of the private support to resident parents, the federal policy from 1984 to 1996. This policy might remove some of the disincentive for nonresident parents to pay and increase the incentive for resident and nonresident parents to cooperate in compliance, and thus could increase formal payments. While little empirical research has been conducted on the effects of the pass-through, anecdotal evidence and recent ethnographic research (Johnson and

Doolittle, 1998) suggest that $50/month may not be a large enough incentive to encourage cooperation. The research suggests that some parents strategically collaborate: In exchange for the resident parent not providing information on the nonresident parent, the nonresident parent agrees to pay child support informally, which allows the resident parent to keep all child support paid (Edin, 1995).

The third possible policy would be to ensure that all resident parents receive all of the child support paid on their behalf. This policy should fully remove the disincentives for nonresident parents to pay, thus increasing formal payments and improving their children's economic well-being. It may also increase the proportion of children who have had paternity formally established, decrease the resident parent's participation in food stamps and Medicaid, promote earnings among resident parents, increase contact between nonresident parents and their children, and eventually improve other aspects of children's well-being. Moreover, this policy would be consistent with the way child support is treated in the private sector (where all support is passed through to the family), making the income support system more consistent with the way the working world operates. The ultimate cost of such a policy will depend on the extent to which these beneficial effects compensate for the loss in revenue previously collected from child support payments to families receiving public support. The cost will also depend on the extent to which low-income parents choose to receive TANF benefits if they can also retain child support.

The state of Wisconsin is unique in pursuing the third option and passing through all child support to resident-parent families. An evaluation of the pass-through policy in Wisconsin is particularly important because the historic PRWORA allows states to set their own pass-through policies. At this time, Wisconsin is the only state choosing to provide full pass-through of child support payments. According to the U.S. Department of Health and Human Services (1997), the majority of states have discontinued the pass-through. All states continuing the pass-through are maintaining the $50 level except for Kansas ($40), Nevada ($75), and Wisconsin. The new Wisconsin policy offers an opportunity to evaluate the potential advantages and disadvantages of this new approach to child support, and the evaluation could be important in helping other states determine which approach to take.

Experimental Design

The federal Department of Health and Human Services has granted Wisconsin a demonstration waiver from the requirement that child support be assigned to the government and that the state forward the federal government its share of any child support received. Under the terms of the waiver, an evaluation of the pass-through policy is being performed. In this evaluation, the control group is subject to a limited pass-through of child support payments, while the experimental group and the remainder of W-2 participants in the state receive all child support paid on their behalf.

Only those W-2 participants receiving cash assistance are subject to having their child support retained by the state. Thus, assignment to the experimental or control group has a direct effect only on those who receive W-2 benefits as caretakers of newborns (eligible for benefit payments for a limited period of time after the birth of a child), and those in Community Service Jobs (CSJ) and W-2 Transitions positions (both of which receive grants from the state in exchange for their participation). For individuals assigned to the control group, participating in these programs results in a reduced pass-through of up to $50 or 41 percent of child support paid, whichever is greater. Control group members receive the full pass-through while participating in W-2 only if they are in subsidized or unsubsidized employment. In contrast, members of the experimental group receive all child support regardless of the level of their participation in W-2. In the absence of a federal waiver Wisconsin could keep or pass through to the resident parent the greater of 41 percent or $50, with the remaining child support going to reimburse the federal government. Thus, although some families (those in the experimental group) benefit more than others from the experiment, no family receives less than it would in the absence of a waiver.

Random assignment of new W-2 cases was conducted in two phases, September 1997 through June 1998, and January through June 1999. About 3,700 individuals who began their W-2 participation in a CSJ, W-2 Transitions, or as a caretaker of newborn were assigned to experimental and control groups. Existing AFDC cases were assigned in September 1997 such that approximately 3,000 cases made an initial transition from AFDC to one of these tiers of W-2.[3] The evaluation will analyze the impact of the demonstration on these cases as well as on cases initially in subsidized or unsubsidized employment, categories in which control-group members are not subject to a reduced pass-through. The evaluation covers a four-year period ending in the fall of 2001.

The evaluation includes three parts: a process and implementation evaluation, an experimental impact evaluation, and a nonexperimental evaluation. We begin with brief comments on the process and implementation evaluation, but the main focus of this paper is the experimental impact evaluation. In the final sections of the paper we discuss some of the limitations of the experimental evaluation and the potential for the nonexperimental evaluation to help us address some of these limitations.

Process and Implementation Evaluation

The process and implementation evaluation has four goals.[4] First, we want information on how the policy was actually implemented in order to assess the findings of the impact evaluation. For example, if nonresident parents did not know about the new pass-through policy, the impact evaluation would find no effect of the demonstration on child support payments. To assess the level of knowledge about the new policy, we are examining printed materials available to W-2 program recipients and observing what resident and nonresident parents are told about the demonstration in eight representative W-2 agencies around the state.[5] Second, implementation details can alter the program that policy makers thought they were designing, and these differences in details may vary among the program sites. We hope to gain a sense of the range of variation, if any, in the way the demonstration is conducted in different areas through two mechanisms: field observation, conducted in the eight agencies, and a survey of front-line staff around the state that includes hypothetical situations, asking what the worker would say to a client in a particular situation. Third, implementation challenges are useful to describe for the benefit of others interested in trying the reform in different jurisdictions. We will attempt to document particular problems and issues faced in implementation that could be useful to other states. Finally, to set the results of the experimental evaluation in context, we will document and describe the economic and political situation in the state during the demonstration.

Impact Evaluation

Before turning to the outcomes of interest, we briefly review the counterfactual, the main evaluation methods, time periods, and data.

Counterfactual and Methods of Analysis

A critical step in evaluating the effect of a new policy is to determine an appropriate counterfactual. A key question is, "What group should be compared to the group that faces the new policy regime?" In the child support demonstration, W-2 cases demographically eligible for child support are randomly assigned into two groups, one group that faces the new policy (receiving all child support paid on their behalf, the "experimental" group), and one group that faces an alternate policy (receiving only a portion of child support paid on their behalf, the "control" group). Because the assignment of cases is being done randomly, the experimental group and the control group should be equivalent, differing only in the type of policy they face (and other differences due to chance). This yields a powerful evaluation design, a simple comparison of outcomes between the two groups. This will be the basic comparison we will make, and to the extent that the two groups are equivalent (and we have information on outcomes among each group) this comparison provides a "pure" test of the policy's effects.

Nonetheless, it is possible that the simple comparison could produce misleading results. One possibility is that there may be substantive differences between the experimental and control groups at the time of random assignment, even if the random assignment were perfectly executed, due to chance. Another possibility is that even though the groups were equivalent upon assignment, when we try to compare them later, we will only have information on subsets of cases, and these subsets may not have been equivalent upon assignment. One way in which this could occur is that individuals requesting information on W-2 were told their potential experimental group status, but we may not have full information on them unless they actually entered W-2. If individuals who anticipated receiving large amounts of child support were told that they would be members of the control group and consequently decided not to enter the program, this "diversion" effect could cause the experimental and control groups to differ on an important dimension.[6]

In the event of significant differences in experimental and control groups, we will use multivariate analyses to adjust our measures of impact. Multivariate analyses will also allow us to evaluate the extent to which the demonstration has different effects for subpopulations. The federal waiver requires that separate analyses be done for two geographic areas (Milwaukee and the rest of the state), presumably because the problems, issues, and policy context are different in large urban areas as compared to other areas, and the policy may have different effects. We want to examine whether there are different effects for other subgroups as well. We will explore whether the demonstration has different effects on those initially in W-2 Transitions, Community Service Jobs, or caring for a newborn. As sample size allows, we propose also examining nonresident parents of different ages, in different counties, cases with various lengths of history with child support and with welfare, paternity cases compared to divorce cases, those with one versus more children, those with preschool versus older children, and those with substantial child support arrearages.

Time Period

The choice of appropriate time period for analysis is complex. Certainly the period needs to be long enough for the policy to affect behavior. For example, even if the new pass-through increases the incentive for nonresident parents to find employment, it may take some time for them to find jobs and then for their employment to be recorded in the data systems, or if it increases the likelihood of paternity establishment, it will take a considerable amount of time for paternity to be formally established. Moreover, because it may take some time before counties become effective at explaining the pass-through policy, an evaluation of effects that takes place too early may find little effect. Furthermore, the policy may have indirect effects; indeed the evaluation design requires an examination of some of these. For example, the policy may *directly* increase child support payments while the increased payments in turn affect child well-being. Indirect effects in particular may take some time to detect.

Because this policy reform is unique, there is no policy experience by which to estimate how long it should take before an effect is found. Moreover, some short-term effects may be of interest as well. Thus, the evaluation is designed to examine both short-term and intermediate-term effects, the examination of short-term effects being concentrated in those areas in which direct effects are most likely (child support payments) and in which measurement of the effect is simplest (using administrative data).

Data

We are using both administrative and survey data for the experimental evaluation. State data from four administrative record databases is being assembled for all those assigned to the experimental and control groups. Data from the Client Assistance for Re-employment and Economic Support (CARES) records include information on W-2 participants (case history, tier placement, benefit history, sanctions); information on public assistance to low-income families, including food stamps, Medicaid, and child care; as well as such demographic information as birth dates, number of children, family composition, marital status, educational background, and residential location. The KIDS Child Support Database contains information on child support orders, payments, and arrearages, the method of payment (wage withholding, tax intercepts), destination of the payment (resident parent, state), demographic information about the parents and children in the case (birth dates, dates of marriage and divorce, paternity adjudication, residential location), and child support case history. KIDS includes some cases without child support orders, but with child support potential: paternity cases in which the paternity adjudication process has begun, and cohabiting paternity cases. Also included are cases in which no child support order has been made due to extenuating circumstances, such as the economic situation of the nonresident parent, problems in locating the nonresident parent, and cases in which the resident parent is determined to have good cause for not establishing an order. In addition to these two sources we are also using the unemployment insurance (UI) wage file for quarterly earnings for individual covered workers,[7] and Wisconsin Department of Revenue (DOR) individual tax data, which contain valuable information on earnings and other income, such as interest, rent, self-employment earnings, as well as personal information, such as marital status and residential location.[8]

Although administrative records will provide much of the data needed for the evaluation, the goals of the evaluation require that records be augmented with a survey. The survey serves several purposes essential to the evaluation: It provides information about independent and dependent variables that are not available in administrative records, about participants' knowledge of the program in which they participate, and information that will provide some capability to assess the administrative records. The survey will include basic demographic information, details on household composition, income, and program participation. In addition, the survey will include questions on: knowledge of policies, including W-2 program and the handling of child support payments; formal and informal child support paid or received; source and costs of child care; contact and conflict between nonresident parent and the resident parent and their child; and measures of child well-being.

We will try to interview 3,000 pairs of parents. Almost two-thirds are being drawn from those cases in which the resident parent was initially a caretaker of newborn or a CSJ or W-2 Transitions participant. The remaining pairs are being drawn from those who initially enter subsidized or unsubsidized employment (in which no child support is retained by the state regardless of experimental or control status). Respondents are interviewed twice: in the spring of 1999 and the spring of 2000. The 50-minute survey is administered by telephone when possible. In-person interviews are attempted for those we are unable to locate by phone.

Outcomes of Interest

A broad range of outcomes is of interest for this evaluation. The primary focus of the policy is child support, and the experimental impact evaluation will examine the impact of the demonstration on formal and informal child support payments. The reforms will also change the benefits of establishing paternity and setting a child support order. A set of secondary effects may also result. Thus, the outcomes of interest also include those less directly affected by the demonstration policy: W-2 and related program costs, self-sufficiency of the resident parent, earnings of the nonresident parent, the nonresident parent's involvement with the child, and overall child well-being. A set of hypotheses related to each of these outcomes has been developed. Below we briefly discuss the primary outcomes of interest, and expected effects. This discussion is taken from more detailed evaluation strategies developed for each topic area by a set of researchers.[9]

Formal Child Support Payments. A primary objective of this reform is to increase child support collections. As discussed earlier, the previous policy contained disincentives to paying child support within the formal system, as child support in excess of $50 per month was used to reimburse the state for welfare expenditures rather than to benefit the resident-parent family. These disincentives were relevant to the behavior of both resident and nonresident parents: Resident parents had little incentive to cooperate with the child support system at any step (i.e., establishing paternity, seeking a support order, cooperating with enforcement efforts), while nonresident parents had little incentive to pay support within the formal system. In light of these disincentives, we hypothesize that this reform will lead to an increase in formal child support collections. Further, we expect the increase in collections to stem both from an increase in compliance with support orders as well as from an increase in the rate of paternity establishment and in the rate and magnitude of support orders.

Existing research has examined factors associated with both the dollar amount of child support collections and a related concept, compliance with child support orders. In a review of this body of research, Meyer and Bartfeld (1996) find two primary factors which affect child support compliance: the nonresident parent's ability to pay support (income, employment status, and the share of income the nonresident parent is asked to pay) and the characteristics of the child support enforcement system. This demonstration will provide further information on the extent to which changes to the enforcement system can affect payments. Ethnographic research (e.g., Edin, 1995; Johnson and Doolittle, 1998) provides a different perspective on child support payments. Such research has found that both resident and nonresident parents are aware of the interplay between child support payments and welfare payments, and that some parents alter their behavior accordingly. As discussed below, some nonresident parents do not want to pay child support when such support does not directly benefit their child(ren), and they may be able to circumvent the formal child support system. Likewise, some resident parents are not interested in pursuing formal child support when this support would primarily benefit the state, preferring to work out informal arrangements with the nonresident parent. The limited research that exists in this area thus implies that the child support reform does indeed have the potential to alter the behavior of resident and nonresident parents with regard to cooperation with the child support system.

We are primarily using administrative data to compare the amount of child support paid, the amount received, and the compliance rate (support payments divided by support owed) among families in the experimental and control groups, using both simple comparisons and multivariate analyses.

Informal Child Support Payments. As discussed above, under AFDC rules nonresident parents had little incentive to pay formal support but much greater incentive to make informal transfers and other material, in-kind contributions to the resident parent and children. Informal and in-kind contributions enable nonresident parents to feel as though they provide directly for their children. These informal contributions also allow nonresident parents to trade financial support to the resident parent in exchange for access to children (e.g., Johnson and Doolittle, 1998).

The W-2 child support reform increases the incentive to pay *formal* support, as compared to the AFDC rules and the rules for the control group. The likely effect on *informal* transfers of the W-2 child support reform is ambiguous. On one hand, nonresident parents may substitute formal for informal payments when formal payments are transferred in full to the resident parents and children. Given the limited resources of nonresident parents whose children are eligible for W-2 participation, the total resources available for child support may restrict nonresident parents' ability to fulfill formal child support responsibilities as well as make informal cash transfers and in-kind contributions (e.g., providing clothing, diapers, or food), and thus informal contributions would decrease. On the other hand, past research suggests that nonresident parents who already pay formal child support are more likely to make informal material contributions than those who do not pay formal child support (Teachman, 1991). Thus if the demonstration increases formal payments, informal contributions may increase as well.[10]

Survey data will be used to analyze informal payments because there is no administrative record.

Orders and Paternity Establishment. The increased incentives to pursue child support and make formal payments are also expected to increase paternity and child support order establish-ment. W-2 child support reform increases the potential benefit of child support to resident parents participating in W-2 by allowing such parents to combine child support with money from W-2 grants. This increases the incentives of both resident and nonresi-dent parents to cooperate with the child support system. Such coop-eration is important at various stages in the process leading to payment of child support. Of particular relevance here, cooperation can influence the likelihood of paternity establishment, order estab-lishment, and order revision, as these steps, to varying degrees, op-timally require the involvement of one or both parents. Thus, we hypothesize that the reform will be associated with higher rates of both paternity establishment and support orders, higher amounts of support obligations, and more frequent revisions of existing or-ders.

We are using administrative data to examine the extent to which paternity is established among experimental and control cases with nonmarital births. Administrative data are also being used to examine the prevalence of child support orders and their amounts.[11]

W-2 and Related Program Costs. The demonstration is ex-pected to increase the establishment of paternity and new child sup-port orders and increase child support collections for both existing and new orders. This increased child support should decrease W-2 recipiency (Meyer, 1993; Sandfort and Hill, 1996). In addition, as de-tailed below, the reform is expected to promote resident-parent em-ployment and earnings. Given the resulting increase in these sources of nonwelfare income, resident parent family reliance on W-2 and other related means-tested programs is generally expected to decline. This decrease in recipiency should decrease governmen-tal costs.

But opposing effects are also possible. In particular, net W-2 costs among the experimental group could be higher than among the control group, since a portion of the child support collected for the control group goes to offset W-2 costs. Another factor that could lead to increased costs for the experimental group is that those in the control group have a larger incentive to move into the top two tiers of W-2 (Trial Jobs or unsubsidized employment) than do those in the experimental group. This is because resident parents in the con-trol group could experience a large increase in their total income package by moving into the top two tiers (because they would then get to keep all child support), an incentive not applicable to those in the experimental group, who keep all child support regardless of W-2 tier. While placement in W-2 tiers depends largely on job-readiness, the speed of transition from one tier to another may be affected by this incentive. Thus, the predicted effect of the demonstration on W-2 tier status and W-2 costs is ambiguous, with more child support tending to lead the experimental group to lower welfare costs at the same time that the control group has lower costs because of child support offsets and because of extra incentives to move into unsubsidized employment.

The effect on food stamps has some similarities to the effect on W-2: decreased likelihood of food stamps and decreased food stamp costs among the experimental group to the extent that the demonstration leads to higher child support or more earnings, but decreased food stamp costs among the control group because these women may move more quickly into unsubsidized employment. The effect on Medicaid is less ambiguous. In part, this stems from the possibility that the demonstration will increase cooperation with the child support system, and this may lead not only to new child support orders but also to a requirement that nonresident parents provide health insurance to their children as part of the child support order. To the extent that the demonstration increases health insurance orders and this insurance is actually provided, Medicaid costs should decrease.[12]

Simple comparisons between the experimental and control groups and multivariate analyses are being conducted on program participation and total cost, using primarily administrative data.

Resident Parent Employment and Earnings. Standard microeconomic theory suggests that an increase in nonlabor income (such as that represented by an increase in child support payments) may reduce work effort. The logic here suggests that an increase in such income makes it less necessary to work and earn in order to attain a given level of well-being. Thus, the increased child support available to the experimental group might be expected to reduce resident parent work effort.

On the other hand, relative to members of the control group, the nonwelfare income of resident parents in the experimental group will be increased by the child support pass-through.

Substantial "fixed" or "start-up" costs are encountered in making the transition from welfare to work, associated with attaining self-sufficiency. These costs take the form of expenses for child care, transportation, clothing, and so on. The increase in income from the additional child support may assist the resident parent in covering these costs, and hence facilitate the move from dependency to self-sufficiency. In addition, an unrestricted increase in income also enables the recipient to "buy" a number of things that both encourage and facilitate work and earnings, especially when the fallback position of reliance on means-tested benefits is no longer available. These work-facilitating purchases often entail the taking of risks, and include items such as arranging higher quality or more reliable child care, enabling the accumulation of savings necessary to purchase an automobile or otherwise reduce travel difficulties, or moving to a location where more jobs are available or where living is more "work-conducive." In addition, more difficult to measure, but potentially equally important, is the impact of the increased support payment in strengthening the belief on the part of the resident parent that the goal of self-sufficiency is actually attainable. Finally, the additional child support may also provide a sufficient "cushion" to enable the resident-parent family to handle financial or other difficulties without disrupting work and to make investments that will increase self-sufficiency.

If these effects dominate the standard labor supply effect, as they may in the absence of available means-tested benefits, the increase in income due to child support payments will encourage resident parents to enter, and sustain their participation in, the labor force, and to secure financial self-sufficiency and independence. In this case, to the extent that resident parents in the experimental group receive more child support, they will have higher rates of employment, more stable employment patterns, higher wage rates, and higher earnings than those in the control group.

Employment rates and patterns and total earnings are all being examined using administrative data; hourly wage rates will be examined using survey data. The survey data will also be used to augment the administrative data because not all earnings are recorded in the administrative records.

Nonresident Parent Employment and Earnings. As we have discussed above, the prior welfare (AFDC) arrangements created an incentive for the nonresident parent to transfer child support through unofficial channels and avoid official child support payments, particularly those in excess of $50 per month. The incentive to avoid formal payments of child support encouraged nonresident parents to seek employment in the informal economy or to frequently change jobs (given that employment in the formal economy will trigger discovery of employment and earnings, and mandatory payment of support). Informal or unstable employment may also lead to lower wages and earnings for nonresident parents. In contrast, under the W-2 child support reform all child support paid is paid directly to the resident parent in the experimental group, reducing the adverse incentives mentioned above and potentially leading to increased work and earnings of the nonresident parent, more stability in work, and the concentration of work in the formal labor market. This change may also encourage the use of the W-2 employment services offered to nonresident parents.

We use administrative data to compare the employment rates and patterns and the earnings of the experimental and control groups. We will use survey data to compare hourly wage rates, to examine the extent of working in the formal sector, and to augment the administrative data because not all earnings are recorded in the administrative records.

Nonresident Parent's Involvement with the Child. This reform is designed to increase nonresident parents' financial ties to their children by passing through the full amount of child support collected on behalf of the family. A growing body of evidence shows that nonresident parents who pay more child support also spend more time with their children (Furstenberg et al., 1983; Seltzer, Schaeffer and Charng, 1989; Seltzer, 1991; McLanahan et al., 1994; Seltzer, McLanahan, and Hanson, 1998; but see Veum, 1993). Nonresident parents who know that their children receive all of the child support paid have more incentive to spend time with the children and to pay attention to how the resident parent spends the child support money (Weiss and Willis, 1985). When all child support paid on a family's behalf is passed through, nonresident parents may see themselves as more effective parents and, as a result, spend more time with their children and try to play a bigger role in making decisions about the children's lives. Nonresident parents whose formal child support payments go in part to the state, as under past AFDC rules and for the evaluation control group, do not feel as though they are supporting their children (Johnson and Doolittle, 1998). In addition, resident parents who receive all of the

288

child support paid for their children may see the nonresident parents' claims to access and influence as more legitimate and, as a result, may facilitate the nonresident parent's greater involvement with their children.

The W-2 child support reform is likely to improve nonresident parents' perceptions of themselves, and they may change other aspects of their behavior to conform to their new image, for instance by pushing to spend more time with their children. If resident parents adopt a more positive view toward nonresident parents, this also may facilitate nonresident parents' greater access to children and participation in all aspects of child rearing, including making decisions about and participating in the child's medical and educational needs.

In contrast to this benign view of increasing nonresident parents' involvement, in which both resident and nonresident parents cooperate to facilitate access to children, an unintended negative effect on families of the W-2 child support reform may be to increase serious disagreements between parents. This might occur if passing through the full amount of child support increases contact between resident and nonresident parents who are unable to organize their joint child rearing responsibilities. The reform may increase conflict about such things as scheduling each parent's time with the children, whether the children spend the night at the nonresident parent's home, how child support money is spent, and other decisions about the children's care. Preliminary evidence suggests that rigorous enforcement of child support responsibilities may increase children's exposure to serious conflict (Seltzer, McLanahan, and Hanson, 1998), and that this may be harmful to children (McLanahan et al., 1994).

In summary, we expect that nonresident parents in the experimental group will spend more time with their children, including more frequent visits, more overnight stays, and greater participation in child care than nonresident parents in the control group. Similarly, compared to those in the control group, nonresident parents in the experimental group will be more involved in children's medical care and education. At the same time, nonresident and resident parents in the experimental group will disagree more frequently and more severely about child rearing matters than nonresident and resident parents in the control group. These outcomes will be examined using survey data.

Child Well-Being. Assuming that the pass-through will result in a change of behavior and, in particular, an increase in child support payments received by the family, we anticipate that this will lead to an increase in resources available to children. Hence, in a number of respects, the relationship between child support and children's well-being provides an important opportunity to test the theory and belief that income support is an effective policy tool to improve the well-being of children. A major question of this aspect of the study is: Do the financial benefits of income support (through child support payments) carry over to promote children's well-being? Having additional child support is expected to lead to increased investment in a child. This may take the form of more money for purchases for the child, such as books, clothing, improved nutrition, and more or better quality medical care, greater ability to pay for better child care and for additional education such as preschool. It may also mean more time spent by parents with the child and better quality time (defined in terms of level of stress of the parent). This time could be provided by the nonresident parent and/or the resident parent, who may reduce work hours, save travel time, work closer to home, or simply be less stressed concerning financial matters. It may also mean better parenting if the parents are more willing to discuss problems with each other about the child. If the receipt of more child support leads to less mobility — changes of residence — there can be additional benefits: School outcomes will improve and there may be added emotional support and stability from peers or teachers. Hence increased resources to the family may lead to a variety of improvements for the child, especially in the areas of health and education and possibly self-esteem. In addition, some prior research has suggested that a greater proportion of child support is likely to be allocated to investments in children than income from other sources. Consequently, the likelihood of self-sufficiency of the children would be expected to increase. Garfinkel, McLanahan, and Robins (1992) report on the impact of child support payments on child well-being and indicate that educational attainment can be affected by child support payments.

The three components of child well-being we intend to investigate are children's physical health (e.g., medical care access and use, health insurance coverage, and a measure of health status), educational development (e.g., school achievement and attainment), and parenting behavior with or on behalf of their children (e.g., parent-child interactions, time spent with the child, and parent involvement in school activities.) We expect that relative to the control group, children from families in the experimental group will have improved health outcomes and enhanced educational development. In addition, children from families in the experimental group are expected to experience greater investments from parents in their health and educational development and to have more nurturing relations with their parents. These topics will be addressed through survey data.

Limitations of the Experimental Impact Evaluation

In this section we discuss the principal challenges faced across most outcomes of interest in evaluating this reform. Of particular concern are factors that may limit the difference in the pass-through policy experienced by the experimental and control groups and the implication of this for the size of any likely effects.

One limitation of this evaluation is that it is compares two pass-through policies that may be of limited interest to other states. This evaluation addresses only the implications of a full pass-through policy relative to the Wisconsin partial pass-through. Neither of these policies is in effect in any other state. This evaluation will not directly assess the impact of a full pass-through in a state that currently has a policy of passing nothing through to the family, or passing through $50/month.

One potential difficulty with this evaluation is that the new pass-through policy faced by the experimental group may not be different enough from the pass-through policy faced by the control group to be able to detect a response. Families in the experimental and control groups receive different amounts of child support only when they are caretakers of newborns and have little other income or are participants in Community Service Jobs and W-2 Transitions (once a resident-parent family "climbs the self-sufficiency ladder" and takes a Trial Job or unsubsidized employment, the experimental and control groups both receive the full amount of child support paid). Even then, the child support received differs only when a payment is over $50/month. Further, even if a payment of over $50 is made during a time a family is in a W-2 category with a lower child support payment, the actual difference in the amount received by the experimental and control groups may not be large.[13]

Finally, many evaluation domains principally involve potential secondary effects. The policy is expected to have a direct effect on payments, paternity establishment, and orders. These changes may, in turn, lead to reduced W-2 costs, greater self-sufficiency for resident parents, greater nonresident parent earnings and involvement, and improved child well-being. Even if direct effects are sufficiently large to be detected, indirect effects may not be discernible.

Another limitation of the design is that this change is occurring simultaneously with many other changes. Indeed, W-2 is a complete redesign of the way low-income families with children are assisted. This may mean that families do not understand the pass-through policy, and thus it would have little effect on their behavior.[14]

While a classical experiment, with families randomly assigned to an experimental group and a control group, is a powerful evaluation tool, the design has limits. Policy changes that hope to affect community norms may be particularly difficult to evaluate with an experimental design because broadcasts of the new policy must be somewhat limited or the control group may become angry and exert political pressure to redesign the experiment.

Another limitation has to do with the dynamic situation of many W-2 child support families. The experimental design responds to the dynamics of W-2 by requiring that families remain in either the experimental or control groups regardless of their W-2 status. But some children may change physical custody, either from primarily living with one parent to primarily living with the other, or to sharing time with both, or to living with someone other than parents (primarily grandparents or other relatives). When these types of changes occur, the parent who is responsible for paying child support may change, and how these families will be treated is not clear.

The final set of limitations discussed here relates to the availability and accuracy of administrative and survey data. While administrative data provide large sample sizes, enable relatively fast turnaround, and provide outstanding information on some domains, there are limitations. Although administrative data provide a complete record of individuals participating in W-2 and food stamps in Wisconsin, the other administrative data sets generally have limited coverage: There is no child support information on families who have not been through the courts nor through the child support office; there is no earnings information on several groups of people in the unemployment records (people who work in other states, are self-employed, work for cash, or work in some types of organizations), and there is no income information for those who do not have to file a tax form. Moreover, even when coverage is complete in that families have records, the records may be lacking: for example, informal child support payments are not captured in administrative data, nor is contact between nonresident parents and their children.

The survey can provide information on the groups and topics that are missing in administrative data, and the survey responses can also be used to help understand the gaps or inconsistencies in the administrative data (Kornfeld and Bloom, 1997). Nonetheless, even survey data will be limited. For example, the evaluation of the effects on nonresident parents' informal payments and in-kind contributions requires that we rely on parents' own reports. Unlike formal child support payments, there is no external criterion (e.g., court records, KIDS) by which to evaluate the quality of self-reports. Social scientists know little about parents' ability to retrospectively report informal transfers, which are often irregular. Finally, we anticipate substantial challenges in our effort to achieve sufficient response rates, especially for the survey of nonresident fathers.

The Role of Nonexperimental Evaluation

Because of these concerns, particularly the concern about the generalizability of a comparison of a full pass-through policy to a $50/41 percent pass-through policy, we are also planning four nonexperimental components. First is a multi-state comparison using administrative data from the federal Office of Child Support Enforcement, in order to explore whether various levels of the pass-through in different states at different times have led to differences in the likelihood or level of child support payments among welfare cases. Second is an individual-level analysis using data from the Current Population Survey. Like the first analysis, these data cover all states over a fairly long period of time; since these data are at an individual level, in this analysis we will be able to control for individual factors that may affect payments. Third is a comparison of payment patterns and AFDC patterns using Wisconsin court record data, to examine whether formal payments change as mothers go on and off public assistance. Fourth is an ethnographic study of nonresident fathers in Milwaukee.[15] The purpose of this component is to give context and understanding to the life experiences of nonresident fathers and resident mothers. The qualitative study component is modest in scope, but offers an opportunity to learn in-depth information directly from those most affected by the child support reform. What is learned will be complementary to the other research efforts of this project, as well as informative and relevant on its own merit. We expect to interview 40 nonresident fathers, conducting several semi-structured interviews with each individual over a period of 18 months. Topics covered will include fathers' conceptions of their roles and responsibilities, their understanding of the reform, the strategies they use to support their children, and their ability to pay support.

Evaluation Products

Quarterly reports on child support payments and W-2 costs are being produced beginning May 1998. The implementation report and first experimental impact report was completed in July 1999. The final process and experimental impact report will be completed by early 2001. A report with the results of the nonexperimental components and a comparison of the experimental and nonexperimental results will be completed by September 2001.

Conclusions

The evaluation effort described here illustrates a number of the issues discussed elsewhere in this volume regarding the focus, methods, and data sources of importance in evaluating comprehensive welfare reform. First, the outcomes of interest identified here are broad, going well beyond the direct effect on child support payments and receipts. Proponents of this reform hope to encourage fundamental changes in family structure and functioning and attitudes regarding parental responsibility. Only a broad evaluation can hope to capture such effects. Second, while the opportunity to mount an experimental evaluation is uncommon, the importance of complementary nonexperimental, process, and implementation evaluations is something likely to be shared by other efforts. Similarly, in the context of complex comprehensive reforms, in-depth ethnographic research is likely to be especially important in helping us interpret other analysis and better understand how participants experience policy change. Finally, this evaluation draws extensively from administrative data. Other welfare reform evaluations are also likely to rely on existing administrative data.

References

Bumpass, Larry L., and James A. Sweet. "Children's Experience in Single-Parent Families: Implications of Cohabitation and Marital Transitions." *Family Planning Perspectives* 21 (1989): 256-260.

Edin, Kathryn. "Single Mothers and Absent Fathers: The Possibilities and Limits of Child Support Policy." *Children and Youth Services Review* 17 (1995): 203-230.

Franklin, D. L. "Race, Class, and Adolescent Pregnancy: An Ecological Analysis." *American Journal of Orthopsychiatry* 58 (1988): 339-354.

Furstenberg, Frank, C. W. Nord, J. L. Peterson, and Nicholas Zill. "The Life Course of Children of Divorce." *American Sociological Review* 48 (1983): 695-701.

Garfinkel, Irwin, Sara McLanahan, and Philip K. Robins, eds. *Child Support Assurance: Design Issues, Expected Impacts, and Political Barriers as Seen from Wisconsin.* Washington, DC: Urban Institute Press, 1992.

Graham, John W., and Andrea H. Beller. "The Effect of Child Support Payments on the Labor Supply of Female Heads: An Econometric Analysis." *Journal of Human Resources* 24 (1989): 665-688.

Johnson, Earl S., and Fred Doolittle. "Low-Income Parents and the Parents' Fair Share Program: An Early Qualitative Look at Low-Income Nonresident Parents and How One Policy Initiative Has Attempted to Improve Their Ability and Desire to Pay Child Support." In *Fathers Under Fire: The Revolution in Child Support Enforcement,* eds. Irwin Garfinkel, Sara S. McLanahan, Daniel R. Meyer, and Judith A. Seltzer. New York: Russell Sage Foundation, 1998.

Kornfeld, Robert, and Howard S. Bloom. "Measuring Program Impacts on Earnings and Employment: Do UI Wage Reports from Employers Agree with Surveys of Individuals?" Paper presented at a conference, "Evaluating State Policy: The Effective Use of Administrative Data," Joint Center for Poverty Research, Northwestern University, June 16-17, 1997.

McLanahan, Sara, Judith A. Seltzer, T. L. Hanson, and Elizabeth Thomson. "Child Support Enforcement and Child Well-Being: Greater Security or Greater Conflict?" In *Child Support and Child Well-Being*, eds. Irwin Garfinkel, Sara McLanahan, and Philip K. Robins. Washington, DC: Urban Institute Press, 1994.

Meyer, Daniel R. "Child Support and Welfare Dynamics: Evidence from Wisconsin." *Demography* 30 (1993): 45-62.

Meyer, Daniel R., and Judi Bartfeld. "Compliance with Child Support Orders in Divorce Cases." *Journal of Marriage and the Family* 58 (1996): 201-212.

Meyer, Daniel R., and Steven Garasky. "Custodial Fathers: Myths, Realities, and Child Support Policy." *Journal of Marriage and the Family* 55 (1993): 73-89.

Sandfort, Jodi R., and Martha S. Hill."Self-Sufficiency: An Underdefined Goal for Public Policy." Paper presented at the annual research conference of the Association for Public Policy Analysis and Management, Pittsburgh, 1996.

Seltzer, Judith A."Relationships between Fathers and Children Who Live Apart." *Journal of Marriage and the Family* 53 (1991): 79-101.

Seltzer, Judith A., Sara S. McLanahan, and Thomas L. Hanson."Will Child Support Enforcement Increase Father-Child Contact and Parental Conflict after Separation?" In *Fathers Under Fire: The Revolution in Child Support Enforcement*, eds. Irwin Garfinkel, Sara S. McLanahan, Daniel R. Meyer, and Judith A. Seltzer. New York: Russell Sage Foundation, 1998.

Seltzer, Judith A., Nora Cate Schaeffer, and H. W. Charng. "Family Ties after Divorce: The Relationship between Visiting and Paying Child Support." *Journal of Marriage and the Family* 51 (1989): 1013-1032.

Teachman, Jay D. "Contributions to Children by Divorced Fathers."
Social Problems 38 (1991): 358-371.

U.S. Bureau of the Census. *Marital Status and Living Arrangements:
March 1998.* Current Population Reports, Series P20-514. Washington, DC: U.S. Government Printing Office, 1998a.

U.S. Bureau of the Census. *Poverty in the United States: 1998.* Current
Population Reports, Series P60-207. Washington, DC: U.S. Government Printing Office, 1998b.

U.S. Department of Health and Human Services, Office of Child
Support Enforcement. *Child Support Report* 19, no. 12 (1997): 3.

Veum, Jon R. "The Relationship between Child Support and Visitation: Evidence from Longitudinal Data." *Social Science Research* 22
(1993): 229-244.

Weiss, Yoram, and Robert J. Willis."Children as Collective Goods
and Divorce Settlements." *Journal of Labor Economics* 3 (1985):
268-292.

Endnotes

1   In addition to applying to new W-2 cases, this policy also applied to AFDC cases before they transitioned to W-2 or closed, beginning in October 1997. Families receiving AFDC in September 1997 were required to make the transition to W-2 no later than March 1998.

2   The Institute for Research on Poverty was awarded a contract by the Wisconsin Department of Workforce Development to evaluate the child support reform (Daniel R. Meyer and Maria Cancian, Principal Investigators; project researchers include Judi Bartfeld, Patricia Brown, Emma Caspar, Judith Cassetty, Thomas Corbett, Robert Haveman, Earl Johnson, Thomas Kaplan, Margaret Krecker, David Pate, Arthur Reynolds, Gary Sandefur, Nora Cate Schaeffer, Judith A. Seltzer, and Barbara Wolfe.) The process, implementation, and impact evaluations described here were approved by the Administration for Children and Families of the U.S. Department of Health and Human Services in February 1998. The nonexperimental evaluation was approved in July 1999.

3   To be included in the count of new and existing cases assigned, individuals must be receiving a cash benefit and must not be exempt from the reduced pass-through. Those who are exempt and thus are excluded from the experimental/control groups include: two-parent cases, cases that have no living nonresident parent, and cases that have "good cause" for not pursuing child support (the experiment can not be expected to affect these cases); and cases that include a child who receives Supplemental Security Income (SSI) (in these cases state regulations prohibit retaining any portion of child support).

4   This section is adapted from a section of the evaluation plan that was written by Thomas Kaplan.

5   Two additional methods of assessing what parents knew about the new policy are described below: a survey of resident and nonresident parents, and qualitative in-depth interviews with nonresident fathers in Milwaukee.

6   Another way in which differences could arise is that resident parents in the experimental group who were considering moving out of state may have realized that the child support policies in other states allowed them to keep substantially less child support, and may have been more likely to stay in Wisconsin than an equivalent parent in the control group. An evaluation using administrative data from Wisconsin may thus find more parents from the experimental group, and the simple comparison of the two groups may no longer be valid. This problem is probably even more severe for comparisons conducted using survey data; we may have more difficulty locating parents in the control group, or they may be less willing to participate in a survey.

7   "Covered" workers include about 91 percent of Wisconsin workers. Excluded workers in Wisconsin are the self-employed, commission sales workers, farmers, church employees, and employees of not-for-profit organizations with fewer than four workers.

8   Because low-income individuals in Wisconsin can file for a refundable Homestead rental tax credit, substantial numbers of low-income families are represented in the Wisconsin tax data who otherwise would not have been required to file an income tax form. Individuals can be identified in the DOR data as either the tax filer or the spouse.

9   The authors of the evaluation strategies in the various domains are as follows: Daniel R. Meyer and Judi Bartfeld for formal child support payments; Judith A. Seltzer and Nora Cate Schaeffer for informal child support payments; Bartfeld and Gary

Sandefur for orders and paternity establishment; Meyer and Maria Cancian for W-2 and related program costs; Cancian and Robert Haveman for the earnings of both the resident and nonresident parent; Seltzer and Schaeffer for the nonresident parent's involvement with the child; and Barbara Wolfe and Arthur Reynolds for child well-being.

10 The previous research finding that informal contributions are higher when there are formal contributions has been unable to determine whether or not this is a causal relationship. For instance, nonresident parents who pay formal child support may consider themselves to be good providers as a result of this behavior. Self-identification as a "good provider" may encourage nonresident parents to contribute to children in other ways in addition to formal child support, such as by providing clothes or presents for the children. Alternatively, paying formal and informal support may each be the result of a common cause. Nonresident parents who make both formal and informal child support contributions, for example, may be more committed to children in the first place, or have a better co-parenting relationship with the children's resident parent than nonresident parents who make neither formal nor informal payments. Commitment to children or the quality of the parents' relationship with each other may account for both formal and informal payments. Finally, nonresident parents who already have a history of providing informally for children may continue to make at least some informal contributions, even if the state increases their incentive to make formal child support contributions, because providing presents for children (one of the most common informal transfers, according to Teachman, 1991), is an established part of their relationship with their children. The financial value of these presents, however, may decline.

11 In addition to a comparison of paternity and support outcomes for families in the experimental and control groups at particular points in time, an event-history analysis will be used to estimate the changing probability of paternity establishment and related outcomes. Potentially important independent variables include earnings capacity of the resident and nonresident parents, actual (time-varying) employment and earnings of the parents, county, and relationship between the parents (potentially available from the survey).

12 In the Medicaid case there is less likely to be an offsetting effect: Even if resident parents move into the top two tiers of W-2, most of them would probably still be eligible for Medicaid because the income eligibility limits for Medicaid are higher than they are for food stamps. Moreover, as long as individuals remain income-eligible, an extra dollar of income for a recipient does not lower Medicaid costs in the way it would lower W-2 costs and food stamp costs.

13 For example, a standard child support order for a nonresident parent of one child working half time at $5.50/hour would be about $81/month. If this were fully paid, the resident-parent family would receive $81/month if they were in the experimental group, and $50/month if they were in the control group, a difference of $31/month. If the resident-parent family were receiving food stamps and/or housing assistance, the child support would decrease these benefits, and the difference in actual total income for the resident-parent family could be less than $15/month. While it is possible that even $15/month may be significant for low-income families, this small change may not generate a detectable behavioral response. (For example, one of the estimates of Graham and Beller (1989) is that a $1,000/year increase in child support would change work hours of resident parents only two hours per year.)

14 The process analysis may help us to identify counties that seem to be doing a particularly outstanding job of explaining the pass-through policy to participants, and we could explore whether the effect of the policy was different in these counties as compared to others.

15 This research is being conducted by Earl Johnson of the Manpower Demonstration Research Corporation and David Pate of the Institute for Research on Poverty.

12

Potential Effects of W-2 on Families Who Have Very Young Children with Disabilities and Special Health Care Needs

George Jesien
Waisman Center
University of Wisconsin — Madison

Caroline Hoffman
Wisconsin Council on Developmental Disabilities

Thomas Kaplan
Institute for Research on Poverty
University of Wisconsin–Madison

Τhis paper explores potential impacts of Wisconsin's W-2 program on families containing very young children with disabilities. The paper provides an overview of Wisconsin's Birth to Three program for children with disabilities and special health care needs, describes how the program is typically implemented at the local level, and then discusses a series of possible indicators that may serve as valid estimators of the impact of W-2 on this special population.

Having a newborn challenges most families to adapt to the demands of the infant by shifting priorities, changing schedules, and garnering the necessary resources to clothe, feed, and take care of the growing infant (Begun, 1996). Having an infant with a physical or mental disability or a special health care need further stresses the resources of any family owing to the additional needs that the infant poses, the time needed to interact with medical staff and developmental therapists, and the emotional strain of wanting to do everything possible to optimize the infant's chances for normal development (Turnbull & Turnbull, 1990). Raising and nurturing an infant or toddler with disabilities or special health care needs in an economically well-off and intact family poses complications and associated stresses sufficient to have persuaded national policy makers to provide assistance in identifying, assessing, and providing services to infants and toddlers with disabilities and their families (Smith & McKenna, 1994). Addressing these needs in poor families or those headed by single or teenage parents poses significant additional obstacles and difficulties to overcome (Erwin, 1996). Families in poverty face the synergistic and additive effects of all three sources of stress: adapting to the new infant, learning about and addressing the needs posed by the disability, and at the same time continuing the struggle for securing food, shelter, and other necessities (Zigler, 1995).

The Birth to Three Early Intervention Program

National policy makers recognized the seriousness of the challenge facing a family with an infant or toddler with a disability by passing Public Law 99-457 in 1986, now referred to as Part H of the Individuals with Disabilities Education Act (IDEA). The legislation changed the "landscape" of services available for very young children with disabilities and has had far-reaching effects on systems of services throughout the country (Jesien, 1996). One of the legislation's main purposes was "to enhance the capacity of families to meet the special needs of infants and toddlers with disabilities" (IDEA, 1991). Policy makers accepted that the needs posed by having a child with a disability were a challenge to all families regardless of socioeconomic or educational levels (Smith & McKenna, 1994).

This legislation gave states the option to develop, over a span
of five years (two annual extensions were subsequently provided), a
comprehensive and coordinated state system for the provision of
family-centered early intervention services (Trohanis, 1994). In
1991, Wisconsin passed its own early intervention legislation pat-
terned after the federal legislation. The Wisconsin law designated
the Department of Health and Family Services (DHFS) as the lead
agency and, in effect, established a mandate for early intervention
services for all eligible children and families.

The eligibility criteria in the federal law targeted children with a
developmental delay, children having a physical or medical condition
that has a high probability of resulting in developmental delay, and —
at the discretion of the state — children who are at risk of having substantial developmental delays if early intervention services are not
provided (IDEA, 1991). The definition of developmental delay was to
be established by each state. Wisconsin defined a developmental delay
as a 25 percent delay in one or more areas of development. The state
did not choose to serve children at risk, but administrative rules implementing the program did allow services for a category of children who
have "atypical development" (HHS 90).

The federal law establishes a set of "core services" which are to
be provided to all families at no cost. These services include:

❖ Evaluation — an interdisciplinary process to determine
   a child's initial and continuing eligibility for early intervention services.

❖ Development of an Individualized Family Service Plan
   (IFSP) — developed in conjunction with the family, detail-
   ing the expected outcomes, providing information on the
   developmental status of the child, and with the parents'
   permission including information on parent resources,
   priorities, and concerns. The IFSP contains the type, frequency, and intensity of services that will be provided and
   also contains transition plans for children as they "gradu-
   ate" out of the program at three. The IFSP is to be redevel-
   oped annually and reviewed every six months.

❖ Service Coordination — provided by an assigned individual for each child and family to monitor and assist in
   the implementation of the IFSP. It is this person's responsibility to link the family with community resources, to help parents identify their own and their

child's needs, and to serve as a monitor to assure that the IFSP is implemented.

❖ Transition Services — preparation of the child for moving into the next environment, whether that is a special education program in the public schools, Head Start, preschool, child care, or home environment.

Other early intervention services are provided based on the IFSP. These services include special instruction, developmental therapies, audiology, nursing care necessary for the child to benefit from early intervention, and parent education and counseling. If parents permit, third party insurance can be billed for therapy services such as occupational, physical, and speech therapies. Medicaid has also been billed for therapy services in many counties. In the early stages of the program, developmental or educational services which were typically not billable to third party insurers or Medicaid were provided at no cost to families by Birth to Three providers. More recently, families with sufficiently high income to have been deemed able to pay a fee have been charged for early intervention services but not the four core services.

Currently, approximately 105 providers of Birth to Three services serve the 72 counties of Wisconsin. The counties are designated as local administrative agents for the program, which is managed at the state level by the Wisconsin Department of Health and Family Services. Counties have flexibility in how they implement the program but are expected to meet state guidelines. Some counties provide direct services to families using county employees, while others provide only service coordination through the county and contract with other agencies for remaining services. Still other counties contract for all services, including evaluation, service coordination, and early intervention services. The number of children served by individual counties varies greatly, ranging from Milwaukee, where more than 2,000 children were served in 1995, to 10 counties that each served fewer than 10 children that year. Dane County served the second highest number of children, with more than 400 children receiving services in 1995.

Children receiving services in the Birth to Three program vary greatly in their type and degree of disability. Some children have a 25 percent delay in speech and language with minimal compromises in other developmental areas; others have disabilities so severe as to render them technologically dependent for food and breathing capability. Some children with multiple and complex needs may be involved with as many as 15 provider agencies and personnel addressing their medical, health, and developmental needs. Many of the children in the program had extensive hospital stays before their referral to the Birth to Three program.

Program services are provided in a range of locations: the home, child developmental center, family or child care setting, hospital or clinical offices. Based on data submitted to the federal government in December of 1995, approximately 45 percent of children in Wisconsin receive most of their services in the home, 35 percent receive most services in a center or classroom for children with disabilities, 15 percent in an outpatient clinic, and 2.5 percent receive the majority of their services in a family or child care setting (Hoffman, 1996). In theory, settings are chosen based on the preferences of the family and the needs of the child, although in actuality, some service settings are determined more on the basis of what is available or where openings exist rather than preferences of the family.

The number of children served in the state has gradually increased. In 1990, approximately 2,233 children were in the program on December 1 (the date required by the federal government for annual program counts); the comparable figure for December 1, 1995, was 3,919 children. The total number of children served during a year is much larger than the December 1 count because children enter and leave programs during the year. For example, the total number of children served in 1995 was 7,205.[1] Approximately 25 percent of Wisconsin children served in the Birth to Three program reside in Milwaukee county and another 5.5 percent reside in Dane County, the two most populous counties in the state.

Description of Local Services and Information Collected

Each child who is referred to the Birth to Three program is evaluated to determine eligibility for early intervention services. An interdisciplinary team of at least two people representing different disciplines (many evaluations are conducted by three or more disciplines) is convened. The team obtains a developmental history and determines functioning level and needs in several domains: communication development, physical development, social

305

development, cognitive development, and adaptive development. Data collection methods and evaluation instruments vary from county to county and provider to provider.

Once the child is determined eligible, an early intervention team — composed of staff from at least two disciplines, a service coordinator (who can also represent one of the disciplines), and the parent — develops the IFSP. The IFSP contains the parents' statements on expectations, goals, and desired outcomes for intervention. Additionally, with parent consent, information on the family make-up, resources, and priorities are obtained, as well as a parental statement of other needs (outside the boundaries of the Birth to Three program) that parents perceive in addressing the needs of their child.

Although the evaluation instruments and format of the IFSP vary greatly, the state does require some consistent data elements to be collected and reported across the Birth to Three programs. The data elements include:

- child's name
- client characteristics (for example, type of disability)
- Social Security number
- parents' name
- county of residence
- birth date
- gender
- ethnicity
- start & end dates of service
- services provided
- location of service (home, center, hospital, etc.)
- discharge reason

Individual Birth to Three programs keep additional information in nonstandard, but generally easily accessible formats. This information includes reason for eligibility, name of service coordinator, type of health insurance (including Medicaid), whether the child receives Supplemental Security Income (SSI) benefits, and native language. Each county is charged to maintain an individual record on each child served by the Birth to Three program and maintain the files for seven years after the child leaves the program. Many counties delegate this responsibility to the provider agencies with whom they contract.

Additional information could be obtained from the provider programs through the service coordinator who works with the family, if appropriate permission can be obtained from the parents and program administrators. These data include whether family members are employed, child care needs, who provides child care and where, levels of parent participation, and program dropouts. Also, for purposes of determining ability to pay under the state fee schedules, programs must have income data on the families served.

Several Birth to Three programs could be contacted about providing information for a potential future study. One of the authors of this paper (Jesien) has contacted many program managers who have expressed interest in potentially participating in a study of the effects of W-2 on families with young children with disabilities. In general, we are convinced that program managers would serve as motivated agents for data collection. The information they obtained could also be expected to be reliable because of their close relationships with families and the high likelihood that a trusting relationship exists.

Two potential counties to participate in a study are Milwaukee and Dane, which serve a large number of families with young children with disabilities, have a fairly large population of ethnically diverse families affected by W-2, and utilize a range of Birth to Three provider structures and organizations. In Milwaukee, the Birth to Three program is administered by the Milwaukee County Human Services Office and contracts with approximately 17 providers serving the county's families. Most services in Milwaukee are conducted in center-based programs that also provide child care services as children are attending their Birth to Three program. Dane County has two large Birth to Three providers, one for metropolitan Madison and one serving families in the rest of the county. Approximately half the families served in the Madison program were on AFDC in the early 1990s.

Potential Effects of W-2 on Birth to Three Programs and Families

Given the additional demands on families' financial, time, and emotional resources that having an infant or toddler with a disability places, the impact of W-2 on this specific and especially vulnerable population should be carefully evaluated. The Wisconsin Council on Developmental Disabilities estimates that of the approximately 7,000 families who have a very young child with a diagnosed disability and are participating in the Birth to Three Program, 2,250 will be required to participate in the work requirements of W-2.

Families with a child with a disability often have additional costs for special foods, clothing, and equipment. Health care is typically a major concern for many families with a child with disability. Many children have conditions that require frequent medical attention, such as children who may be gavage fed, have a tracheotomy for breathing, or require either oxygen support or heart and breathing monitors. Often parents must learn specific procedures that are necessary for the care of the child. Adequate and affordable health insurance is an ongoing and persistent challenge for many families. Child care, in many cases, poses a special challenge: Willing and qualified providers who can meet the needs of the child with a disability are rare. Last, parents of children with disabilities need greater flexibility in work situations, because they often have to take their children to medical and therapeutic appointments for assessment, care, or intervention. Children with disabilities may be more susceptible to bacterial and viral infections, and parents may need more excused time from work to take care of a sick child or to meet with health, social service, or early intervention staff.

The manner in which the W-2 program is implemented and the degree of flexibility that is available to parents of children with disabilities will in large part determine the degree to which parents are able to balance the demands of specialized care for their child and the requirement under W-2 to work. Significant impacts are likely in three areas: a) ability of the family to remain intact; b) availability of parents in attending to the special needs of their child and working with Birth to Three program personnel; and c) the physical and developmental well-being of children. Each of these potential impacts and possible measurable indicators are described below.

Ability of Family to Remain Intact

A possible consequence of W-2 may be an increased likelihood that a parent of a young child with a disability would feel compelled to place the child in foster care, kinship care, or a child caring institution, or even terminate parental rights and give up the child for adoption. This would be most likely to occur in large families.

Parents who are needed at home because of the illness or incapacity of another member of the family will probably not be required to work outside the home under W-2. They can be placed in a W-2 Transitions assignment and given a required activity of caring for the child. Nevertheless, the W-2 benefit provided at this level ($628/month, regardless of family size) may be insufficient to care for a child with a disability or special health care need and other members of the family, especially in larger families. With the additional costs of raising an infant with a disability, parents may feel forced to place their child outside the home in order to be able to meet the needs of the other children in the family. A potential indicator of this effect is frequency of out-of-home placements, such as foster care, child care institutions, or adoptions.

Parent Availability to Participate in Services/ Programs for the Child with a Disability

Parents seeking higher incomes than are available at the W-2 Transitions level may enter a Community Services Job or find unsubsidized employment. Because of work schedules, these parents may have less time to spend with their children and may have less time available to address the specific needs associated with a disability. Parents may be unable to make the appointments with early intervention staff or medical or therapeutic staff. Parents may also become less in touch with the developmental progress of their child and be less aware that a developmental delay even exists.

Potential indicators include:

- ❖ Changes in delivery of services models with trend toward center-based and away from home-based services
- ❖ Decreased rates of attendance at IFSP meetings, transition meetings, parent education opportunities such as support groups, and informational meetings
- ❖ Decreased rates of follow-through on clinic appointments, well-baby checks, therapy sessions, and reevaluation
- ❖ Decreased implementation of developmental intervention strategies proposed by Birth to Three staff

❖ Lower rates of referrals from parents and possibly even public health nurses and pediatric clinics and increased rates of referrals from child care providers

❖ Increased rates of children dropping out of the Birth to Three program

❖ Increased rates of eligible families rejecting Birth to Three services

❖ Decline in rates at which IFSP goals are achieved based on annual reviews

Maintaining the Health and Well-Being of a Child with Disabilities

Group child care can be a significant benefit for many children, but not for all. Placing medically fragile children in child care situations may expose a significant number of infants to increased health risks. Quality infant care is difficult to find under the best of conditions. Quality infant care for infants and toddlers with disabilities and special health care needs is rare in most Wisconsin communities. The lack of quality care and potential decreased attention of parents may put the health of many children at risk. Changes in health care for W-2 participants may limit the amount and extent of health services that children and families receive. Additionally, adding stressors to already stretched and struggling families without the provision of supports may result in increased child abuse incidents.

Potential indicators include:

❖ Increased hospitalizations for preventable illnesses

❖ Increased emergency hospitalizations

❖ Lower immunization and well-baby visit rates for young children

❖ Increased reports of unsubstantiated and substantiated child abuse and neglect

❖ Increased requests for out-of-home placements

Possible Methods for Studying Impacts of W-2

Determining the impact of W-2 in these areas is likely to require the kind of pre-post comparisons suggested in the chapters by Haveman and by Kaplan and Meyer in this volume. That is, the condition of families with children in Birth to Three programs under W-2 will likely have to be compared to the condition of families with children in the programs under AFDC in the early 1990s. Fortunately, good program records for the earlier period exist in the Milwaukee and Dane County W-2 programs. We hypothesize that the effects described above will be most pronounced in large families and in families with older children. In comparison to AFDC, small families with a young child still in a Birth to Three program may actually be better off. Under AFDC, if the child with the disability did not qualify for SSI, a single parent with such a child plus one other child received $517 per month; under W-2, a single parent wishing to remain in the home to take care of the child would receive the $628 benefit under the W-2 Transitions program, regardless of the number of other children in the family. Only families containing five or more people would receive less money under W-2 than under AFDC, assuming the parent remains in the home to care for a child with a disability and receives the W-2 Transitions grant.

Although any negative effects of W-2 (in comparison to AFDC) are likely to be greatest on large families with a disabled child, smaller families in which the child with a disability has aged out of the Birth to Three programs and entered a nearly full-time public school program could also be affected. As the child grows older and becomes appropriate for more hours each day in a school program, W-2 agencies are increasingly likely to require the parent to leave the W-2 Transitions program and enter another part of W-2 or an unsubsidized job. Whereas under AFDC the parent could have continued to receive a grant without entering the labor market until the child with a disability turned 18, the parent may now have to enter the labor market when the child is much younger. If that happens, the potential effects we note above could occur.

Determining whether W-2 policy changes actually resulted in these effects will be complicated by other changes in the policy environment that occurred at about the same time as the W-2 changes. One alteration that occurred approximately simultaneously was a change in eligibility criteria for children under the federal SSI program. As a result of the U.S. Supreme Court's Zebley decision and subsequent congressional action, criteria for SSI eligibility have grown much more restrictive. In Wisconsin, 6,570 child SSI cases were reviewed after congressional action to tighten eligibility standards, and two-thirds of these reviews resulted in denial of further eligibility for SSI. Moreover, federal child welfare laws have also undergone recent changes which have made it easier in some cases for terminations of parental rights and adoptions to occur.

The likelihood that W-2 will have systematically different effects on families with more and older children than on smaller families with young children may help researchers control for other policy changes that occurred simultaneously and thereby estimate the independent impact of W-2. We propose to measure changes in the indicators suggested above for families containing children with disabilities and not likely to have been affected by W-2 (smaller families in which the child with a disability is young) to obtain an estimate of the effect of the other changes in the policy environment. We hypothesize that much of any differential change we observe in larger families or families in which the child graduated from the Birth to Three program several years earlier will be an effect of the W-2 program.

We propose three basic approaches to obtain information on the impact of W-2 welfare reforms on families and young children with disabilities. These include: (a) a case study approach, (b) a panel study of a cohort of families experiencing the changes, and (c) collection and analysis of existing data from selected program sites. The primary pre-post comparison will have to derive from the collection and analysis of existing data, because only that approach allows for an establishment of a baseline under AFDC. The other two approaches will add context to the study. The following section briefly discusses each option.

Case Study

A case study approach can be used to understand any number of aspects of the impact of welfare reform on the families' routines and resource utilization, and impact on the care of the child with a disability. A case study approach would provide a depth of information from which a greater understanding of the complicated factors at play could be obtained, and variables for potential future studies could be identified. Cross-sectional descriptive case studies in which families are selected based on blocking variables such as type and severity of disability, size of family, and need for services could be used to obtain both qualitative and quantitative information on the differential effects of various elements of W-2.

A variation of Yin's (1994) case study methodology could be used to obtain both process and outcome data associated with the care of children with disabilities, work requirements of W-2, and changes in health care availability. According to Yin, case studies are the "preferred strategy . . . when the focus is on a contemporary phenomenon within some *real-life context*" (p. 1, emphasis added). A multiple case study design could be used, with families selected based on the principal variables associated with potential impacts of W-2. Five of the main blocking variables could include severity of the disability measured by level of delay or level of need for services, size of family, ethnicity, age of the disabled child, and length of time on previous AFDC program. A common case study protocol format could be used for the conduct of the case studies across program sites.

Panel Study

A second option is to develop a panel study of families in selected program sites. Families could be surveyed either through structured personal or telephone interviews to gather data on factors such as level of care for the child with a disability, use of specialized services, child care arrangements, child health status, family well-being, participation in the early intervention program, amount and intensity of therapeutic services, typical daily routines, and transition process into programming after early intervention. These same factors could be sampled in six to eight month intervals over the following two or three years to establish short- and longer-term trends of change within families and the manner in which the child with disability's development is nurtured. Impacts of various elements of the W-2 program as parents go through training and the various employment options can be monitored along with the progress of the child and the services that he or she receives.

Personnel to conduct the panel study could be selected either from outside or within the early intervention programs. Service coordinators are a possible choice. They could be trained and reliability rates could be established. Personnel hired from outside of the program may be seen as more objective, yet may have greater difficulty in obtaining information from families participating in early intervention who may be reluctant to speak openly to unknown interviewers. Service coordinators typically have well-established relationships and rapport with families in the program.

Review of Records

The third approach involves a review of administrative records. Programs that have sizable populations potentially affected by welfare reform could be selected. Past records could be reviewed to determine baseline data on rates of a series of program participation and family indicators. Possible data elements include rates of referral, program dropout, refusals of services, "no shows" for therapy and home visits, suspected child abuse reports, referral for out-of-home placements, attendance at IFSP, suspension of services because of hospitalizations, parent meeting participation, and intervention outcome goals achieved. Once baseline information on data elements has been established, these same factors could be tracked to identify systematic changes over time.

Summary

Given the interest that W-2 has generated among both parents and providers of Birth to Three Early Intervention services, there would likely be a great deal of motivation by program staff to participate in any evaluation of the impact of W-2 on families and the service system. Birth to Three staff could serve as a valuable resource to obtain information from parents and their communities. The children and families enrolled in Birth to Three programs are a well-defined population who have regular and sustained contact with services and providers in their communities. Families who have eligible children and are in poverty are in an especially vulnerable state, facing multiple needs and challenges simultaneously. The study of the impact of W-2 on these families is critical to help assure that public policy designed to optimize the chances for financial independence does not create the opposite effect by mitigating the impact of community developmental, medical, and social support efforts and endangering the continued development of very young children with special needs.

References

Begun, A. L. "Family Systems and Family-Centered Care." In *Partnerships in Family-centered Care: A Guide to Collaborative Early Intervention*, eds. P. Rosin, A. D. Whitehead, L. I. Tuchman, G. S. Jesien, A. L. Begun, and L. Irwin. Baltimore: Paul H. Brookes Publishing Co., 1996.

Erwin, E. *Putting Children First: Visions for a Brighter Future for Young Children and Their Families.* Baltimore: Paul H. Brookes Publishing Co., 1996.

Hoffman, C. "Data on Young Children with Special Needs." Wisconsin Council on Developmental Disabilities, Madison, WI, 1996.

HSS 90: Early Intervention Services for Children from Birth to Age 3 with Developmental Needs. Wisconsin Administrative Code. Register, No. 450, June 1993.

Individuals with Disabilities Education Act (IDEA) of 1990, PL 102–119. (October 7, 1991). Title 20 U. S. C. 1400 et seq: *U. S. Statutes at Large*, 105, 587–608.

Jesien, G. "Challenges for the Future of Early Intervention." In *Partnerships in Family-centered Care: A Guide to Collaborative Early Intervention*, eds. P. Rosin, A. D. Whitehead, L. I. Tuchman, G. S. Jesien, A. L. Begun, and L. Irwin. Baltimore: Paul H. Brookes Publishing Co., 1996.

Smith, B. J. and McKenna, P. "Early Intervention Public Policy: Past, Present and Future." In *Meeting Early Intervention Challenges: Issues from Birth to Three*, eds. L. J. Johnson, R. J. Gallagher, M. J. La Montagne (2nd ed., pp. 251-264). Baltimore: Paul H. Brookes Publishing Co., 1994.

Trohanis, P. "Continuing Positive Changes Through Implementation of IDEA." In *Meeting Early Intervention Challenges: Issues from Birth to Three*, eds. L. J. Johnson, R. J. Gallagher, M. J. La Montagne

(2nd ed., pp. 167-182). Baltimore: Paul H. Brookes Publishing Co.,
1994.

Turnbull, A. P. & Turnbull, H. R. *Families, Professional and
Exceptionality: A Special Partnership.* New York: Merrill Publishing,
1990.

Yin, R. K. *Case Study Research: Design and Methods* (2nd ed.). Thousand Oaks. CA: Sage Publishing Co., 1994.

Zigler, F. E. "Meeting the Needs of Children in Poverty." *American
Journal of Orthopsychiatry* 65, no. 1 (1995): 6-9.

Endnotes

1   Data on the number of children served by year and county was provided by State
    Birth to Three Program staff in the Wisconsin Department of Health and Family
    Services, Division of Supported Living.

13

Welfare Reform and Child Welfare Services: Issues of Concern and Potential Evaluation Strategies

Mark E. Courtney
Institute for Research on Poverty
School of Social Work
University of Wisconsin — Madison

The possible impact of welfare reform — including Wisconsin's W-2 program — on the child welfare services system is a cause of concern. There has been considerable speculation about the potential of welfare reform to result in an increase in child maltreatment and the movement of large numbers of children into out-of-home care (OOHC) settings (e.g., foster homes, kinship foster homes, group homes, and children's institutions). Little empirical evidence exists, however, on which to base firm predictions. The poor understanding of how the child welfare system and its clients will fare in the new era raises a number of questions. In what ways might welfare reform affect the demand for child welfare services? What existing data sources might be used to try to assess such effects? What measures beyond the use of existing data might need to be taken to ensure an adequate evaluation of welfare reform's impact on the child welfare system? In this paper I try to answer these questions using

Wisconsin's W-2 proposal as an example of welfare reform, and in the process, to inform the discussion of the evaluation of state-level welfare reform in general. I conclude that it will be very difficult to evaluate the impact of welfare reform on the demand for child welfare services in Wisconsin, and most likely in other states as well.

The Nature of Child Welfare Services

An appreciation of how welfare reform might affect the child welfare system requires a basic understanding of the purposes and functioning of the system. By and large, children come to the attention of the child welfare system because of parental neglect or abuse, though a relatively small number enter OOHC due to parent-child conflict.[1] Public child welfare agencies are charged with investigating reports of child maltreatment, protecting children from maltreatment, and finding children permanent homes when they must be removed from the care of their parents.

Depending on what is discovered during the initial child maltreatment investigation, the agency has several options, including: deciding not to intervene any further; informally referring the family to social service providers in the community; offering the family voluntary services provided by the agency itself; requiring the family to participate in court-ordered services in order to retain custody of their child; and placing the child in OOHC, at least temporarily, for the child's protection. In most cases when a child is placed in OOHC the child welfare agency endeavors to help the family to be able to safely parent the child so as to reunify the family. When this is not possible the agency tries to find the child another permanent home, preferably through adoption.

Historically, OOHC has consisted of foster family care and group care ranging from small group homes to large children's institutions. In recent years kinship foster care (i.e., foster care by relatives of children in OOHC) has become the second most common form of OOHC after traditional foster family care. The growth of kinship care is a result of many factors including a greater acceptance of the role of extended family in caring for maltreated children, a shortage of foster family homes, and federal and state court decisions and legislation providing kin with access to financial reimbursement for providing foster care. States vary to some extent in their efforts to seek out relatives to provide foster care and in their kinship care reimbursement policies. In Wisconsin, kin who are able and willing to meet foster care licensing regulations are paid the same foster care boarding rate as unrelated foster parents. Kin who for one reason or another are not licensed as foster parents may still care for children who have been removed from home, but they are not eligible for foster care reimbursement. Prior to implementation of W-2, unlicensed kinship caregivers were eligible for a child-only payment under Aid to Families with Dependent Children (AFDC), known in Wisconsin as NLRR (non-legally responsible relative) payments. NLRR payments were lower than foster care payments.

Potential Effects of W-2 on Children and Families and on the Child Welfare System

W-2 is likely to significantly change the circumstances of the children of poor families in Wisconsin in ways that are difficult to predict at this time. Some children may benefit if W-2 contributes to improving the financial condition of families by moving parents into the workforce. In contrast, some children may suffer if W-2 leads to the cutoff of benefits to families who fare poorly under the program's work requirements or if families are unable to acquire adequate child care. Several issues stand out as important to consider in developing a method to assess the consequences of W-2 for Wisconsin's children.

Trends in Out-of-Home Care in Wisconsin and Their Relationship to the AFDC Program

Between 1988 and 1995 the statewide OOHC caseload grew by 77 percent, from 4,891 in 1988 to 8,649 at the end of 1995.[2] About four-fifths of this growth took place in Milwaukee County, which now accounts for about half of all placements in Wisconsin. These numbers do not include unlicensed kinship foster care, which best estimates suggest accounts for about 1,500 placements in Milwaukee County. Historically, over half of children in OOHC in Wisconsin came from families that were eligible for AFDC at the time the child was placed in such care. If Wisconsin is similar to other states, the vast majority of children entering OOHC whose families were not eligible for AFDC came from families with near-poverty incomes. In other words, children in OOHC come almost exclusively from poor or near-poor families. This is not to say that all, or even a large proportion, of poor families maltreat their children. In fact, in Wisconsin fewer than one in twenty families who receive AFDC have a child placed in OOHC.

This rapid growth in OOHC took place during the same time that restrictions were being placed on public assistance programs in Wisconsin and AFDC caseloads were declining. It is unclear what role, if any, AFDC program changes and benefit reductions have played in the growth of OOHC during this period. It is clear, however, that caseload reductions in public assistance programs in Wisconsin have not led to a commensurate decrease in the number of children needing to be placed out of their homes.

Although only a small proportion of families receiving public assistance abuse or neglect their children, there is a strong association between material deprivation of families, child maltreatment, and the placement of children in OOHC. The incidence of abuse and neglect is approximately 22 times higher among families with incomes below $15,000 per year than among families with incomes over $30,000 per year.[3] Moreover, a time series analysis of the number of referrals to child protective services in Los Angeles County that controlled for the overall trend and seasonal variation in reports found that a 2.7 percent cut in benefit levels in 1991 was associated with an increase of about 12 percent in the monthly number of protective services referrals, while a 5.8 percent cut in AFDC benefits implemented in two phases during late 1992 was associated with an approximate 20 percent increase.[4] The relationship between poverty and child maltreatment is most pronounced in the area of child neglect, which is the most common form of child maltreatment and the primary reason children are placed out of home. Thus, if W-2 or any other welfare reform program results in a significant increase in poverty, it is likely to contribute to increased demand for child welfare services. Conversely, lifting families out of poverty would be expected to reduce the demand for such services.

Changes in the Economic Well-Being of Families

The impact of W-2 on the economic well-being of families is likely to vary depending on the circumstances of families. In some cases W-2 will result in a net improvement in family resources due to enhanced earnings combined with government support for child care and health care. These benefits will most likely accrue to families with relatively well-functioning wage earners and relatively fewer children. In other cases, W-2 will result in a decrease in family resources. Even full participation in W-2 subsidized jobs, community service jobs, and W-2 Transitions activities will result in a net decrease in income for large families. More important, some parents will be unable or unwilling to participate in required W-2 activities. These families will be "sanctioned," resulting in a loss of income. The time-limit provisions of W-2, if fully implemented, will also eventually result in some number of families being denied assistance.

Impact on Children of Work Requirements of W-2

Many parents who would not work at all or would work part time under current public assistance arrangements will choose to work full time because of the incentives/sanctions structure of W-2. The impact on children of this change in parental involvement in the workforce is difficult to predict but will almost certainly vary depending on family circumstances.

Some parents will adapt well to work. This could lead to an improvement in parental self-esteem and parenting behavior. It might also serve as a source of improved self-esteem for the children in these families. In some cases, children placed in child care when their parents are working may receive better care than they did in their own homes. Families with strong support systems to help with child care responsibilities (e.g., extended family and friends) are likely to cope best with the added responsibility of work.

Other parents will have difficulty coping with the combination of parenting responsibilities and work. Some parents are marginal caregivers when providing full-time care of their children. Many of them may neglect or abuse their children when faced with the combined stress of parenting and work. In some cases a lack of parental supervision may lead children to experience decreased school performance, be subjected to extrafamilial abuse, or engage in delinquent behavior. In addition, some parents may have difficulty finding safe and affordable child care for their children. Isolated parents with poor or nonexistent support systems will probably fare worst in balancing the demands of work and parenting. (Of course, as mentioned above, some parents will simply fail to work and will be denied benefits under W-2.)

Consequences for Children of the Apparent Contradiction between the Goals of W-2 and Those of the Child Welfare Services System

W-2 and the recently enacted federal welfare reform legislation are primarily concerned with encouraging parents to work instead of relying on public assistance. Families are rewarded for work both financially and through government support for child care and health care. When parents refuse to work or do not appropriately participate in work activities (e.g., are late for work), W-2 sanctions families through denial of benefits. The purpose of the child welfare system is to protect children from maltreatment while preserving the integrity of families whenever possible, based on the assumption that a child's family is generally the best place for a child to be raised. Though material deprivation often contributes to the circumstances bringing families in contact with the child welfare system, poverty alone is not grounds for placement of children in OOHC. Nevertheless, in the process of trying to preserve families, the child welfare system often provides support to families in the form of targeted financial assistance (e.g., help with paying utilities or rent), in-kind benefits (e.g., child care), and various social services. Whatever its limitations, the cash-based public assistance system complemented the child welfare services system: It provided minimal financial support to poor families regardless of whether or not they chose or were able to work.

In contrast, provision of assistance to poor families by the child welfare system may be seen to undercut the work-related sanctions of W-2, even though the present child welfare system does not have the resources to give ongoing financial support to poor families. Moreover, employees of W-2 agencies which are working under performance contracts may see the child welfare system as a vehicle for ridding themselves of responsibility for parents who are poor prospects for work.

It is impossible to anticipate at this time how the child welfare system may evolve in response to rapid changes in the social safety net for families, or how the managers of W-2 programs will attempt to make use of child protective services. If W-2 results in a noticeable increase in child poverty and neglect, political pressure may result in increased intervention to protect children through placement in OOHC. Alternatively, in the absence of new resources, the system may be forced to narrow its grounds for intervention and respond only to extremely desperate situations. Given Wisconsin's decentralized administration of child welfare programs, the response to change is likely to vary widely from county to county.

The Uncertain Role of Kinship Care Under W-2

To date, Wisconsin has made little concerted effort to develop policy in the area of kinship foster care, despite the fact that licensed and unlicensed kinship foster homes account for between 25 and 35 percent of all OOHC placements in Wisconsin. Currently kinship care appears to account for over half of OOHC in Milwaukee County.

W-2 calls for the development of a new category of kinship care. Presumably this is at least partly a response to the perceived need for out-of-home placement resources for children whose parents are not able to care for them when confronted by the requirements of W-2. Currently the W-2 kinship care reimbursement rate is slightly lower than the rate paid previously to non-legally responsible relatives under the AFDC program. Procedural requirements for approving kinship homes and reviewing the care of children in these homes are much less stringent than existing permanency planning requirements for children in OOHC.

Changes in kinship care arrangements proposed under W-2 raise a number of questions. For example, what effect will changes in regulation and reimbursement of kinship care have on the supply of kinship care providers in Wisconsin? Will the altered context of kinship care contribute to changes in the number of children entering OOHC? How will children fare in kinship care settings?

There is no way to know in advance if, or how, W-2 will affect the rate of child maltreatment and need for child welfare services. Nevertheless, the issues raised above call for close attention to the child welfare system in evaluating of the consequences of W-2.

Variables of Interest in Evaluating the Impact of W-2 on Child Welfare Services

A full discussion of the range of potential indicators of the impact of welfare reform on child maltreatment, the child welfare system, and its clients is beyond the scope of this paper. For the purposes of illustration I will use two indicators of change in the demand for child welfare services: the incidence of child maltreatment and the incidence of child placement in OOHC.[5] For reasons discussed above, the incidence of child maltreatment, particularly child neglect, may be altered by W-2 and any significant change in child maltreatment owing to W-2, whether for better or worse, is worthy of interest. Methodological problems inherent in trying to reliably measure the incidence of child maltreatment are considerable and a discussion of them is far beyond the scope of this paper. Suffice it to say that there are no reliable historical data on the actual incidence or prevalence of child maltreatment in Wisconsin, and that this is almost certainly true for every other state.[6]

The only indicator of child maltreatment that is likely to be available for purposes of evaluating welfare reform will be child maltreatment reports made to child welfare agencies. This indicator has the advantage of being based on a legal definition of what forms of parental behavior constitute child abuse or neglect. Child abuse reports are also the primary source of demand for child welfare services. Still, child abuse reports are obviously a crude measure of actual child maltreatment if for no other reason than the fact that an unknown amount of child abuse and neglect goes unreported for a host of reasons. Moreover, just because a report is made does not mean that a child was harmed. Evaluators will probably want to rely on "substantiated" reports, those for which an investigator from a child welfare agency has determined that legally prohibited child maltreatment has actually taken place. Using child maltreatment reports as an indicator of change in the level of child maltreatment is problematic for other reasons that will be discussed below.

The incidence of OOHC placement should, in principle, be somewhat easier to measure given that child welfare agencies ought to have a clear idea of how many children enter care during any given period of time. Measurement of change can be complicated, however, for reasons that will be discussed below.

Basis of Comparison for Evaluating the
Impact of W-2 on the Child Welfare System

In this volume Haveman has examined the comparative advantages and disadvantages of the experimental, pre-post, and comparison site designs for state-based evaluation of welfare reform. I generally accept his assessment of the advantages and disadvantages of each design strategy. I will not discuss the experimental design here because of the "fatal flaw" Haveman notes in this design (i.e., the difficulty of identifying a within-state control group immune from the incentives of the new policy) and the fact that I am not aware of any plans to analyze welfare reform impacts on child welfare services using an experimental design. As noted by Haveman, the comparison site design also suffers from flaws which render it of limited usefulness in the current policy context. Moreover, although there is some discussion of multi-state studies of the impact of welfare reform on child welfare systems, these proposals really amount to a series of pre-post studies rather than true cross-site comparisons. Thus, to the extent that the pre-post design offers some promise, and some child welfare researchers intend to examine the impact of welfare reform using pre-post designs, I will briefly take up this approach here.

In principle, it is possible to evaluate the impact of welfare reform on child maltreatment reports and foster care entries by examining the rate of reported child maltreatment and foster care entry among the population of interest *prior to* and *after* implementation of the reform program. This assumes that the population of interest (i.e., those families who are affected by the reform in a manner likely to alter the probability that they will need child welfare services) can be identified and that the "pre" and "post" periods can be delineated. The pre-post design also assumes that the evaluator can secure comparability in the "state of the world" characteristics between the pre-reform period and the post-reform period. It is important to note here that the state of the world does not merely include the social and economic conditions emphasized in Haveman's discussion. When considering the potential impact of welfare reform on the demand for social services, such as child welfare services, the evaluator will also be faced with the problem of securing comparability of policy and practice *within the service system of interest* between the pre-reform and post-reform periods. The low probability of accomplishing this with respect to child welfare services will be discussed below. In summary, if the evaluation design is able to meet the assumptions described above, then changes in the demand for child welfare services in the wake of welfare reform can be inferred to be the result of the new welfare policy.

Data Sources

Existing management information systems and data systems to be implemented under W-2 could provide for an assessment of changes over time in child maltreatment and the transition of children from poor families receiving public support to out-of-home care. Before summarizing the potential use of these systems for evaluating W-2, a description of the systems and their strengths and weaknesses is in order.

Data on Child Maltreatment

Wisconsin collects data on reported child maltreatment via the completion of the Division of Community Services #40 form (DCS-40) by county child welfare workers. Unique child identifiers are not recorded on the DCS-40, meaning that it is impossible to link data on child maltreatment reports to data from public assistance, child support, or OOHC data systems. This implies that evaluators will not be able to use administrative data in Wisconsin to assess change over time in the incidence of child maltreatment reporting within the population of interest to W-2 evaluators (i.e., families affected in some significant way by W-2). Therefore, about the only possible use of the DCS-40 data for evaluation purposes would be to measure aggregate change over time in the number of maltreatment reports, and even that possibility is limited by other problems with the DCS-40, including intercounty variation in completion of the form. In particular, the standard for reporting maltreatment as "substantiated" (i.e., meeting the criteria listed in statute) appears to vary from county to county. Moreover, there is some reason to believe that reporting numbers can be affected by resource constraints. For example, preliminary data from the 1993 National Incidence Study of Child Abuse and Neglect indicate that the proportion of maltreated children whose situations were investigated by child protective services authorities nationally declined from 44 percent in 1986 to 28 percent in 1993.[7] This was during a period of rapid growth nationally in the number of child maltreatment reports. In a number of cases media attention to sensational child maltreatment cases has been shown to lead to rapid, though generally transitory, increases in child maltreatment reports. All of these problems call into question the meaning of changes in the number of reports over time.

County-level data could conceivably be used to evaluate in selected counties the impact of welfare reform on the incidence of child maltreatment and the provision of child welfare services to families. Counties sometimes maintain their own child welfare data systems, and some of these systems may have more reliable data than that obtained from statewide data systems. In addition, child maltreatment data in some counties could include child identifiers, facilitating the linkage of data on child maltreatment to data on OOHC and/or family participation in public assistance programs. Last, some county data systems collect information on purchased services that are provided to families during their involvement with child protective services. Unfortunately, there do not appear to be any counties in Wisconsin with data systems that improve in any significant way on available state child maltreatment data systems.[8]

Data on Out-of-Home Care

The state collects data on out-of-home care placements via the completion of the Human Services Reporting System (HSRS) Substitute Care module by county child welfare workers and clerical staff. All out-of-home care placements, with the exceptions of placements in secure detention facilities and unlicensed kinship care, are recorded in the HSRS data. (It may be possible to obtain some historical data on AFDC-supported kinship care through the AFDC reporting system, but the AFDC data system does not distinguish between NLRR cases involved with the child welfare system and those having no involvement with the system.) The HSRS system does not generate payments to providers, and there is fairly minimal monitoring of county compliance. As a result, while it is believed by those operating the system that nearly all children who are placed out of home for at least a few days show up in the HSRS system, cases are sometimes not closed in a timely manner, and data fields that are not subject to system edits (e.g., family income and some child characteristics) are not routinely filled out by workers. HSRS could be linked to historical AFDC data. Moreover, HSRS will continue to operate under W-2 and might therefore be used to monitor movement of children from families participating in W-2 into out-of-home care.

As in the case of child maltreatment reports, it is conceivable that county data could be used to fill in gaps in HSRS data (e.g., cost data on services provided to children and families and inclusion of data on kinship foster care placements). Unfortunately, no county has a data system that significantly improves on the limitations of HSRS that are noted above.

Potential Evaluation Strategies

Discussion of the potential uses of existing administrative data to evaluate the impact of W-2 on the child welfare system and its clients illustrates the strengths and weaknesses of this approach. There are two advantages to using administrative data. First, it is a relatively inexpensive and timely source of information. Second, in some cases it makes possible the comparison of data from before the implementation of W-2 with data generated after implementation, thus facilitating a pre-post evaluation design. In particular, data on child maltreatment reports and OOHC — with all of their problems — are available from the late 1980s onward and will continue to be available in the foreseeable future.

In contrast, there are no survey data on child maltreatment or foster care entry available in Wisconsin that could be used for a pre-post welfare reform study. General surveys undertaken in Wisconsin such as the Current Population Survey or the Survey of Income and Program Participation are not up to the task for a variety of reasons, including inadequate sample sizes at the state level to study rare events such as foster care entry, a lack of survey items pertaining to participation in child welfare programs, and the inability through self-report data to capture events such as substantiated child maltreatment reports.

There are several disadvantages to using administrative data to evaluate the impact of W-2 on child welfare services. The statewide data are of somewhat questionable reliability. The OOHC data do not cover unlicensed kinship care and do not distinguish between licensed kinship homes and foster family homes. Considering the prominent role of kinship care under W-2, this is a serious limitation. Most important, a simple interrupted time series of child maltreatment reports or OOHC entries — the most likely use of administrative data — will be hard to interpret meaningfully. As has already been mentioned, many factors can significantly affect maltreatment reports, and the same can be said for OOHC caseloads.

In particular, a problem noted above involves the potential difficulty posed for a pre-post evaluation design by changes in policy or practice within a service system (e.g., child welfare services) that might be affected by a change in policy within another system (e.g., the public assistance system). For example, a problem in the current context is the recent enactment of significant changes in the Wisconsin child protection statutes that define child maltreatment. Without a clear understanding of how changes in the definition of child maltreatment might have affected the number of reports in the absence of W-2, it will be impossible to estimate the net effect of W-2 on reports. Similarly, W-2 is being implemented at the same time that the Wisconsin Department of Health and Family Services is taking over the operation of the child welfare services system in Milwaukee County. The plan calls for a major overhaul of child welfare practice in an area now accounting for over half of the OOHC caseload. Other states have adopted a range of other child welfare "reforms" in recent years, any of which might have an impact on demand for services. Perhaps most importantly, the enactment by Congress of the Adoption and Safe Families Act of 1997 could result in major changes in the functioning, and outcomes, of the child welfare system in every state. This is not to say that there is no use in monitoring changes in reports or caseloads over time, only that alternative explanations of any observed changes will abound.

Wisconsin is not necessarily a good model for using a pre-post design to assess the impact of welfare reform on the child welfare system, given Wisconsin's relatively poor child welfare data capacity. A few states already have the ability to track children's paths through the child welfare system, from child abuse reports through a variety of transitions within the system to eventual exit. In some cases these states can also link data from their public assistance systems to child welfare services data. Moreover, federal financial support for the development of statewide automated child welfare information systems (SACWIS)[9] currently exists under the Omnibus Budget Reconciliation Act of 1993 and has been extended for one year under the Personal Responsibility and Work Opportunity Reconciliation Act of 1996. This support is being used by many states to develop much more sophisticated data management systems than those currently in existence, many of which integrate child welfare, public assistance, child support, and juvenile court data. Needless to say, such integrated data systems will increase the potential use of administrative data in assessing the impact of welfare reform on children in general, and on the child welfare system in particular.

Nevertheless, the variety of problems described above casts a long shadow over any hopes for a meaningful pre-post evaluation of the impact of welfare reform on the child welfare system. Data systems in child welfare are generally so poor that basic measures of interest to evaluators will simply be impossible to obtain in the near future, let alone retrospectively. Even in jurisdictions with relatively good data, observers will have a host of explanations for change in child welfare caseloads, and little hope of ruling out any reasonable hypothesis about the reasons for change. Given that child welfare scholars have not been able to come to any firm conclusions about the impact of changes in child welfare policy over the past few years on child maltreatment reports and foster care entries, why should anyone believe that analysis of such caseload change will become *easier* in the context of welfare reform?

Assessing the Relationship Between Welfare Reform and the Child Welfare System

I have argued that an impact evaluation of W-2 (and most likely other welfare reforms as well) will have little chance of providing useful knowledge about the effect of welfare reform on the child welfare system. This does not mean that I believe that there is no reason to attend to the potential relationship between W-2 and the child welfare system. The ways in which W-2 *could* impact child welfare are simply too great to ignore. Whereas the magnitude of the net impact of W-2 on the demand for child welfare services will be difficult if not impossible to judge, it may be possible to identify the mechanisms by which W-2 contributes to demand for child welfare services. This would look more like an implementation study or close monitoring effort than an impact evaluation, but it could still have significant benefits. Many child welfare authorities in

Wisconsin and around the country are apprehensive about how welfare reform will affect the child welfare system. Getting a good picture of the ways in which families involved in W-2 and other reform programs come into contact with the child welfare system, and the ways in which the two systems themselves interact, may go a long way toward minimizing this anxiety, or at least giving program administrators a better idea of what they should really be worried about.

Unfortunately, existing administrative data will probably be of limited use in such monitoring efforts. Although administrative data can generally be used to monitor certain events of interest in a person's life, they are usually not very helpful in assessing the *reasons* for these events. Administrative data tell us very little about how a child comes to be maltreated, draws the attention of child welfare authorities, or is found in need of OOHC. Yet the reasons for all of these events might change under welfare reform.

One alternative to the use of administrative information for evaluating the relationship between W-2 and child welfare services would be the collection of data over time on the circumstances of families participating in W-2. Even better would be data collection from the low-income population as a whole, since some families who would have previously taken advantage of public assistance may choose not to do so in the new era and W-2 participants would be a subset of this larger group. This could take the form of surveys or interviews. A cohort or panel design would be preferable, so that changes in family and child status could be measured over time. This approach would have the advantage of measuring changes in more detail than is possible using administrative data. Furthermore, at least in theory it offers the opportunity to examine the intervening variables that contribute to particular outcomes, a crucial missing link in administrative data. For example, interviews with program participants might show that a substantial proportion of families participating in W-2 have children placed in OOHC due to "lack of supervision" and that this occurs almost exclusively among families who are not able to obtain stable child care for their children while the parents are working. Clearly this would be more interesting, and a more policy relevant finding, than simply noticing that OOHC placements had gone up over time. Although such a finding could not be used to indicate that W-2 "caused" the children to be placed in OOHC, it could help to identify a group of families that might be at high risk of neglecting their children. Policy responses might include changes in the W-2 child care program or in the response of child welfare agencies to such family situations. There are many other examples of findings that might emerge from a monitoring effort aimed at the circumstances under which low-income families, particularly those involved in W-2, experience contact with the child welfare system.

A panel study is no panacea. Collection of survey or interview data is much more logistically difficult and costly than analyzing administrative data. Moreover, conducting a panel study would most likely require adequate administrative data to select and track an appropriate sample. It is very unlikely that a panel study would be undertaken solely to monitor the impact of W-2 on child welfare services. As a result, any panel created would need to be large enough to generate adequate statistical power when it comes to outcomes such as child maltreatment and OOHC to achieve the purposes suggested here. For example, if 5 percent of AFDC families have a child placed in OOHC (over five times the placement rate for the overall population), even a doubling of the OOHC placement rate for W-2 families would still mean that only 10 percent of children in W-2 families are removed from the care of their parents. Thus, it would take a large sample of families to measure even major overlaps between W-2 and child welfare services populations.

Perhaps the use of a combination of administrative data and selective analysis of additional data on families who receive child welfare services could realize the benefits of administrative data while filling in some gaps. Analysis of entries to OOHC can serve as an example. HSRS data can now be linked to AFDC data to identify children who are removed from families who receive AFDC. Similarly, it is likely that it will be possible to link data on W-2 participation of families to data on children being placed in OOHC from these families. Given the limitations of statewide child maltreatment reporting data, it will not be possible to selectively augment administrative data analysis in order to assess the impact of W-2 on child maltreatment for Wisconsin as a whole. It may be possible, however, to conduct in several counties the sort of analysis discussed above, to the extent that the counties have the capacity to uniquely identify maltreated children in a manner that allows for linking child maltreatment data to AFDC and W-2 participation.

Analysis of the circumstances of families should be complemented by qualitative analysis of how the two service systems —

W-2 and child welfare services — interact. This could shed light on a number of important questions. How do W-2 workers react when they perceive that parents are not only unable to meet their work requirements, but are also having difficulty adequately caring for their children? Are W-2 workers trained in how the child protection system functions and what their responsibilities are regarding the reporting of child maltreatment? Do child welfare workers see the W-2 office as an obstacle to their efforts, or as a supportive resource for low-income families, and therefore for the workers' efforts to preserve the integrity of families? In short, in what ways do the two systems work together, and in what ways are they at cross purposes? Observational studies and focus groups come to mind as two possible methods to be used in this part of an implementation study and monitoring effort.

Ironically, one of the most interesting possibilities for using experimental evaluation designs in developing W-2 is in the manipulation of the interface between W-2 agencies and child welfare programs. For example, the state could choose to randomly assign counties to groups that would receive funding to implement specified but distinct approaches to dealing with the relationship between W-2 and child welfare services. Some counties would be randomly assigned to a "control" group that would not receive such funding. For example, currently families become ineligible for W-2 support if all of their children are placed in OOHC, since only families with children may participate in W-2. This could clearly limit the ability of child welfare agencies to work toward reunification of children with their families. An interesting experiment would involve giving some randomly-selected counties the ability to continue W-2 benefits to a family for a time-limited period if the parents were actively working toward family reunification. Another useful experiment would involve training W-2 workers to identify families with certain characteristics that place their children at high risk of being maltreated (e.g., parental substance abuse, social isolation, domestic violence in the home, very young children in the home). When such families were identified, their cases could be referred to a special W-2 unit that works closely with child welfare authorities to assess the family's needs and offer appropriate services or supports. The purpose of these kinds of experiments would be to assess the extent to which various approaches to integrating W-2 and child welfare services affect the demand for, and outcomes of, child welfare services.

Such experiments would not be immune to methodological problems of their own, of course. Still, Wisconsin, like many other states, currently has a relatively large amount of money to spend on each family involved in W-2 as a result of caseload reductions in recent years combined with stable funding under the Temporary Assistance to Needy Families block grant. Given the great cost of OOHC, experimentation with the interface between child welfare and workfare programs would appear to be money well spent.

Conclusion

Much concern over the implementation of welfare reform has focused on the possibly negative impact on children. Perhaps some of the large-scale surveys being undertaken will be able to provide some kind of "before-after" perspective on the overall impact of welfare reform on child well-being, but the specific impact on child maltreatment and OOHC will most likely not come into clear view. Nevertheless, creative use of administrative data, targeted surveys, qualitative studies, and county-level experimental program evaluation could help to provide a better understanding of how poor children and families come into contact with the child welfare system. Most importantly, such work could inform how workfare and child welfare programs can best be designed to minimize the need for coercive child welfare services intervention with poor families.

References

Courtney, Mark and Linda Park. *Out-of-Home Care in Wisconsin, 1995*. Madison, WI: School of Social Work, University of Wisconsin: 1996.

Courtney, Mark and Raymond C. Collins. "New Challenges and Opportunities in Child Welfare Outcomes and Information Technologies." *Child Welfare* 7, no. 5 (1994): 359-378.

U.S. Department of Health and Human Services, "Survey Shows Dramatic Increase in Child Abuse and Neglect." Press release, September 18, 1996.

Endnotes

1   The terms "out-of-home care" and "foster care" are used interchangeably in this paper to refer to all forms of out-of-home care. Youth are also placed in OOHC settings because of delinquency, but their care is generally supervised by juvenile justice authorities rather than child welfare agencies. This discussion pertains only to children placed in OOHC due to child maltreatment.

2   Mark E. Courtney and Linda Park, *Out-of-Home Care in Wisconsin: 1995* (Madison, Wis.: School of Social Work, University of Wisconsin, 1996).

3   The 1993 National Incidence Study of Child Abuse and Neglect provides data on the relationship between family income and the incidence of child maltreatment. See press release from the U.S. Department of Health and Human Services, "Survey Shows Dramatic Increase in Child Abuse and Neglect," September, 18, 1996.

4   Robert E. Sherman, unpublished report to Norm Zimlich, of the Institute for Human Services Management, (Seattle, WA, April 5, 1995).

5   Potential entry effects on the demand for child welfare services owing to welfare reform have received the most attention in discussions of the subject. My choice of indicators reflects this focus. Nevertheless, there are many other ways in which welfare reform could affect the child welfare system. For example, welfare reform that results in a decrease in the availability of economic assistance to families whose children have been placed in OOHC may limit social workers' ability to reunite children with their families, thus increasing the length of stay of children placed in OOHC. It is therefore possible that welfare reform could affect the overall demand for child welfare services without having a significant entry effect.

6   To this author's knowledge the national studies directed at estimating child maltreatment incidence and prevalence rates cannot be used to estimate state-level rates.

7   U.S. Department of Health and Human Services, 1996.

8   At a Madison, Wisconsin, meeting on September 20, 1996, for Wisconsin county officials interested in evaluating the impact of W-2 on children and families, none of the officials (including several from larger counties in the state such as Dane, Milwaukee, and Rock) believed that any county had a data system capable of child-specific tracking of child maltreatment reports, out-of-home placement histories, or service provision to families and children.

9   See Courtney and Collins 1994.

Index

337